American Inside Out Evolution

Teacher's Book

Upper Intermediate

SUE KAY
VAUGHAN JONES

macmillan education

Macmillan Education
Companies and representatives throughout the world
American Inside Out Evolution. Teacher's Edition Upper Intermediate

Written by Helena Gomm
Adapted by Catherine Smith
Content Writers: Ben Naismith, James Michael Ubriaco and Lavaughn John
Macmillan is a registered trademark.
First edition published 2018

ISBN: 978-607-473-615-1

Based on New American Inside Out Teacher's Edition Upper Intermediate

Director of Languages Brazil: Patrícia Souza
Editorial Manager: Patricia Muradas
Art Editor: Jean Aranha
Content Editors: Cintia Zaitune and Larissa Vannucci
Digital Editor: Ana Paula Girardi
Concept design: Martha Tadaieski
Page make-up: Figurattiva Editorial
Illustrations: Gustavo Gialuca
Graphic Production: Kelly Gobbo and Tatiane Romano
Proofreaders: Edward Willson and Larissa Vazquez
Photographic research: Cintia Zaitune, Denis Araujo, Jean Aranha and Marcia Sato
Image Processing: Denis Araujo and Jean Aranha
Cover concept and design: Jean Aranha
Cover photo: Songquan Deng | Dreamstime.com

The authors and publishers would like to thank the following for permission to reproduce the photographic material: **iStockphoto**/pseudodaemon p.xx
We are grateful for permission to reprint the following copyright material: Page vi: Quotation from Language and Problems of Knowledge by Noam Chomsky copyright © Noam Chomsky 1988 Massachusetts Institute of Technology, reprinted by permission of The MIT Press, Cambridge, Massachusetts. Page vi: Quotation - Reproduced by permission of Oxford University Press. From Oxford Applied Linguistics: Understanding Second Language Acquisition by Rod Ellis © Rod Ellis 1985. New Edition OAL: A Study of Second Language Acquisition published 2008.

CANIEM No. 2275

Macmillan Publishers S.A. de C.V.
Insurgentes Sur 1886
Col. Florida, CP 01030
Álvaro Obregón
Ciudad de México
Tel: +52 (55) 5482 2200
elt@grupomacmillan.com

www.grupomacmillan.com
www.macmillan.com.mx
www.macmillanenglish.com

Printed in Brazil

This book was printed in June, 2018 by: Eskenazi Indústria Gráfica Ltda, Avenida Miguel Frias Vasconcelos, 1023 - Jaguaré - São Paulo - SP.

Contents

Teacher's notes

Student's Book Content Map

	Units & topics	Speaking & Writing	Reading & Listening	Grammar, Vocabulary, & Pronunciation
Page 8	**1 Impressions** **Events** **Adam Levine** **Self-image**	S Famous events **Anecdote:** A person who made a big impression on you S Adam Levine S People's self-image, clothes W ***Extra*** Introduction emails WB W Writing a short biography	▶ Four people talking about memorable events ▶ Two people meeting in a coffee shop R Staying on Top ▶ Four men talking about their self-image **Language for Life:** Talking about people's appearance **Life Skills** Communication: Making a good first impression	G Verb structures. Auxiliaries. Tag questions. Indirect questions V Collocations to do with appearance. Word formation: prefix *re*. Clothing idioms P Intonation in tag questions
Page 18	**2 Generations** **International exchanges** **Interviews between two generations** **Employers and employees**	S Ages and stages S International exchanges S Interview for a job **Anecdote:** Somebody's home you have stayed in	R How I learnt English R The Generation Gap ▶ Interview with employers ▶ Interview with a prospective employee ▶ Conversation between friends ▶ Conversation between friends about a job interview ▶ An au pair talking about her experience **Language for Life:** Showing someone around your home **Life Skills** Communication: Intergenerational Communication	G Verb patterns (1). Adjective structures V Language learning. Relationships. Describing people. Sayings. Social register V ***Extra*** Learning about words P Single vowel sounds
Page 28	**3 Gold** **The 1849 Gold Rush** **Making money** **Treasured possessions**	S Spending money S Having money S If you governed your country **Anecdote:** Your most treasured possession W ***Extra*** Description WB W Writing a story from pictures	R California - The Golden State ▶ Sam Brannan: California's first millionaire ▶ Father and daughter discussing money R School's out for shopping! ▶ Three people discussing money R Shop till you drop from the comfort of your home ▶ Three people talking about their most treasured possessions **Language for Life:** Shopping: money expressions; explaining what you want **Life Skills** Social Skills: Negotiating	G Reported speech. Unreal conditionals V *have*, *make*, *take* collocations. Metaphor. Money expressions P The schwa /ə/ in sayings about money
Page 38	**Review A**	Pages 38, 39 **Grammar / Vocabulary / Pronunciation review**		

	Units & topics	Speaking & Writing	Reading & Listening	Grammar, Vocabulary, & Pronunciation
Page 40	**4 Challenge** **Expeditions** **Charities** **Health** **Diet**	S Challenging situations **Anecdote:** A challenge you have faced S Doing things for charity S The future S Health and exercise S Healthy eating	R Cross country on a budget ▶ Gap year travel R Personal challenges: Charity Night Run ▶ Four people talking about exercise R A change of habit **Language for Life:** Common ailments: showing sympathy; recommendations and advice **Life Skills** Social Skills: Advice on dealing with challenges	G Narrative tenses. Future progressive and future perfect V Word formation: prefix *self-*; suffixes *able* / *ible*. Collocations in a text. Phrasal verbs V ***Extra*** Phrasal verbs P Sounding sympathetic
Page 50	**5 Ritual** **Superstitions** **Habits** **Weddings**	S Personal rituals S Habits and routines (past and present) S Marriage and romance **Anecdote:** A wedding you've been to W ***Extra*** Article: expressing an opinion WB W Writing an email of complaint	R The Morning Ritual ▶ A woman talking about her father and his car R Falling in Love and Making Ends Meet ▶ Four people talking about wedding rituals R Whatever Can Go Wrong, Will Go Wrong ▶ Four people talking about romance **Language for Life:** Annoying habits **Life Skills** Communication: The Practice of Gratitude	G *will*, *would*, and *used to* for present and past habits. Verb patterns (2) V Guessing from context. Collocations. Weddings P Sounding annoyed
Page 60	**6 Eat** **Restaurants** **Food trends** **Vegetarianism** **Food waste**	S Restaurant experiences S Food **Anecdote:** Your favorite restaurant S Vegetarianism W Using linkers S Food waste	▶ A man talking about a bad experience at a restaurant R Table customs around the world ▶ Interview with a restaurant critic R Food Trends R Becoming a vegetarian R What a Waste! **Language for Life:** Complaints in a restaurant; food idioms **Life Skills** Empathy: Turning off and Tuning in	G Present perfect: simple and progressive. Passives review V Food collocations. Guessing from context. Linkers. Numbers V ***Extra*** Exploring synonyms P Pronouncing numbers
Page 70	**Review B**	Pages 70, 71 **Grammar / Vocabulary / Pronunciation review**		

Student's Book Content Map

Introduction

In ***American Inside Out Evolution***, meaning is central to everything we ask the students to do. Instead of basing lessons on invented people in imaginary situations, we present target language in real contexts and authentic texts. We believe that the richest "source of meaning" in any lesson is what each student brings into the classroom—their thoughts, ideas, opinions, experiences, and feelings. Our materials are therefore designed to help the teacher exploit this resource and make important and memorable connections between the target language and the students' own lives.

In addition to this fundamental core principle, here are three more important beliefs that have guided us in our teaching and writing over the years:

Sue Kay and *Vaughan Jones*

- Vocabulary should share center stage with grammar. Words are the basic building blocks of any language.
- Language skills are best acquired through lots of practice. You learn to read by reading; you learn to speak by speaking, etc. Attempts to identify and then practice discrete sub-skills are not convincing.
- There can never be enough practice activities!

Engaging Content

The American linguist and philosopher Noam Chomsky once said:
"The truth of the matter is that about 99% of teaching is making the students feel interested in the material. Then the other 1% has to do with your methods."

While we might want to quibble with the percentages, we would nevertheless agree whole-heartedly with the central message in Professor Chomsky's assertion: namely, students learn best when they're interested in the material. It's as simple as that. A text might contain six beautifully crafted examples of the simple past, a good spread of high frequency lexical items, and exemplify some useful functional language, but if it doesn't engage the students, if they can't relate to it, if it feels alien to them, then the most important ingredient for successful learning is missing.

In *American Inside Out Evolution*, we've drawn on our own classroom experience, and that of our colleagues around the world, to select topics, texts, and tasks that engage students both emotionally and intellectually. Students are our richest resource. They come to class with their own knowledge of the world, their own tastes, feelings, and opinions. It's up to us to exploit this rich resource by organizing learning around topics that they can relate to—topics that are part of their life experience.

Structured Support

We all know that learning a language is a messy, non-linear business. We're dismayed when there seems to be little correlation between what is taught and what is learned! However, there is plenty of evidence to suggest that "instructed" learners (those who attend classes or follow a course of study) learn faster, and ultimately attain a higher level of proficiency than "non-instructed" learners.

In *American Inside Out Evolution*, new language input is carefully controlled: we aim to maximize exposure to high frequency language appropriate to this level. Students are encouraged to notice new grammar and new vocabulary in contexts where the meaning is clear. They are then given opportunities to manipulate the new language and try it out in different situations. They discover why using one particular form rather than another one actually matters: not just because it's right or wrong, but because it does or doesn't communicate a meaning successfully. The emphasis is always on what students can do with the language rather than what they know about the language. The new language is systematically reviewed and recycled until finally the students feel confident enough to use it to make their own meanings. It becomes part of their available repertoire. It has been "learned."

Real-World Tasks

We're strong believers in the old adage: "practice makes perfect." *American Inside Out Evolution* emphasizes output, particularly speaking, and there are a huge number of tasks that are designed to develop fluency. Students practice functional language in sections entitled *Language for Life*. But for the most part, the speaking tasks simply encourage the students to talk about things that actually matter to them, rather than playing roles or exchanging invented information. One of our main objectives is to ensure that the language our students spend time rehearsing in the classroom is transferable to the real world. By orchestrating tasks that require the students to use grammar and vocabulary to make meaningful utterances, this objective becomes obtainable. As the linguist and academic Rod Ellis reminds us:

"It is the need to get meanings across and the pleasure experienced when this is achieved that motivates second language acquisition."

www.insideout.net
"the art of communication"

Components of the Course

Student's Components

Student's Book with access code to Digital Student's Book see pages viii-x

Workbook with access code to Digital Workbook see page xi

- Companion website: macmillan.com.br/americaninsideoutevolution
- Free app

Teacher's Components

- Teacher's Edition with access code to Teacher's Presentation Kit with Extra Resources
- Test Generator
- Class audio CDs
- Companion website: www.macmillan.com.br/americaninsideoutevolution

For the Student:
A typical Student's Book unit

READING
Contemporary reading texts have been adapted and graded to suit the level. They have been selected not only for their language content but also for their interest and appropriacy.

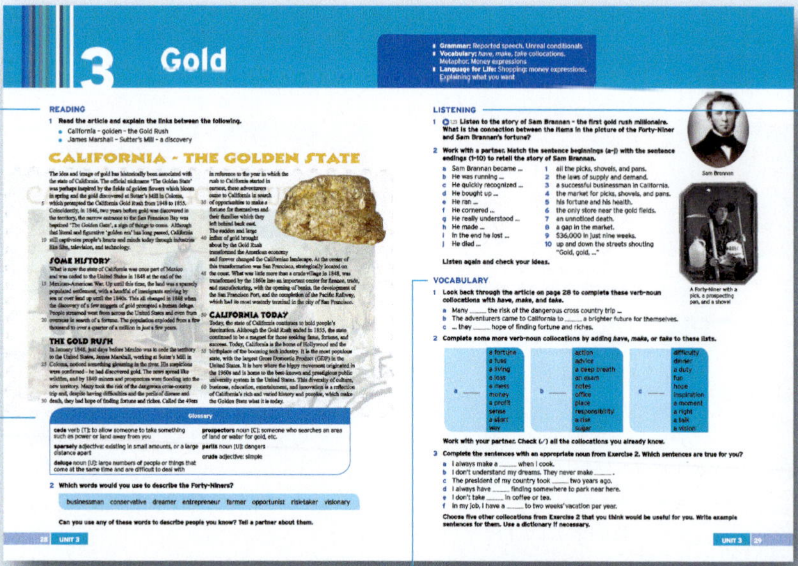

Glossaries give simple definitions for more challenging words. This minimizes interruptions and helps students read more fluently.

LISTENING
The listenings include texts specially written for language learning – dialogues, conversations, and monologues. They were carefully designed to develop real-life listening skills.

VOCABULARY
- Vocabulary is presented in context.
- Practice acitivities will help expand students' knowledge of selective lexical items and will give them the opportunity to use vocabulary in meaningful exchanges.

SPEAKING
Students are encouraged to relate the topics to their own life, views, and feelings.

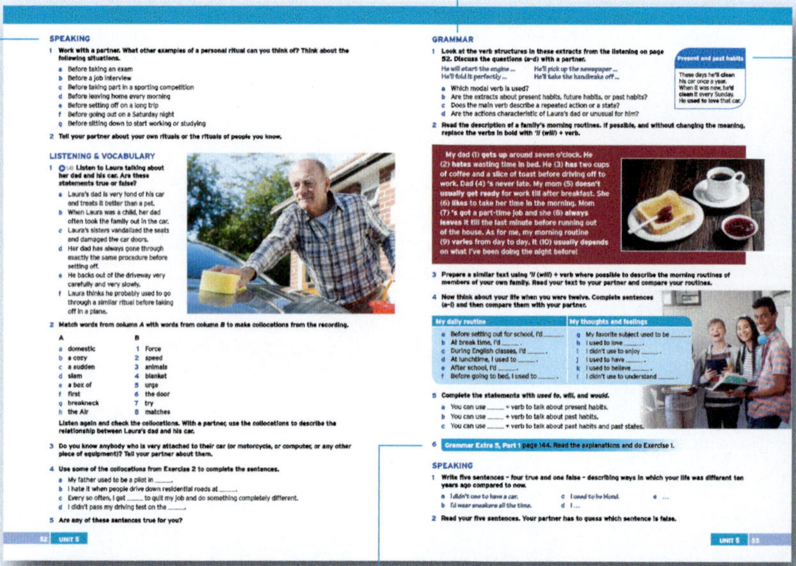

GRAMMAR
- Here students will explore new grammatical structures that have been contextualized in the reading / listening sections. They will focus on the way language works.
- A brief summary of the grammar point is provided in the box.
- Language is explored in realistic and meaningful practice exercises.
- Students will use target language in controlled and personalized practice.

The Grammar Extra pages at the back of the Student's Book extend explanations and provide further practice.

LANGUAGE FOR LIFE

The Language for Life section gives students a portable toolkit of functional language. Here, they notice how language is more than just form. They will see language in fun and engaging social situations.

VOCABULARY EXTRA

The Vocabulary Extra pages at the end of every second unit recycle the key vocabulary items taught in the units. This provides an activated wordlist and a useful bank of vocabulary.

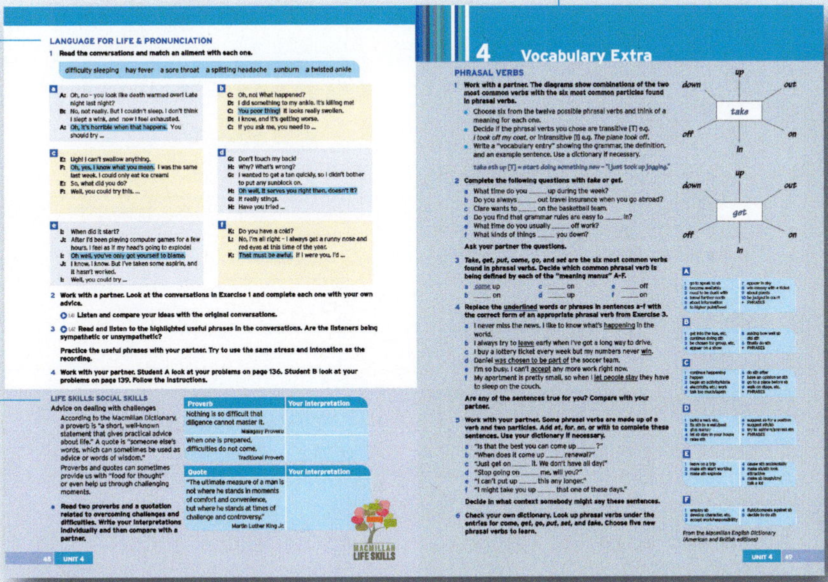

LIFE SKILLS

Developing life skills alongside language skills is an essential requirement to meet the demands of the contemporary world.

American Inside Out Evolution has a Life Skills section in every unit. Life Skills presents activities that require students to reflect on and discuss the skills necessary for social and work situations in today's world.

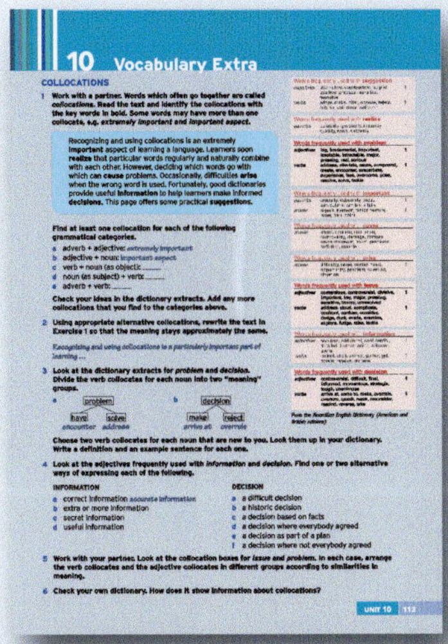

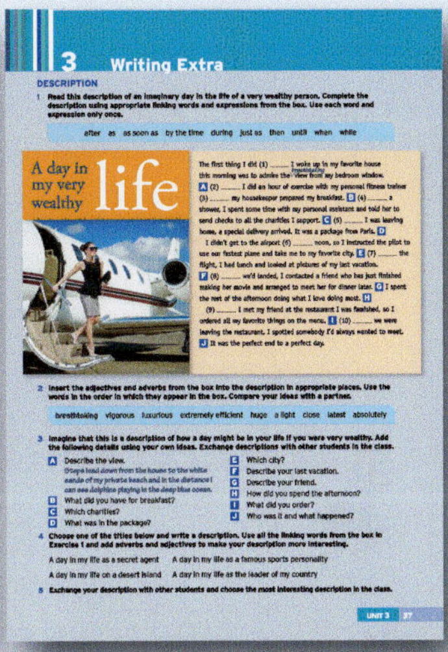

The Vocabulary Extra pages alternate with the Writing Extra pages at the end of each unit.

The Writing Extra pages develop important writing skills in a variety of genres.

The Vocabulary Extra pages explore key lexical areas such as collocations, metaphor, phrasal verbs, etc. They provide detailed practice activities and help promote useful dictionary skills.

REVIEW

There are Review units in the Student's Book. They review the new structures and vocabulary taught in the previous units.

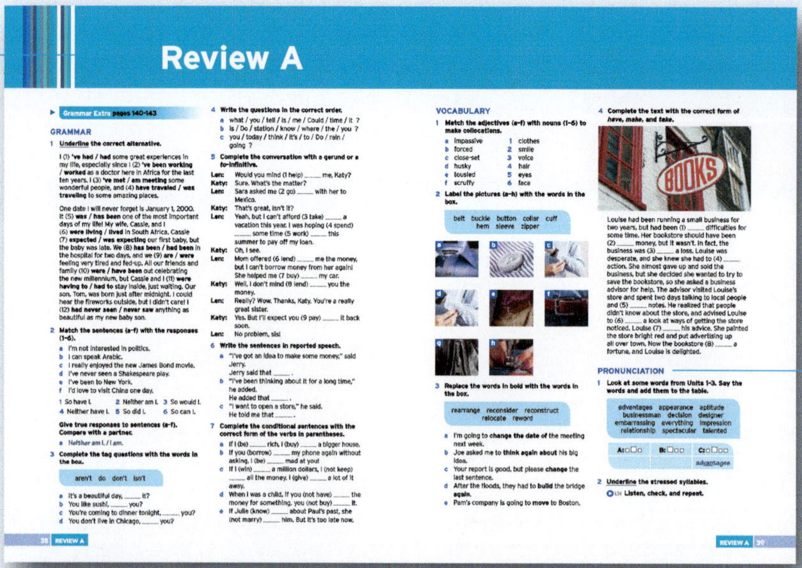

PRONUNCIATION

Pronunciation work on particular areas of sound, stress, and intonation is integrated into every unit.

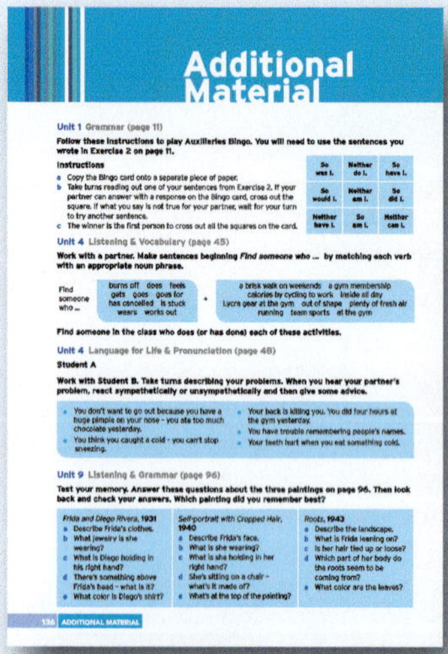

The Additional Material section includes pairwork activities as well as answers to quizzes and activities from the units.

GRAMMAR EXTRA

The Grammar Extra pages at the back of the Student's Book provide extended explanations and further practice.

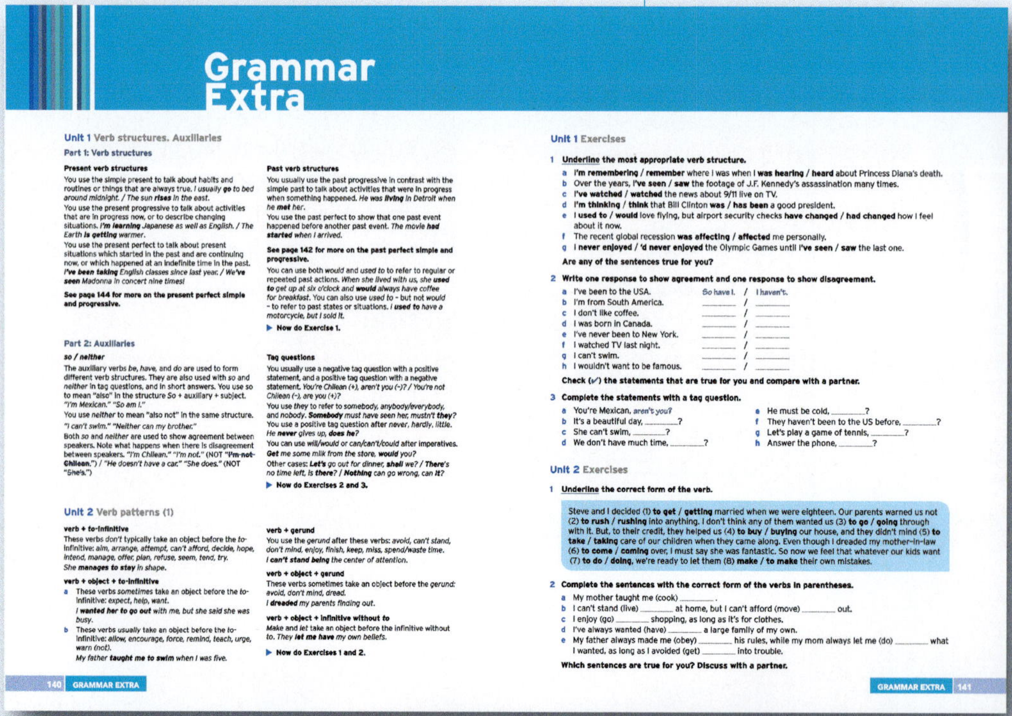

The Workbook provides a review of all the main points in the Student's Book, plus extra listening practice, pronunciation work, and a writing program.

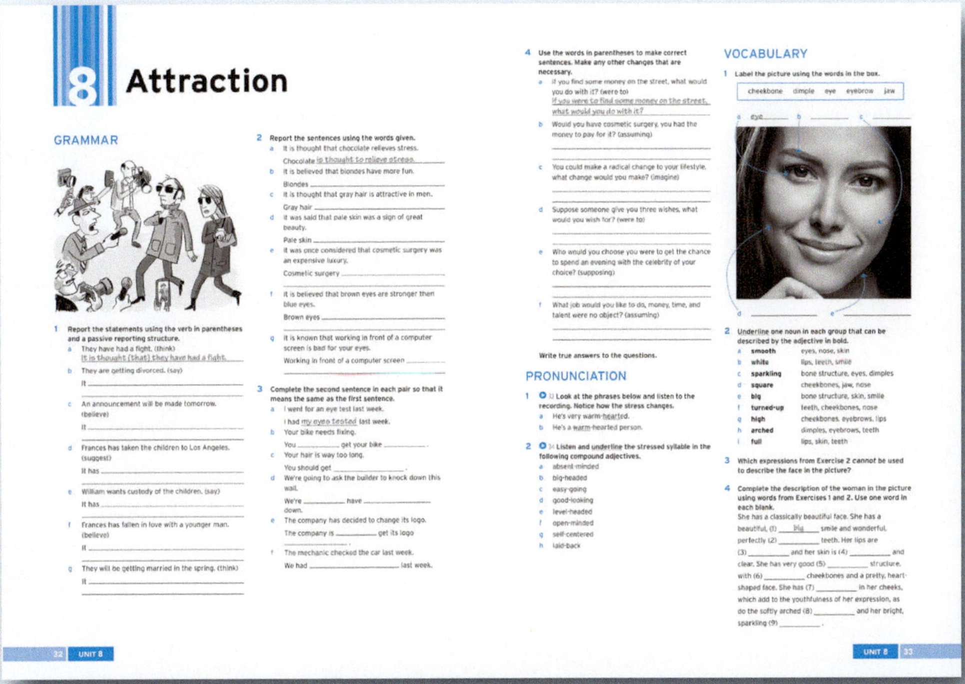

- The **Digital Student's Book** is a version of the Student's Book in digital. It includes all the student's pages plus the audio tracks for the listening activities. It can be accessed online and offline on computers and tablets.
- The **Digital Workbook** is a version of the Workbook in digital. It includes all the workbook pages plus the audio tracks for the listening activities. It can be accessed online and offline on computers and tablets.
- A free **app** gives students the opportunity for extra classroom practice on the move.
- The **companion website** www.macmillan.com.br/americaninsideoutevolution contains information about the course, its authors, and access to resources.

For the Teacher

Teacher's Edition

The Teacher's Edition contains:

An Introduction

Practical Methodology

Common European Framework of Reference (CEFR) checklists

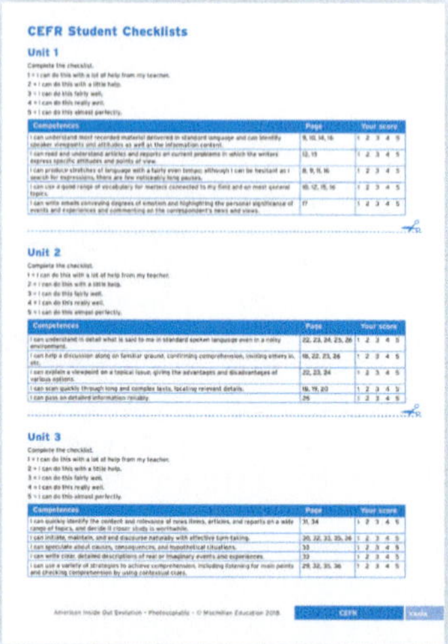

Complete teaching notes with answer keys

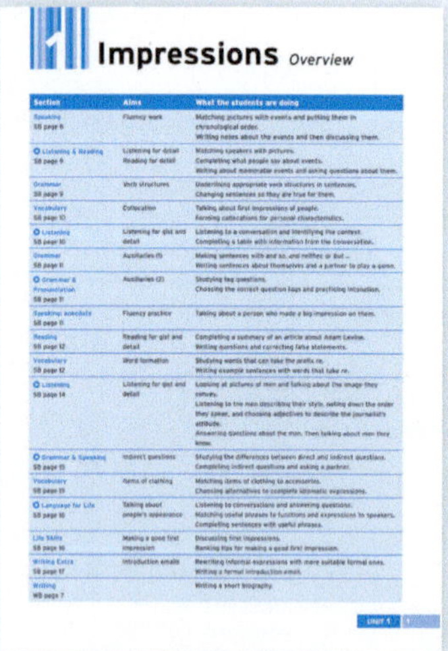

Class CD set

The Class CDs contain:

- The dialogues and listening activities from the Student's Book
- Pronunciation activities
- Recordings of the reading texts

- The **Teacher's Presentation Kit** contains the Student's Digital Book with audio and answers, and tools that can be used with an Interactive Whiteboard or Data Projector.
- The **Test Generator** is a tool for teachers to edit their own tests.
- The **Extra Resources** are links to tests and a bank of extra photocopiable grammar, vocabulary, and communicative activities.
- The **companion website** www.macmillan.com.br/americaninsideoutevolution contains information about the course, its authors, and access to resources.

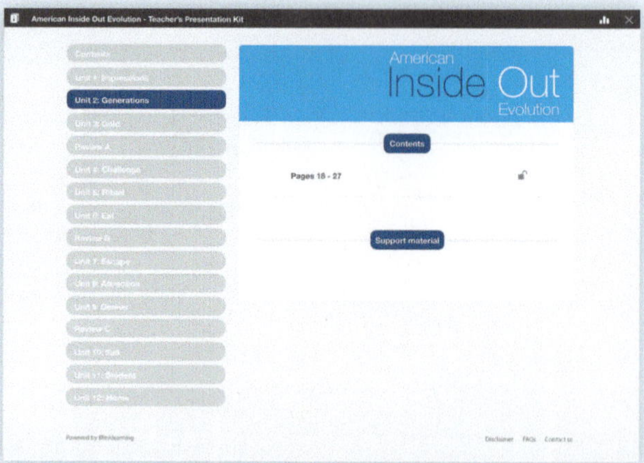

Practical Methodology

Teaching Upper Intermediate Students

A student who has reached the Upper Intermediate level is to be congratulated. Having managed to move off the so-called "intermediate plateau," the student is well on his or her way to becoming a competent communicator at an advanced level. The CEFR descriptor for B2 is a useful summary of what a student at this level is aiming for:

*Can understand the main ideas of complex text both on concrete and abstract topics, including technical discussions in his/her field of specialization. Can interact with a degree of fluency and spontaneity that makes regular interaction with native speakers quite possible without strain for either party. Can produce clear, detailed text on a wide range of subjects and explain a viewpoint on a topical issue giving the advantages and disadvantages of various options.**

Progress towards this highly desirable goal is not necessarily automatic. Because Upper Intermediate students can get by in nearly every situation, and because they're more interested in expanding the quantity rather than the quality of their language knowledge - more "new" words rather than more about "old" words - there's a danger that "half-learned" language will "fossilize": i.e. that their language deficiencies will become permanent features of their competence.

In *American Inside Out Evolution Upper Intermediate* we've tried to balance the natural inclination to race ahead and learn more and more "brand new" language with an analytical approach which encourages students to notice more complex aspects of language they already "know." We believe that time spent learning more about "half-known" words - things such as collocation, range, connotation, and register - can help iron out any residual problems students may have without compromising a sense of progress and forward momentum.

In common with all the teaching materials in the *American Inside Out Evolution* series, there's a relentless focus on meaning - in particular, the aim to help students make their own meanings in ever more communicatively competent and socially acceptable ways. This is built in to every stage of the learning process. It's this core feature of *American Inside Out Evolution* which helps students maintain their enthusiasm and motivation.

Right from the start

Every teacher has their own way of setting up their classroom, interacting with their students, and conducting their lessons. Here are a few things that we have found useful to bear in mind.

The right atmosphere

It's important to do everything you can to create a supportive learning environment. Start by memorizing every student's name and learn as much information as you can about them. Make sure students learn each other's names, too, and that they all get to know things about each other early on in the course.

Make sure you find time to "chat" with individual students or small informal groups of students before or after class. More formally, it's a good idea to devote at least one lesson per term to counsel your students individually and discuss their progress.

The right environment

Your class might be the only exposure to English that students get. Make that exposure as rich as you can by decorating the walls with maps and posters. Have several monolingual dictionaries available to refer to - a class set if possible. Also, try to have a selection of English-language books, newspapers, and magazines lying around that students can pick up and browse before and after class. Here are some further ideas:

- Institute the "Class Scribe" idea. One student in the class is given the role of recording any new language that comes up during the lesson that isn't necessarily the target language of that lesson. This unique record is then kept in a folder in the class and provides the teacher with valuable data for review activities. The role of class scribe is rotated so that each student gets a turn at being responsible for recording the lesson. This shared responsibility can help promote positive group dynamics.

* Council of Europe, 2001. *Common European Framework of Reference for Languages: Learning, Teaching, Assessment* p. 24.

- Promote graded readers. There's a huge selection of readers available at the Upper Intermediate/ Advanced level: both simplified classics and original stories. Many of them now come as "talking books" or apps. Ask the students to always bring their reader to the lesson and occasionally set aside a ten-minute slot for them to talk about what they're reading. Alternatively, just devote ten minutes to silent reading. Most Upper Intermediate students will be best suited to readers where the basic vocabulary is in the range 2,200-3,000 words. Some may feel that they want to tackle unsimplified, original versions. This is fine, but make sure the students understand that it's much better to read and enjoy ten easy books than struggle through one difficult one. Get your students hooked on books!

The right learning skills

Students will always benefit from help with learning strategies. Here are some thoughts:

- Encourage students to ask questions about language. If you have created the right atmosphere in your classroom, then students will be more likely to take an active approach in their own learning, and this is important. Students should never feel intimidated about asking questions.
- Spend time encouraging students to experiment with how they record words and phrases from the lesson. Make sure they note the part of speech - verb, noun, adjective, etc. Tell them to find a way of noting the pronunciation of the word, either using phonetic script or by developing their own system. Ask them to write complete personalized sentences putting the new word or phrase in a real context and thereby making it more memorable.
- A dictionary is a very important language learning tool, and most students will have one. Usually students prefer a bilingual dictionary, but at the Upper Intermediate level they need to think seriously about investing in a good advanced monolingual dictionary. The Vocabulary Extra pages at the end of Units 2, 4, 6, 8, 10, and 12 in *American Inside Out Evolution Upper Intermediate* have been designed to give students valuable dictionary practice and make them aware of all the useful "extra" information that is available in a good monolingual dictionary.

The right amount of practice

In our experience, the most successful lessons consist of a manageable amount of new input, and then a lot of meaningful practice. For this reason, we've tried to provide maximum practice activities in *American Inside Out Evolution*, both in the Student's Book and in the other supporting components. But there is never enough time in the lessons alone. Always assign homework, even if it's just reading a chapter from a reader, and make homework feedback or correction an integral part of the lesson.

The top 10 activities for Upper Intermediate Students

These tried and trusted activities can be used as lead-ins, warmers, fillers, pair-forming activities, or for reviewing and recycling. Most of them require very little or no preparation and can be adapted to cover a wide variety of different language points. The emphasis is on vocabulary review, as we all know that it's only through repeated, systematic exposure to new words and expressions that students are likely to transform "input" into "intake." You may be familiar with some of the ideas, and others may be new. In any event, we hope they provide a useful extension to your teaching repertoire. They certainly get used and re-used in our own classrooms!

It's always useful to have a stock of small white cards and access to a collection of pictures. Magazine pictures are ideal and can be filed in alphabetical order according to topics.

1 Board bingo

Aim

This activity is good for reviewing any type of vocabulary.

Preparation

Write down twelve to fifteen words you want to review on the board. They could be words from the last lesson, words from the unit you've just finished, or a random selection of words covering the whole term.

Procedure

- Ask the students to choose five of the words and write them down. When they've done that, tell the students that you're going to read out dictionary definitions of the words in random order and that they should cross out their words if they think they hear the definition. When they've crossed out all five words, they shout *Bingo!* Make sure you keep a record of the word definitions you call out so that you can check the students' answers.
- If you teach a monolingual class, you could read out a translation of each word rather than an English definition. Alternatively, you could turn it into a pronunciation exercise by working on the recognition of phonetic script. Hold up cards with phonetic transcriptions of the words in random order. Students cross out their words if they think they've seen the corresponding phonetic transcription.

2 My criteria

Aim

This activity can be used to review almost any vocabulary.

Preparation

Choose up to ten words that you want to review. You might want to start with recognizable lexical sets and then move on to groups of random words.

Procedure

- Write the words on the board in no particular order. Put the students in pairs or small groups. The activity consists of writing out the words in a specific order according to a particular criterion of the students' choosing. Each pair or group keeps their criterion secret. They then give their list to another pair or group who have to work out what they think the criterion is.

  For example, let's say you want to review words for items you find in the home from Unit 12. You write eight items on the board: e.g. *coat hooks, a doormat, a rug, shutters, a knocker, a dustpan, an ironing board, blinds*. The students then rearrange the list according to the criterion that they've thought of. The criterion can be anything from "alphabetical order": i.e.
  1 *blinds*, 2 *coat hooks*, 3 *a doormat*, etc., to "useful": i.e., 1 *coat hooks*, 2 *a dustpan*, 3 *an ironing board*, etc.

- Sometimes the criterion clearly suggests only one possible order (i.e. "alphabetical order"). If the criterion is "useful," then the order of items might be open to debate. This is fine and can lead to some interesting discussion. To get the students used to this activity, in the first instance, you might want to give them different criteria to choose from. Here are some more possible criteria for household items: *expensive, big/small, easy to find in stores, things I use or have*. Alternatively, you might want to give them just one criterion - one where the order is not obvious - and see if each group comes up with the same order.

- Here are some more ideas for lexical sets and criteria:

  1 Phrasal verbs (Unit 4 page 47)

  Possible criteria: *frequent, useful, largest number of meanings, most idiomatic*

  2 Facial features (Unit 8 page 82)

  Possible criteria: *attractive, distinctive, feminine/masculine, likely to age*

  3 Professions (Unit 9 page 99)

  Possible criteria: *creative, well-paid, useful to society, easy, fun*

3 Category dictation

Aim

This activity can be adapted to review almost any vocabulary. It can also be used to review certain pronunciation and grammar points.

Preparation

Choose the language you want to review and devise a way of categorizing it into two or more categories.

Procedure

- Write the category headings on the board and ask the students to copy them onto a piece of paper. Two simple categories is usually best. More than four can get complicated. Then dictate the words (ten to twelve maximum) slowly and clearly, and ask the students to write them down in the correct category.

  For example, you might want to review verb-noun collocations from Vocabulary Exercise 2 on page 29. So, write the following on the board and ask the students to copy it.

have	make	take

- Then dictate some noun collocates, e.g. *a loss, a think, action, sense, a laugh*, etc. The students write the words in the correct category. When you've dictated ten or twelve words, ask students to compare their lists. When they've done this, ask them to call out their answers and write them on the board in the correct category, so that they can check the spelling. Alternatively, you could ask the students to take turns writing the answers on the board. This simple activity can be used to review more or less any verb-noun collocation involving "de-lexical" verbs such as *do, put, give, get*, etc.

- Here are some more ideas for categories:

  1 Review verb patterns (Unit 2 page 21)
  Suggested categories: *verb + gerund* or *verb + to-infinitive*; *verb + object* or *verb + no object*

  2 Review word formation. How to make adjectives negative (Unit 7 page 77)
  Suggested categories: *"dis"* or *"in"* or *"un."* Read aloud the positive forms of the adjective, i.e. *loyal, appropriate, willing*, etc.

  3 Review ways of saying "hello" and "goodbye" (Unit 12 page 132)
  Suggested categories: *hello* or *goodbye*. Read out different useful phrases, i.e. *Drive safely, Long time no see, Keep in touch*, etc.

4 Whose dialogue?

Aim

To imagine what people in pictures are saying to one another and to write a short dialogue.

Preparation

You will need a selection of eight to ten magazine pictures. Each picture should show two people who could be talking to one another. Try to get pictures of as widely varying contexts as possible.

Procedure

- Divide the students into pairs or small groups. Display the pictures on the board, on the wall, or on the floor where everybody can see them. Ask each pair or group to secretly choose a picture, but without pointing or touching it. The students then write a short dialogue between the people in the picture they've chosen. When they've finished, ask them to act out their dialogue to the other members of the class without indicating which picture it's based on. The other students guess which picture the dialogue goes with.
- This activity is particularly suited to reviewing some of the functional language from the *Language for Life* sections in the Student's Book. You could write six or more useful phrases on the board and tell the students that their dialogues must include at least one (or two, or three) of them. The useful phrases could be part of a recognizable set (i.e. Unit 4 page 48: *Oh, you poor thing*; *Oh yes, I know what you mean*; *Oh well, it serves you right then?*, etc.). Alternatively, they could just be random (i.e. *It can't be her*; *Make yourself at home*; *I'm not made of money*, etc.).
- Alternatively, you could choose any ten to twelve words you want to review and write them on the board. Then tell the students that they must include at least three (or four, or five) of the words in their dialogues.

5 Random letters

Aim

This activity is good for reviewing any type of vocabulary.

Preparation

None

Procedure

- Ask the students to call out any seven letters from the alphabet. (It doesn't have to be seven letters: anything between seven and twelve is fine.) Write the letters scattered on the board.

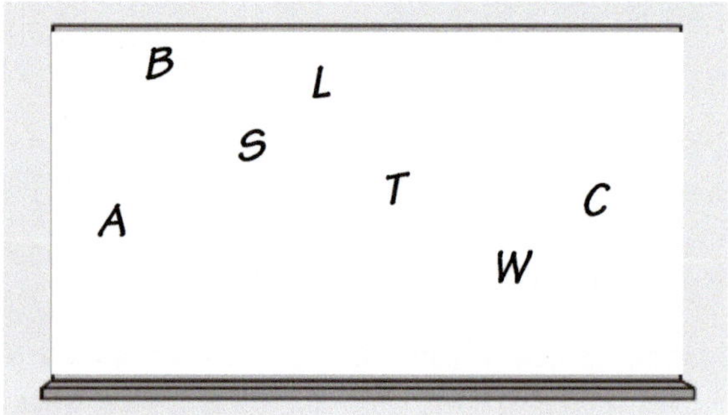

- Then ask the students in pairs to think of a word beginning with each letter on the board. The most obvious criteria is to review words from a specific lexical set that you have taught recently. Alternatively, you could simply ask them for words they've noted down in lessons over the past two weeks.
- Another possibility would be to find the most interesting words they can from the Student's Book unit that you've just finished. If the lexical set you want them to review is particularly rich, you could ask the students to think of as many words for each letter as they can in, say, three minutes: make it into a contest to find the most words.
- There are lots of possible variations using different criteria for words from the letters on the board. Here are a few:
  1. Use the same criteria as above, but ask the students to think of words ending with the letter on the board.
  2. Ask the students to write only nouns, or adjectives, or irregular verbs, or some other part of speech.
  3. Ask the students to write only words with three syllables or words with the same vowel sounds.
  4. Ask students to write only words that start with the same letter in their own language or only words that start with a different letter.

6 Five favorites

Aim

This activity is good for reviewing any words learned recently.

Preparation

None

Procedure

- Students look back through their lesson notes for the last two weeks and select from the words they've recorded five words that they think are particularly useful. They compare their list with a partner, and together they produce a common list of five words from the combined list of ten. To do this they'll have to argue for and against words on the combined list until they are both satisfied that they have the most useful five.

- If you wanted to continue the activity, you could then have each pair join up with another pair as a group of four and repeat the procedure. Depending on the size of your class, you might continue until you have established a list of "five favorites" for the whole class.
- The value of this activity lies in the students looking back through their notes, choosing the words, and then arguing for them to be part of the combined list. The whole procedure gives them valuable repeat exposure to words recently learned.
- A possible extension activity after each pair has formed their common list of five words is to collect the lists and redistribute them so that each pair has a different list. The pairs then write a dialogue or short story incorporating the five words they have on the list they've just received. You could then ask them to read aloud their dialogues or stories and the other students guess what the five listed words were.

7 Crosswords

Aim

This activity is good for reviewing lexical sets and can help with spelling.

Preparation

Choose a lexical set you want to review. For example: *nouns that go with "make"* (or *"take"* or *"have"*) (Unit 3); *words on the topic of weddings* (Unit 5); *food* (Unit 6); *positive adjectives to describe personality* (Unit 8), etc.

Procedure

- Students work in pairs. They'll need a piece of paper, preferably graph paper with squares.
- Choose a topic, e.g., *food*.
- Student A writes "across" words, and Student B writes "down" words.
- It's a good idea to provide the first word across, and make sure that it's a long one (e.g. *vegetables*). Student B then adds another food word down the paper from top to bottom. This word must intersect with the food word written across the page.
- Student A then writes another food word across that intersects with the word Student B has written down. Students continue taking turns writing their words.

- Students build up a crossword until they can't think of any more food words. (You could make it into a game by saying that the last person to write a food word is the winner.) Note that students must leave one square between each word – this is why it's better and clearer to use graph paper.
- At this level, with a topic as big as *food*, it might be advisable to narrow the category: i.e. *fruit and vegetables* or *meat and fish* or *food you put in the refrigerator* or ...

8 Which one doesn't belong?

Aim

This activity can be used to review almost any language.

Preparation

Think of the vocabulary, pronunciation, or grammar point you want to review.

Procedure

- Write five words on the board and ask students which one doesn't belong. The students then explain why. This is usually related to the meaning of the word.

milk	cheese	cream	butter	sugar

- Here *sugar* doesn't belong because the other words are all dairy products.
- Note that it doesn't matter if the students can't explain in perfect English why *sugar* doesn't belong. The important thing is that they're looking at and thinking about the words you want them to review.
- You can use this format to practice and review all kinds of things. Here are some examples:

  1 For meaning:
  sister / nephew / daughter / wife / mother
  nephew doesn't belong because it's a man. The other words describe women.

2 For spelling:
pen / book / bag / phone / story
story doesn't belong because you spell the plural *ies*. With the other words you just add *s*.

3 For pronunciation: sounds
A / I / H / J / K
I doesn't belong because the vowel sound is different.

4 For pronunciation: stress
hospital / banana / potato / Italian / computer
hospital doesn't belong because the stress is on the first syllable. The other words have the stress on the second syllable.

5 For collocation: *do* or *make*
your homework / the laundry / a job / an appointment / the grocery shopping
an appointment doesn't belong because you use *make*. For the others you use *do*.

6 For grammar:
agree / promise / want / can't stand / offer
can't stand doesn't belong because it is followed by a gerund – the other words are followed by a *to*-infinitive.

- You should tell the students what the criteria is, e.g. "Think about meaning" or "Think about the sounds." To make the activity a little more challenging, instead of writing the words on the board, you can dictate them. As a follow-up, ask the students to write their own examples.

9 Making sentences

Aim

This activity is good for reviewing any type of vocabulary. It works best if the words are a fairly random selection and not part of a tight lexical set.

Preparation

Choose twelve words you want to review and write them in a circle (like a clockface) on the board.

Procedure

- Students work in pairs. They choose two or more of the words and try to make a sentence with them.

  Example sentences:

  My brother is doing [yoga] *in the* [park].

  The [snowboarder] *eats* [organic vegetables] *on* [Friday].

  I [saw] *an* [ambitious] [puppy] *in the* [canal] *with a* [blue] [neck].

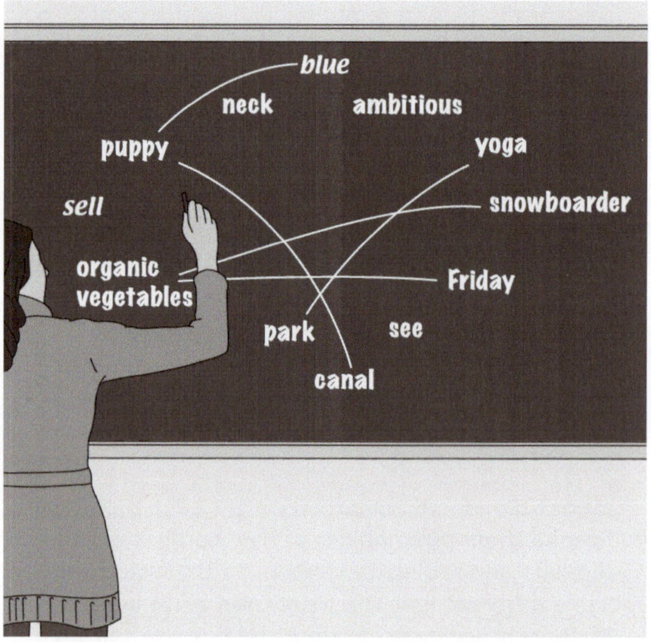

- The students then read out their sentences and you connect the words they have used on the board. You can correct the grammar as necessary or you can make it more difficult for the students by only accepting grammatically correct sentences. (You could make it into a game by saying that the pair who form the sentence including the highest number of words on the board is the winner.) It doesn't matter how bizarre the sentences are; the important thing is that students spend time looking at and remembering the vocabulary.

10 Spell check

Aim

To review any vocabulary and focus particularly on spelling.

Preparation

Choose the words you want to review. They can be lexical sets or words at random. Eight to ten words is best.

Procedure

There are various different ways you can approach this, but the following four ways seem to work best:

1 The missing letter
Students work in pairs. Write the words on the board with a letter missing from each one, e.g. *samon*, *egplant*, *rasberry*, etc. The students have to decide which is the missing letter in each case and rewrite the word correctly then give a definition.

2 The extra letter
Students work in pairs. Write the words with an extra letter in each one, e.g. *unfaithfull*, *sosciable*, *tollerant*, etc. The students have to decide which is

the extra letter in each case and rewrite the word correctly then give a definition.

3 The wrong letter
Students work in pairs. Write the words with a wrong letter in each one, e.g. *nefhew*, *cousen*, *neece*, etc. The students have to decide which is the wrong letter in each case and rewrite the word correctly then give a definition.

4 Anagrams
Students work in pairs. Write the words as anagrams. The students have to unscramble the anagram and rewrite the word correctly. This is the most challenging version of "Spell check," so it's best to give the students a clue, e.g.: "These are all ways of describing hair," for *lurcy*, *ssemy*, *cidenger*, etc. (*curly*, *messy*, *receding*). They then have to give a definition.

Anecdote tasks

American Inside Out Evolution Upper Intermediate includes a number of extended speaking tasks, where students tackle a longer piece of discourse. We've called these "anecdotes." They are based on personal issues, for instance, memories, stories, people you know. When you learn a musical instrument, you can't spend all your time playing scales and exercises: you also need to learn whole pieces in order to see how music is organized. Anecdotes give students a chance to get to grips with how discourse is organized. We have found the following strategies helpful in getting our students to tell their anecdotes.

1 Choose global topics that everybody can relate to

One of the main objectives of an anecdote is to encourage students to experiment with and hopefully grow more competent at using language at the more demanding end of their range. It therefore seems only fair to ask them to talk about subjects they know something about. With familiar subject matter, students can concentrate on how they're speaking as well as what they're speaking about. The anecdote topics in *American Inside Out Evolution Upper Intermediate* have been carefully selected to appeal to the widest range of students, while at the same time fitting in to the context of the unit.

Unit 1	A person who made a big impression on you
Unit 2	Somebody's home you have stayed in
Unit 3	Your most treasured possession
Unit 4	A challenge you have faced
Unit 5	A wedding you've been to
Unit 6	Your favorite restaurant
Unit 7	A childhood family vacation
Unit 8	The most positive (or negative) person you know
Unit 9	Your favorite historic place
Unit 10	A movie you have seen
Unit 11	Your favorite (or least favorite) teacher at school
Unit 12	Your favorite room

As soon as you have gotten to know your students well enough, you'll be able to choose other anecdote topics suited to their particular interests and experiences.

2 Allow sufficient preparation time

Students need time to organize their thoughts and think about the language they'll need. The anecdotes are set up through evocative questions. Students read or listen to a planned series of questions and choose what specifically they'll talk about; shyer students can avoid subjects they feel are too personal. This student preparation is a key stage and should not be rushed. Research by Peter Skehan and Pauline Foster, among others, has shown that learners who plan for tasks attempt more ambitious and complex language, hesitate less, and make fewer basic errors.

The simplest way to prepare students for an anecdote is to ask them to read the list of questions in the book and decide which they want to talk about. This could be done during class time or as homework preparation for the following lesson. Ask them to think about the language they'll need. Encourage them to use dictionaries and make notes – but not to write out what they'll actually say. Finally, put them into pairs to exchange anecdotes.

A variation is to ask the students to read the questions in the book while, at the same time, listening to you read them aloud. Then ask them to prepare in detail for the task, as above.

Alternatively, ask the students to close their books – and then to close their eyes. Ask them to listen to the questions as you read them aloud and think about what they evoke. Some classes will find this a more involving process. It also allows you to adapt the questions to your class: adding new ones or leaving out any you think inappropriate. After the reading, give them enough time to finalize their preparation before starting the speaking task.

3 Monitor students and give feedback

It's important for students to feel that their efforts are being monitored by the teacher. Realistically, it's probably only possible for a teacher to monitor and give feedback to one or two pairs of students during each anecdote activity. It's therefore vital that the teacher adopts a strict rotation system, and makes sure that everyone in the class is monitored over the course of a term. Constructive feedback helps students improve their delivery.

4 Provide a "model anecdote"

It's always useful for the students to hear a model anecdote at some stage during the anecdote task cycle. The most obvious model is you, the teacher. Students will enjoy hearing real stories from your own life experience. Alternatively, you might ask a teaching colleague or friend to talk to the students, or record one of them telling an anecdote and play it back in class.

5 Repeat the same anecdote with a new partner at regular intervals

Consider going back to anecdotes and repeating them in later classes. Let the students know that you're going to do this. This will reassure them that you're doing it on purpose, but more importantly, it will mean that they'll be more motivated to dedicate some time and thought to preparation. When you repeat the task, mix up the class so that each student works with a new partner, i.e. one who has not previously heard the anecdote.

In our experience, most students are happy to listen to their partner's anecdotes. If, however, any of your students are reluctant listeners, you might think about giving them some kind of "listening task." Here are three examples:

- Ask the listener to check the prompt questions that the "anecdote teller" answers while telling the anecdote.
- Ask the listener to time the "anecdote teller." In *Teaching Collocations* (page 91), Michael Lewis suggests reducing the time allowed to deliver the anecdote each time it's repeated: for example, in the first instance the student has five minutes; for the second telling they have four minutes; and the third three minutes.
- Ask the listener to take brief notes about the anecdote and use them to write a summary for homework. Then give the summary to the "anecdote teller" to check.

The pedagogic value of getting students to retell anecdotes – to repeat a "big chunk" of spoken discourse – cannot be overstated. Repeating complex tasks reflects real interactions. We all have our set of jokes and stories, and we tend to refine and improve them as we retell them. Many students will appreciate the opportunity to do the same thing in their second language. Research by Martin Bygate, among others, has shown that given this opportunity, students become more adventurous and at the same time more precise in the language they use.

You can also use the anecdotes to test oral proficiency and thereby add a speaking component to accompany the tests in the Teacher's Edition.

Key concepts

The following excerpts are from *An A-Z of ELT* by Scott Thornbury (Macmillan Books for Teachers, 2006). They give clear authoritative definitions and explanations of some of the most important concepts in this textbook.

Contents

Note: SLA = Second Language Acquisition

Scott Thornbury

classroom interaction
methodology

Classroom interaction is the general term for what goes on between the people in the classroom, particularly when it involves language. In traditional classrooms, most interaction is initiated by the teacher, and learners either respond individually, or in unison. Teacher-centered interaction of this kind is associated with transmissive teaching, such as a lecture or presentation, where the teacher transmits the content of the lesson to the learners.

In order to increase the amount of student involvement and interaction, teacher-learner interaction is often combined with **pairwork** and **groupwork**, where learners interact among themselves in pairs or small groups. Other kinds of interaction include mingling or milling. Pairwork and groupwork are associated with a more **learner-centered** approach. Rather than passively receiving the lesson content, the learners are actively engaged in using language and discovering things for themselves. The value of pairwork and groupwork has been reinforced by the belief that **interaction** facilitates language learning. Some would go as far as to say that it is all that is required.

The potential for classroom interaction is obviously constrained by such factors as the number of students, the size of the room, the furniture, and the purpose or type of activity. Not all activities lend themselves to pairwork or groupwork. Some activities, such as reading, are best done as individual work. On the other hand, listening activities (such as listening to an audio recording, or to the teacher) favor a whole class format, as do grammar presentations. The whole class is also an appropriate form of organization when reviewing the results of an activity, as, for example, when spokespersons from each group are reporting on the results of a discussion or survey.

The success of any classroom interaction will also depend on the extent to which the learners know what they are meant to be doing and why, which in turn depends on how clearly and efficiently the interaction has been set up. Pair- and groupwork can be a complete waste of time if learners are neither properly prepared for it, nor sure of its purpose or outcome.

Finally, the success of pair- and groupwork will depend on the kind of group **dynamics** that have been established. Do the students know one another? Are they happy working together? Do they mind working without constant teacher supervision? Establishing a productive classroom dynamic may involve making decisions as to who works with whom. It may also mean deliberately staging the introduction of different kinds of interactions, starting off with the more controlled, teacher-led interactions before, over time, allowing learners to work in pairs and finally in groups.

collocation
vocabulary

If two words *collocate*, they frequently occur together. The relation between the words may be grammatical, as when certain verbs collocate with particular prepositions, such as *depend on*, *account for*, *abstain from*, or when a verb, like *make*, *take*, or *do*, collocates with a noun, as in *make an arrangement*, *take advantage*, *do the shopping*. The collocation may also be lexical, as when two **content words** regularly co-occur, as in a *broad hint*, a *narrow escape* (but not *a *wide hint* or *a *tight escape*). The strength of the collocation can vary: *a broad street* or a *narrow path* are weak collocations, since both elements can co-occur with lots of other words: a *broad river*, a *busy street*, etc. *Broad hint* and *narrow escape* are stronger. Stronger still are combinations where one element rarely occurs without the other, as in *moot point*, *slim pickings*, and *scot free*. Strongest of all are those where both elements never or rarely occur without the other, such as *dire straits* and *spick and span*. These have acquired the frozen status of *fixed expressions*.

Unsurprisingly, learners lack intuitions as to which words go with which, and this accounts for many errors, such as *You can <u>completely</u> enjoy it* (instead of *thoroughly*), *On Saturday we <u>made</u> shopping* (instead of *went*), and *We went the <u>incorrect</u> way* (for *wrong*). Using texts to highlight particular collocations, and teaching new words in association with their most frequent collocations are two ways of approaching the problem. Nowadays learners' dictionaries also include useful collocational information.

communicative activity
methodology

A communicative activity is one in which real communication occurs. Communicative activities belong to that generation of classroom **activities** that emerged in response to the need for a more **communicative approach** in the teaching of second languages. (In their more evolved form as **tasks**, communicative activities are central to **task-based learning**). They attempt to import into a practice activity the key features of "real-life" communication. These are:

- *purposefulness*: speakers are motivated by a communicative goal (such as getting information, making a request, giving instructions) and not simply by the need to display the correct use of language for its own sake
- *reciprocity*: to achieve a purpose, speakers need to interact, and there is as much need to listen as to speak
- *negotiation*: following from the above, they may need to check and **repair** the communication in order to be understood by each other
- *unpredictability*: neither the process, nor the outcome, nor the language used in the exchange, is entirely predictable
- *heterogeneity*: participants can use any communicative means at their disposal; in other words, they are not restricted to the use of a pre-specified grammar item.

And, in the case of spoken language in particular:

- *synchronicity*: the exchange takes place in real time.

The best known communicative activity is the *information gap* activity. Here, the information necessary to complete the task is either in the possession of just one of the participants, or distributed among them.

In order to achieve the goal of the task, therefore, the learners have to share the information that they have. For example, in a *describe-and-draw* activity, one student has a picture which is hidden from his or her partner. The task is for that student to describe the picture so that the partner can accurately draw it. In a *find-the-difference* task, both students of a pair have pictures (or texts) that are the same apart from some minor details. The goal is to identify these differences. In a *jigsaw activity*, each member of a group has different information. One might have a bus timetable, another a map, and another a list of hotels. They have to share this information in order to plan a weekend break together.

Information gap activities have been criticized on the grounds that they lack **authenticity**. Nor are information gap activities always as productive as might be wished: unsupervised, learners may resort to **communication strategies** in order to simplify the task. A more exploitable information gap, arguably, is the one that exists between the learners themselves, i.e., what they don't know—but might like to know—about one another (➔**personalization**).

context

linguistics

The context of a language item is its adjacent language items. In the absence of context, it is often impossible to assign exact meaning to an item. A sentence like *Ben takes the bus to work*, for example, could have past, present, or future reference, depending on the context:

> I know this guy called Ben. One day Ben *takes the bus to work*, and just as ...
>
> Most days Ben *takes the bus to work*, but sometimes he rides his bike ...
>
> If Ben *takes the bus to work* tomorrow, he'll be late, because there's a strike ...

Likewise, a sentence like *You use it like this* is meaningless in the absence of a context. By the same token, a word or sentence in one context can have a very different meaning in another. The sign *NO BICYCLES* in a public park means something different to *NO BICYCLES* outside a bicycle rental shop. It is sometimes necessary to distinguish between different kinds of context. On the one hand, there is the context of the accompanying text, sometimes called the *co-text*. The co-text of this sentence, for example, includes the sentences that precede and follow it, as well as the paragraph of which it forms a part. It is the co-text that offers clues as to the meaning of unfamiliar vocabulary in a text.

The situational context (also context of situation, context of use), on the other hand, is the physical and temporal setting in which an instance of language use occurs. The typical context for the spoken question *Are you being served?* is in a shop, for example. Both co-text and context influence the production and interpretation of language. **Discourse analysis** studies the relationship between language and co-text, including the way that sentences or utterances are connected. **Pragmatics** studies the relationship between language and its contexts of use, including the way meaning can be inferred by reference to context factors. Various theories have been proposed in order to account for the ways that language choices are determined by contextual factors. One of the best known of these is Michael Halliday's **systemic functional linguistics**. Halliday distinguishes three variables in any context that systematically impact on language choices and which, together, determine a text's **register**:

- the field: what the language is being used to talk about, and for what purposes
- the tenor: the participants in the language event, and their relationship
- the mode: how language is being used in the exchange, e.g. is it written or spoken?

For example, this short text shows the influence of all three factors:

> Do u fancy film either 2nite or 2moro? Call me.

The field is "making arrangements about leisure activities", hence the use of words like *film*, *2nite* (*tonight*), *2moro* (*tomorrow*). The tenor is one of familiarity and equality (accounting for the informal fancy and the imperative: *call me*); and the mode is that of a written text message, which explains its brevity, its use of abbreviated forms (*u*, *2nite*) and the absence of salutations. A change in any of these contextual factors is likely to have a significant effect on the text.

Language learners, it is argued, need to know how these contextual factors correlate with language choices in order to produce language that is appropriate to the context. One way of doing this is to ask them to make changes to a text (such as the text message above) that take into account adjustments to the field, tenor, or mode.

drill

methodology

A drill is repetitive oral practice of a language item, whether a sound, a word, a phrase, or a sentence structure. Drills that are targeted at sentence structures are sometimes called *pattern practice drills*. Drills follow a prompt-response sequence, where the prompt usually comes from the teacher, and the students respond, either in chorus (*a choral drill*) or individually. An *imitation drill* simply involves repeating the prompt, as in:

> **Teacher:** They have been watching TV.
> **Student:** They have been watching TV.

A *substitution drill* requires the students to substitute one element of the pattern with the prompt, making any necessary adjustments:

> **Teacher:** They have been watching TV.
> **Student:** They have been watching TV.
> **Teacher:** She
> **Student:** She has been watching TV.
> **Teacher:** I
> **Student:** I have been watching TV.
> etc.

A *variable substitution drill* is the same, but the prompts are not restricted to one element of the pattern:

Teacher:	They have been watching TV.
Student:	They have been watching TV.
Teacher:	She
Student:	She has been watching TV.
Teacher:	radio
Student:	She has been listening to the radio.
Teacher:	We
Student:	We have been listening to the radio.

etc.

Drills were a defining feature of the **audiolingual** method, and were designed to reinforce good language "habits." The invention of language laboratories allowed sustained drilling without the need for a teacher to supply the prompts. With the demise of audiolingualism, drilling fell from favor. However, many teachers—even those who subscribe to a **communicative approach**—feel the need for some form of repetition practice of the kind that drills provide. This may be for the purpose of developing **accuracy**, or as a form of **fluency** training, i.e., in order to develop **automaticity.**

Hence, communicative drills were developed. A communicative drill is still essentially repetitive, and focuses on a particular structure or pattern but it has an *information gap* element built in. Learners can perform the drill in pairs, or as a *milling activity* (**classroom interaction**) and they are required to attend to what they hear as much as what they say. The milling activity popularly known as *Find someone who ...* is one such activity. Students are set the task of finding other students in the class who, for example, can ride a horse, can speak French, can play the guitar, etc. They mill around, asking questions of the type *Can you ...?* until they have asked all the other students their questions, and then they report their findings.

dynamics: group, classroom
methodology

Dynamics are the actions and interactions, both conscious and unconscious, that take place between members of a group, whether the whole class or subgroups. Group dynamics are instrumental in forging a productive and motivating classroom environment. They are determined by such factors as: the composition of the group (including the age, sex, and relative status of the members, as well as their different attitudes, beliefs, learning styles, and abilities); the patterns of relationships between members of the group, including how well they know each other, and the roles they each assume, such as group leader, spokesperson, etc; physical factors such as the size of the group and the way it is seated; and the tasks that the group are set, e.g.: Does the task require everyone to contribute? Does it encourage co-operation or competition? Are the goals of the task clear to the group members?

Ways that the teacher can promote a positive group (and class) dynamic include:

- ensuring all class or group members can see and hear one another, and that they know (and use) each other's names
- keeping groups from getting too big—three to six members is optimal
- setting—or negotiating—clear rules for groupwork, such as using only the target language, giving everyone a turn to speak, allowing individuals to "pass" if they don't want to say anything too personal
- using "ice-breaking" activities to encourage interaction, laughter, and relaxation
- ensuring that group tasks are purposeful, interactive, and collaborative
- personalizing tasks, i.e., setting tasks that involve the sharing of personal experiences and opinions
- defining the roles and responsibilities within the group, and varying these regularly, e.g. by appointing a different spokesperson each time
- monitoring groupwork in progress, and being alert to any possible conflicts or tensions between members, and reconstituting groups, if necessary
- discussing the importance of groupwork with learners, and getting feedback on group processes

fluency
SLA

If someone is said to be fluent in a language, or to speak a language fluently, it is generally understood that they are able to speak the language idiomatically and accurately, without undue pausing, without an intrusive accent, and in a manner appropriate to the context. In fact, research into listeners' perceptions of fluency suggests that fluency is primarily the ability to produce and maintain speech in *real time*.

To do this, fluent speakers are capable of:

- appropriate pausing, i.e.,:
  - their pauses may be long but are not frequent
  - their pauses are usually filled, e.g. with **pause fillers** like *erm, you know, sort of*
  - their pauses occur at meaningful transition points, e.g. at the intersections of clauses or phrases, rather than midway in a phrase
- long runs, i.e., there are many syllables and words between pauses

All of the above factors depend on the speaker having a well-developed grammar, an extensive vocabulary, and, crucially, a store of memorized chunks. Being able to draw on this store of chunks means not having to depend on grammar to construct each utterance from scratch. This allows the speaker to devote **attention** to other aspects of the interaction, such as planning ahead. Speakers also use a number of "tricks" or *production strategies* to convey the illusion of fluency. One such strategy is disguising pauses by filling them, or by repeating a word or phrase.

Some proponents of the **communicative approach** redefined fluency so as to distinguish it from **accuracy**. Fluency came to mean "communicative effectiveness", regardless of formal accuracy or speed of delivery. Activities that are communicative, such as information-gap activities, are said to be *fluency-focused*. This is the case even for activities that produce short, halting utterances. Separating accuracy and fluency, and defining the latter as *communicative* language use, is misleading, though. There are many speech events whose communicativeness depends on their accuracy. Air traffic control talk is just one. Moreover, many learners aspire to being more than merely communicative.

Classroom activities that target fluency need to prepare the learner for real-time speech production. Learning and memorizing lexical chunks, including useful conversational gambits, is one approach. **Drills** may help here, as will some types of **communicative activity** that involve repetition. Research has also shown that fluency improves the more times a **task** is repeated. Fluency may also benefit from activities that manage to distract learners' attention away from formal accuracy so that they are not tempted to slow down. (This has been called "parking their attention"). Some interactive and competitive language **games** have this effect. **Drama** activities, such as roleplays, recreate conditions of real-time language use, and are therefore good for developing fluency. Finally, learners can achieve greater fluency from learning a repertoire of **communication strategies**, i.e., techniques for getting around potential problems caused by a lack of the relevant words or structures.

focus on form
SLA

When learners focus on form, they direct conscious attention to some formal feature of the language **input**. The feature may be the fact that the past of *has* is *had*, or that *enjoy* is followed by verb forms ending in *-ing*, or that adjectives do not have plural forms in English. The learners' attention may be self-directed, or it may be directed by the teacher or by another learner. Either way, it has been argued that a focus on form is a necessary condition for language learning. Simply focusing on the **meaning** of the input is not enough. Focusing on form is, of course, not a new idea: most teaching methods devote a great deal of time to the forms of the language, e.g. when new grammar items are presented. But the term *focus on form* captures the fact that this focus can, theoretically, occur at any stage in classroom instruction. Thus, **correction**, especially in the form of negative **feedback**, is a kind of focus on form. In fact, some researchers argue that the most effective form focus is that which arises incidentally, in the context of communication, as when the teacher quickly elicits a correction during a classroom discussion. This incidental approach contrasts with the more traditional and deliberate approach, where teaching is based on a **syllabus** of graded structures (or *forms*), and these are pre-taught in advance of activities designed to practice them. This traditional approach is called—by some researchers—a *focus on forms*.

function
linguistics

The function of a language item is its communicative purpose. Language is more than simply forms and their associated meanings (i.e., **usage**). It is also the communicative **uses** to which these forms and meanings are put. These two sentences, for example, share the same forms, but function quite differently:

[in an email] Thank you for sending me the disk.
[a notice in a taxi] Thank you for not smoking.

The function of the first is expressing thanks, while the second is more like a prohibition. Likewise, the same function can be expressed by different forms:

[a notice in a taxi] Thank you for not smoking.
[a sign in a classroom] No smoking.

Thus, there is no one-to-one match between form and function. Assigning a function to a text or an utterance usually requires knowledge of the **context** in which the text is used. The study of how context and function are interrelated is called **pragmatics**.

Communicative functions can be categorized very broadly and also at increasing levels of detail. The "big" functions, or macrofunctions, describe the way language is used in very general terms. These include the use of language for *expressive* purposes (e.g. poetry), for *regulatory* purposes (e.g. for getting people to do things), for *interpersonal* purposes (e.g. for socializing), and for *representational* purposes (e.g. to inform). More useful, from the point of view of designing language syllabuses, are microfunctions.

These are usually expressed as **speech acts**, such as *agreeing* and *disagreeing*, *reporting*, *warning*, *apologizing*, *thanking*, *greeting*, etc. Such categories form the basis of **functional syllabuses**, a development associated with the **communicative approach**. They often appear as one strand of a coursebook **syllabus**. Functions differ from notions in that the latter describe areas of meaning—such as *ability*, *duration*, *quantity*, *frequency*, etc.—rather than the uses to which these meanings are put.

One way to teach functions is to adopt a "phrasebook" approach, and teach useful ways of expressing common functions (what are called *functional exponents*), such as *Would you like ...?* (*inviting*) and *Could you ..., please?* (*requesting*). More memorable, though, is to teach these expressions in the contexts of **dialogues**, so that the functional exponents are associated not only with common situations in which they are used, but with related functions (such as *accepting* and *refusing*). The term *function*, in contrast to **form**, is also used in linguistics, specifically with regard to the functions of the different elements of a **clause** (such as subject and object).

grammar teaching

methodology

Like the word **grammar** itself, the topic of grammar teaching is a controversial one, and teachers often take opposing views. Historically, language teaching methods have positioned themselves along a scale from "zero grammar" to "total grammar", according to their approach to grammar teaching. Proponents of *natural methods*, who model their approach to teaching second languages on the way that first languages are acquired, reject any explicit teaching of grammar at all. (They may, however, teach according to a grammar **syllabus**, even if no mention of grammar as such is made in the classroom). This implicit approach is common both to the direct **method** and to **audiolingualism**. Through exposure to demonstrations, situations or examples, learners are expected to pick up the rules of grammar by **inductive learning**. At the other end of the spectrum, there are approaches, such as **grammar-translation**, that adopt an explicit and **deductive learning** approach. From the outset, learners are presented with rules which they study and then practice. Occupying a midway point between zero grammar and total grammar is the approach called **consciousness-raising**. Instead of being given rules, learners are presented with language data which challenge them to re-think (and *restructure*) their existing mental grammar. This data might take the form of **input** that has been manipulated in some way. For example, pairs of sentences, such as the following, have to be matched to pictures, forcing learners to discriminate between them, and, in theory, **notice** the difference (**➔noticing**):

The Queen drove to the airport.
The Queen was driven to the airport.

(This is sometimes called a *grammar interpretation task* or *structured input*.) In order to do the task, learners have to process not just the individual words, but also their grammatical form. That is why this approach to teaching grammar is sometimes called *processing instruction*. There are other researchers who argue that it is by means of manipulating the learner's output, e.g. through productive practice, that mental restructuring is best effected.

The **communicative approach** accommodates different approaches to grammar teaching. Proponents of **task-based learning**, for example, argue that, if the learner is engaged in solving problems using language, then the mental grammar will develop of its own accord. However, advocates of the weaker version of the communicative approach (and the version that is most widespread) justify a role for the pre-teaching of grammar in advance of production. This view finds support in **cognitive learning theory**, which suggests that conscious attention to grammatical form (called **focus on form**) speeds up language learning, and is a necessary corrective against premature **fossilization**. There is some debate, though, as to whether this form focus should be planned or incidental. Incidental grammar teaching occurs when the teacher deals with grammar issues as and when they come up, e.g. in the form of **correction**, or task **feedback**.

In this way (it is argued) grammar teaching follows the learner's own "syllabus." Such an approach attempts to address one of the dilemmas of grammar teaching: the fact that the learner's mental grammar, and the way it develops, bears only an accidental relation to a formal grammar syllabus.

Nevertheless, the research into these different choices is still inconclusive. It may be the case that some items of grammar respond better to explicit teaching, while others are more easily picked up through exposure. There are also different learner types: some prefer learning and applying rules, while others are happier with a more "deep-end" approach (**➔learning style**). Most current teaching materials hedge their bets on these issues. They offer both deductive and inductive grammar presentations, and opportunities for incidental as well as for planned learning.

learner-centered instruction, learner-centeredness
methodology

Learner-centered instruction aims to give learners more say in areas that are traditionally considered the domain of the teacher or of the institution. Learner-centered instruction is true to the spirit of progressive education, including the movement towards providing learners with greater **autonomy**. For example, a learner-centered **curriculum** would involve learners in negotiating decisions relating to the choice of syllabus content, of materials, of activity-types, and of assessment procedures. Learner-centeredness also describes ways of organizing **classroom interaction** so that the focus is directed away from the teacher, and on to the learners, who perform tasks in pairs or small groups. This contrasts with traditional, teacher-centered, classroom interaction. Some writers believe that the dichotomy between learner-centered (= good) and teacher-centered (= bad) is a false one. It might be more useful to talk about *learning-centered instruction*, i.e., instruction which prioritizes sound learning principles. In a learning-centered approach there would be room for both learner-centered and teacher-centered interactions.

learning style
psychology

Your learning style is your preferred way of learning. This style may be influenced by biographical factors (such as how you were taught as a child) or by innately endowed factors (such as whether you have a "good ear" for different sounds). Types of learning style are often presented in the form of polarities (some of which may overlap), such as:

- analytic versus global (or holistic) thinkers, i.e., learners who tend to focus on the details, versus learners who tend to see "the big picture"
- rule-users versus data-gatherers, i.e., learners who learn and apply rules, versus those who prefer exposure to lots of examples
- reflective versus impulsive learners
- group-oriented versus solitary learners
- extrovert versus introverted learners
- verbal versus visual learners
- passive versus active learners

Attempts have been made to group these polarities and relate them to brain lateralization. So, a bias towards left-brain processing correlates with analytic, rule-forming and verbal learners, while a bias towards right-brain processing correlates with their opposite. A less binary view of learning style is that proposed by the psychologist Howard Gardner. He identified at least seven distinct intelligences that all individuals possess but to different degrees. These include the *logical/mathematical*, the *verbal/linguistic*, and the *visual/spatial*. Similarly, proponents of **neuro-linguistic programming** distinguish between different sensory orientations, including the *visual*, *aural*, and *kinesthetic* (i.e., related to movement, touch). So far, though, there is no convincing evidence that any of these dispositions correlates with specific learning behaviors. Nor has it been shown that a preference in one area predicts success in language learning. In fact, it is very difficult to separate learning style from other potentially influential factors, such as personality, intelligence, and previous learning experience. Nor is it clear to what extent learning style can be manipulated, e.g. through **learner training**. The best that can be said is that, if the learner's preferred learning style is out of synch with the type of instruction on offer, then success is much less likely than if the two are well matched. This supports the case for an **eclectic** approach, on the one hand, and the individualization of learning, on the other.

listening
methodology

Listening is the skill of understanding spoken language. It is also the name given to classroom activities that are designed to develop this skill—what are also called *listening comprehension* activities—as in "today we're going to do a listening". Listening is one of the four language **skills**, and, along with **reading**, was once thought of as being a "passive" skill. In fact, although receptive, listening is anything but passive. It is a goal oriented activity, involving not only processing of the incoming speech signals (called *bottom-up processing*) but also the use of prior knowledge, contextual clues, and expectations (*top-down processing*) in order to create meaning. Among the sub-skills of listening are:

- perceiving and discriminating individual sounds
- segmenting the stream of speech into recognizable units such as words and phrases
- using **stress** and **intonation** cues to distinguish given information from new information
- attending to **discourse markers** and using these to predict changes in the direction of the talk
- guessing the meaning of unfamiliar words
- using clues in the text (such as vocabulary) and context clues to predict what is coming

- making inferences about what is not stated
- selecting key information relevant to the purpose for listening
- integrating incoming information into the mental "picture" (or **schema**) of the speech event so far

Also, since listening is normally interactive, listeners need to be capable of:

- recognizing when speakers have finished their turns, or when it is appropriate to interrupt
- providing ongoing signals of understanding, interest, etc. (*back channeling*)
- asking for clarification, asking someone to repeat what they have just said, and repairing misunderstandings

These sub-skills exist across languages, so, in theory, learners should be able to transfer them from their first language into their second. In fact, there are a number of reasons why this does not always happen. One is that speakers of different languages process speech signals differently, depending on the phonetic characteristics of the language they are used to. This means that speakers of some languages will find it harder than others to match the spoken word to the way that the word is represented in their mind. They simply do not recognize the word. Another problem is lack of sufficient L2 knowledge, such as vocabulary or grammar. A third problem is that learners may lack the means (and the confidence) to negotiate breakdowns in understanding. Finally, many learners simply lack exposure to spoken language, and therefore have not had sufficient opportunities to experience listening. These problems can be compounded in classrooms for the following reasons:

- Listening to audio recordings deprives the learners of useful visual information, and allows the learners no opportunity to interact and repair misunderstandings.
- Classroom acoustics are seldom ideal.
- If learners do not know what they are listening for (in the absence, for example, of some pre-set listening task) they may try to process as much information as possible, rather than being selective in their listening. This can lead to listening overload, which in turn can cause inhibiting anxiety.
- Listening texts that have been specially written for classroom use are often simplified. But if this simplification means eliminating a lot of redundant language, such as speaker repetitions, pause fillers and vague language, the density of information that results may make it harder—not easier—to process.

For this reason, the use of audio recordings to develop listening skills needs to be balanced against the advantages of using other media, such as video, and face-to-face interaction with the teacher or another speaker.

Nevertheless, the use of audio recordings is an established part of classroom practice, so it is important to know how to use them to best advantage. The following approach is one that is often recommended:

- Provide some minimum contextual information, e.g. who is talking to whom about what, and why. This helps to compensate for lack of visual information, and allows learners to activate the relevant mental **schema**, which in turn helps top-down processing, including the sub-skill of prediction.
- Pre-teach key vocabulary: this helps with bottom-up processing, although too much help may mean that learners don't get sufficient practice in guessing from context.
- Set some "while-listening" questions. Initially, these should focus on the overall gist of the text. For example: true/false questions, selecting, ordering or matching pictures, ticking items on a list, following a map.
- Play a small section of the recording first, to give learners an opportunity to familiarize themselves with the different voices, and to trigger accurate expectations as to what they will hear.
- Play the recording right through, and then allow learners to consult on the answers to the pre-set task. Check these answers. If necessary, re-play the recording until satisfied that learners have "got the gist."
- Set a more demanding task, requiring more intensive listening, such as listening for detail, or inferring speakers' attitudes, intentions, etc. If the recording is a long one, it may pay to stage the intensive listening in sections. Again, allow learners to consult in pairs, before checking the task in open class.
- On the basis of the learners' success with these tasks, identify problem sections of the recording and return to these, playing and re-playing them, and perhaps eliciting a word-by-word transcription and writing this on the board.
- Distribute copies of the transcript of the recording (if available) and re-play the recording while learners read the transcript. This allows the learners to clear up any remaining problems, and also to match what they hear to what they see.

The above approach can be adapted to suit different kinds of recorded texts and different classroom needs. For higher-level learners, for example, it may be counterproductive to make listening too easy. The approach can also be adapted to the use of video, and even to live listenings, such as listening to the teacher or a guest.

motivation
psychology

Motivation is what drives learners to achieve a goal, and is a key factor determining success or failure in language learning. The learner's goal may be a short-term one, such as successfully performing a classroom task, or a long-term one, such as achieving native-like proficiency in the language. With regard to long-term goals, a distinction is often made between *instrumental motivation* and *integrative motivation*. Instrumental motivation is when the learner has a functional objective, such as passing an exam or getting a job. Integrative motivation, on the other hand, is when the learner wants to be identified with the target language community. Intersecting with these two motivational *orientations* are two different *sources* of motivation: *intrinsic* (e.g. the pleasure of doing a task for its own sake) and extrinsic (e.g. the "carrot and stick" approach). Another motivational source that has been identified is success: experience of succeeding can result in increased motivation (called *resultative motivation*), which raises the question as to whether motivation is as much a result as a cause of learning.

Various theories of motivation have been proposed. Most of these identify a variety of factors that, in combination, contribute to overall motivation, such as:

- *attitudes*, e.g. to the target language and to speakers of the language
- *goals*, both long-term and short-term, and the learners' *orientation* to these goals
- how much *value* the learner attaches to achieving the goals, especially as weighed against *expectancy of success*; expectancy of success may come from the learners' assessment of their own abilities, and how they account for previous successes or failures
- *self-esteem*, and the need to achieve and maintain it through *intrinsic interest*, *pleasure*, *relevance* or *challenge* of the task
- *group dynamic*: is it competitive, collaborative, or individualistic?
- *teacher's attitudes*, e.g. what expectations does the teacher project about the learners' likelihood of success?

As the last point suggests, teachers can play a key role in motivating learners, not just in terms of choosing activities that are intrinsically motivating, but in the attitudes they project. Two researchers on motivation offer the following advice for teachers:

Ten commandments for motivating language learners:

1. Set a personal example with your own behavior.
2. Create a pleasant, relaxed atmosphere in the classroom.
3. Present the tasks properly.
4. Develop a good relationship with the learners.
5. Increase the learners' linguistic self-confidence.
6. Make the language classes interesting.
7. Promote learner autonomy.
8. Personalize the learning process.
9. Increase the learners' goal-orientedness.
10. Familiarize learners with the target language culture.

noticing
SLA

If you notice a feature of the language that you are exposed to, it attracts your attention and you make a mental note of it. For example, a learner might notice (without necessarily understanding) the sign *Mind the gap*, repeated several times on a railroad station platform. That same day, the learner hears the teacher say *would you mind* in the context of making a request in class. A day or two later, the same learner hears someone else say *I don't mind*. Each successive "noticing" both primes the learner to notice new occurrences of mind, and at the same time contributes to a growing understanding of the use and meaning of *mind*. Proponents of **cognitive learning theory** believe that noticing is a prerequisite for learning: without, it input would remain as mere "noise." The *noticing hypothesis*, then, claims that noticing is a necessary condition for acquisition, although not the only one. Some kind of mental processing of what has been noticed is also necessary before the **input** becomes *intake*, i.e., before it is moved into long-term **memory**.

Teachers obviously play an important role in helping learners to notice features of the language. They do this when they repeat words or structures, write them on the board, or even drill them. One way of increasing the chance of learners noticing an item is to include it lots of times in a text, a technique called *input flood*. For example, learners read a text with the word *mind* included several times. They then categorize these examples according to their meaning. A set of **concordance** lines for a particular word can be used in the same way.

There is another type of noticing, called *noticing the gap*. This is when learners are made aware of a gap in their language knowledge. This might happen when they do a **dictation**, for example. When they compare their version with the correct version, they may notice certain differences, such as the lack of past tense endings, which represent a gap in their **interlanguage**. It has been argued that noticing the gap can trigger the **restructuring** of interlanguage. That is, "minding the gap" leads learners to "fill the gap."

personalization
methodology

When you personalize language you use it to talk about your knowledge, experience, and feelings. Personalization of the type *Now write five true sentences about yourself using "used to"* is often motivated by the need to provide further practice of pre-taught grammar structures. But it is also good preparation for the kinds of situations of genuine language use that learners might encounter outside the classroom. These advantages are lost, though, if the teacher's response is to treat the exercise as *only* an exercise, and correct the learners' errors without responding to the content.

The influence of **humanistic approaches** has given a fresh impetus to personalization, both in terms of providing a more coherent rationale and suggesting a broader range of activity types. For a start (it is argued), personalization creates better classroom **dynamics**. This is because groups are more likely to form and bond if the individuals in them know more about one another. And the mental and emotional effort that is involved in finding personal associations with a language item is likely to make that item more memorable. This quality is called cognitive and affective *depth*. Finally, lessons are likely to be more interesting, and hence more motivating, if at least some of the content concerns the people in the room, rather than the characters in course books. On these grounds, some writers have suggested that personalization should not be considered simply as an "add-on," but should be the principle on which most, if not all, classroom content should be based. One teaching approach that is committed to this view is **community language learning**. In this approach, all the content of the lesson comes from the learners themselves. Personalization is not without risks, though. Teachers need to be sensitive to learner resistance: learners should have the right to "pass" on questions that they consider too intrusive. And teachers should be authentic in the way that they respond to learners' personalizations. This means that they should respond to what their learners are saying, not just how they say it.

practice
methodology

If you practice a skill, you experience doing it a number of times in order to gain control of it. The idea that "practice makes perfect" is fundamental to **cognitive learning theory**. It is through practice that the skill becomes automatic. **Sociocultural learning theory** finds room for practice too. Performing a skill with the assistance of someone who is good at it can help in the **appropriation** of the skill. At issue, then, is not so much whether practice is beneficial, but what form it should take, when, and how much of it is necessary. In addressing these questions, it is customary to distinguish between different kinds of practice, such as *controlled practice vs. free practice*, *mechanical practice vs. meaningful/communicative practice*, and *receptive practice vs. productive practice*.

Controlled practice is associated with the second P of the **PPP** instructional model. Practice can be controlled in at least two senses: *language control* and *interactional control*. In the first, the language that is being practiced is restricted to what has just been presented (hence it is also called restricted practice). For example, if the first **conditional** has been presented, learners practice this, and only this, structure, and in a repetitive way, e.g. through a sequence of **drills**. Practice is also said to be controlled if the learners' participation is overtly managed and monitored by the teacher, such as in open-class work, as opposed to closed **pairwork** or **groupwork**. One reason for this degree of control is that it maintains a focus on accuracy, and pre-empts or corrects errors. *Free practice*, on the other hand, allows learners a measure of creativity, and the opportunity to integrate the new item into their existing language "pool." It is also less controlled in terms of the interactions, with pairwork and groupwork being favored. Typical free practice activities might be **games**, **discussions**, or **drama**-based activities.

Mechanical practice is a form of controlled practice, where the focus is less on the meaning of an item than on manipulating its component parts. Mechanical practice can be either oral or written: many traditional **exercises** are mechanical in this sense, such as when learners transform sentences from active into passive, or from direct speech into reported speech. The arguments in favor of controlled and mechanical practice have lost their force since the decline of **behaviorism** and its belief that learning is simply habit-formation.

Meaningful practice requires learners to display some understanding of what the item that they are practicing actually means. One way of doing this is through **personalization.** *Communicative practice* involves the learners interacting in order to complete some kind of task, such as in an *information gap activity* (**➔communicative activity**). Proponents of a communicative approach argue that it is only this kind of practice that is truly effective. This is because learners are not simply practicing language, but are practicing the behaviors associated with the language, and this is a pre-condition for long-term behavioral change.

Finally, some practice activities are purely *receptive*. They involve the learners in identifying, selecting, or discriminating between language items, but not actually producing them. Many **consciousness-raising** activities are receptive, on the grounds that learners first need to understand a new structure before they can properly internalize it. Receptive practice is also associated with comprehension-based approaches to teaching. Productive practice, on the other hand, requires learners to produce the targeted items (either orally or in writing), and is associated with output-based models of learning.

There is fairly general agreement nowadays that the most effective practice activity combines at least some of the following features:

- It is meaningful, which may mean that it is personalized.
- It is communicative, thus it will require learners to interact.
- It involves a degree of repetition—not of the mindless type associated with imitation drills, but of the type associated with many games.
- It is language-rich, i.e., learners have to interpret or produce a lot of language.
- Learners can be creative and take risks, but support is at hand if they need it.
- Learners are pushed, at least some of the time, to the limits of their competence.
- Learners get **feedback**.

pronunciation teaching
phonology

Pronunciation is the general term for that part of language classes and courses that deals with aspects of the **phonology** of English. This includes the individual sounds (**phonemes**) of English, sounds in **connected speech**, word and sentence **stress, rhythm,** and **intonation.** These components are customarily divided into two groups: the *segmental* features of pronunciation, i.e., the individual sounds and the way they combine, and the *suprasegmental* features, i.e., stress, rhythm, and intonation. **Paralinguistic** features of speech production such as voice quality, tempo, and loudness, are also classed as suprasegmental.

Effective pronunciation teaching needs to consider what goals, course design, and methodology are most appropriate for the learners in question. The goal of acquiring a native-like **accent** is generally thought to be unachievable for most learners (and perhaps even undesirable). Instead, the goal of **intelligibility** is nowadays considered more realistic, if less easily measurable. It is often claimed that suprasegmental features play a greater role in intelligibility than do segmental ones. Unfortunately, however, some of these suprasegmental features, such as intonation, are considered by many teachers to be unteachable. Moreover, learners intending to interact with native speakers may need to set different goals from those learners whose purpose is to learn **English as an international language (EIL).** For this latter group, the so-called **phonological core** is a checklist of those pronunciation features considered critical for intelligibility in EIL.

In terms of the design of course content, a basic choice is whether the pronunciation focus is *integrated* or *segregated.* In an integrated approach, pronunciation is dealt with as part of the teaching of grammar and vocabulary, or of speaking and listening. In a segregated approach it is treated in isolation. A classical segregated exercise is the **minimal pairs** task, in which learners are taught to discriminate and produce two contrasted phonemes (as in *hit* and *heat*). There are doubts as to whether this item-by-item approach to pronunciation reflects the way that the features of pronunciation are interconnected. Nor does it reflect the way that they jointly emerge over time ("as a photo emerges in the darkroom"). A related issue is whether pronunciation teaching should be *pre-emptive* or *reactive*. That is to say, should pronunciation teaching be planned around a syllabus of pre-selected items, or should the focus on pronunciation emerge out of practice activities, in the form, for example, of **correction**? There is evidence that the latter approach is more effective than the former.

In 1964, the writer (and former language teacher) Anthony Burgess wrote, "Nothing is more important than to acquire a set of foreign phonemes that shall be entirely acceptable to your hosts." However, there is generally less emphasis given to pronunciation teaching nowadays. Indeed, some teachers are skeptical as to the value of teaching pronunciation at all. This view is reinforced by research that suggests that the best predictors of intelligible pronunciation are "having a good ear" and prolonged residence in an English-speaking country. On the other hand, faulty pronunciation is one of the most common causes of misunderstandings. This is an argument for demanding higher standards than the learners can realistically achieve, in the hope that they will meet you "halfway."

reading

methodology

Reading is a receptive **skill**. But the fact that it is receptive does not mean that it is passive: reading is an active, even interactive, process. Readers bring their own questions to the text, which are based on their background knowledge, and they use these to interrogate the text, modifying their questions and coming up with new ones according to the answers they get. In order to do this, they draw on a range of knowledge bases. They need to be able to decode the letters, words, and grammatical structures of the individual sentences—what is called *bottom-up processing*. But they also enlist *top-down processes*, such as drawing on **discourse** and schematic knowledge, as well as on immediate contextual information. Discourse knowledge is knowing how different text-types—such as news reports, recipes, or academic papers—are organized. Schematic knowledge is the reader's existing knowledge of the topic. Reading involves an interaction between these different "levels" of knowledge, where knowledge at one "level" can compensate for lack of knowledge at another.

Readers also bring their own *purposes* to texts, and these in turn determine the way they go about reading a text. The two main purposes for reading are for *information* (such as when consulting a directory), and for *pleasure* (such as when reading a novel), although these purposes may overlap. Different ways of reading include:

- *skimming* (*skim-reading, reading for gist*): rapidly reading a text in order to get the gist, or the main ideas or sense of a text. For example, a reader might skim a film review in order to see if the reviewer liked the film or not.
- *scanning*: reading a text in search of specific information, and ignoring everything else, such as when consulting a bus timetable for a particular time and destination.
- *detailed reading*: reading a text in order to extract the maximum detail from it, such as when following the instructions for installing a household appliance.
- *reading aloud*: such as when reading a prepared speech or lecture, or reading a story aloud, or an extract from the newspaper.

A reader's purpose usually matches the writer's intentions for the text. Readers seldom read telephone books from cover to cover, for example. Nor do they normally skim through a novel looking for names beginning with *Vron* .... In classrooms, however, texts are frequently used for purposes other than those for which they were originally intended. They are often used not so much as vehicles of information or of pleasure, but as "linguistic objects," that is, as contexts for the study of features of the language. A distinction needs to be made, therefore, between two types of classroom reading: reading as *skills development*, and reading as *language study*. There is no reason why the same text cannot be used for both purposes.

Another distinction that is often made is between *intensive reading* and *extensive reading*. The former applies to the way short texts are subject to close and detailed classroom study. Extensive reading, on the other hand, means the more leisurely reading of longer texts, primarily for pleasure, or in order to accumulate vocabulary, or simply to develop sound habits of reading. This is typically done outside class, using graded **readers**, authentic texts, or literary texts.

A third important distinction is between testing reading and teaching reading. Traditional reading tasks usually involve reading a text and then answering **comprehension questions** about it. This is the testing approach. A teaching approach, on the other hand, aims to help learners to become more effective readers by training them in the *sub-skills* of reading, and by teaching them reading strategies. Some of the sub-skills of reading are:

- understanding words and identifying their grammatical function
- recognizing grammar features, such as word endings, and "unpacking" (or **parsing**) the syntax of sentences
- identifying the topic of the text, and recognizing topic changes
- identifying text type, text purpose, and text organization, and identifying and understanding **discourse markers** and other cohesive devices
- distinguishing key information from less important information
- identifying and understanding the gist
- inferring the writer's attitude
- following the development of an argument
- following the sequence of a narrative
- paraphrasing the text

Activities designed to develop these sub-skills include: underlining topic-related words; contrasting different text-types; comparing different examples of the same text type and identifying *generic* features; circling and categorizing discourse markers; identifying what the pronouns refer to; predicting the direction the text will take at each discourse marker; choosing the best summary of a text; putting a set of pictures in order; extracting key information on to a grid; writing a summary of the text, etc. *Strategy training* involves training learners in ways of overcoming problems when they are reading. Some useful strategies include:

- using contextual and extra-linguistic information (such as pictures, layout, headlines) to make predictions regarding what the text is about
- brainstorming background (or schematic) knowledge in advance of reading
- skimming a text in advance of a more detailed reading
- keeping the purpose of the text in mind
- guessing the meaning of words from context
- using the dictionary

There is some argument, however, as to the value of a "skills and strategies" approach to teaching reading. Most adult learners of English come to English texts with already well-developed reading skills in their own language. They already know how to skim, scan, use context clues, enlist background knowledge, and so on. Theoretically, at least, these skills are transferable. What makes reading difficult is not so much lack of reading skills as lack of *language knowledge*. That is, learners lack sufficient vocabulary and grammar to unpack sentences, and they cannot easily identify the ways that sentences are connected. This can result in "tunnel vision," with readers becoming distracted by unfamiliar words, at the expense of working out meaning from context. On the other hand, it can also result in an over-reliance on guesswork, and on superficial "text attack" strategies such as skimming. This suggests that texts need to be chosen in a way that does not overstretch learners' ability to read them fluently. At the same time, texts should not be so easy that learners can process them simply by skimming. It also means that tasks need to be chosen so that they both match the original purpose of the text, and encourage learners to transfer their first language reading skills. Such tasks are likely to be those that motivate learners to want to read the text. This might mean activating interest in the topic of the text, through, for example, a pre-reading quiz. At the same time, classroom reading texts should be exploited, not just for their potential in developing reading skills, but as sources of language input. This will involve, at some point, detailed study of the text's formal features, such as its linking devices, its collocations, or its grammar.

speaking

methodology

Speaking is generally thought to be the most important of the four **skills**. The ability to speak a second language is often equated with proficiency in the language, as in *She speaks excellent French*. Indeed, one frustration commonly voiced by learners is that they have spent years studying English, but still can't speak it. One of the main difficulties, of course, is that speaking usually takes place spontaneously and in real time, which means that planning and production overlap. If too much **attention** is paid to planning, production suffers, and the effect is a loss of **fluency**. On the other hand, if the speaker's attention is directed solely on production, it is likely that **accuracy** will suffer, which could prejudice **intelligibility**. In order to free up attention, therefore, the speaker needs to have achieved a degree of **automaticity** in both planning and production. One way of doing this is to use memorized routines, such as **formulaic language**. Another is to use *production strategies*, such as the use of **pause fillers**, in order to "buy" planning time. The situation is complicated by the fact that most speaking is interactive. Speakers are jointly having to manage the flow of talk. The management of interaction involves *turn-taking skills*, such as knowing how and when to take, keep, and relinquish speaker turns, and also knowing how to repair misunderstandings.

For language learners these processing demands are magnified through lack of basic knowledge of grammar and vocabulary. For the purposes of most day-to-day talk, however, the grammar that is required is not as complex nor need be as accurate as the grammar that is required for writing. Nor do speakers need an enormous vocabulary, especially if they have developed some **communication strategies** for getting round gaps in their knowledge. A core vocabulary of 1000–1500 high frequency words and expressions will provide most learners with a solid basis for speaking.

Activating this knowledge, though, requires **practice**. This, in turn, suggests that the more speaking practice opportunities that learners are given, and the sooner, the easier speaking will become. Speaking practice means more than simply answering the teacher's questions, or repeating sentences, as in grammar practice activities. It means interacting with other speakers, sustaining long turns of talk, speaking spontaneously, and speaking about topics of the learners' choice.

Approaches to teaching speaking vary. Traditionally, speaking was considered to be a byproduct of teaching grammar and vocabulary, reinforced with work on **pronunciation.** This view has been replaced by approaches that treat speaking as a skill in its own right. One such approach is to break down the speaking skill into a number of discrete sub-skills, such as *opening and closing conversations, turn-taking, repairing, paraphrasing, interrupting,* etc. Another approach is to focus on the different purposes of speaking and their associated **genres,** such as *narrating, obtaining service, giving a presentation, making small talk,* etc. This approach is particularly well suited to learners who have a specific purpose for learning English. A third is to adopt a topic-based approach, where learners are encouraged to speak freely on a range of topics, at least some of which they have chosen themselves. This is the format used in many conversation classes. Typical activity types for the teaching of speaking include: **dialogues, drama** activities (including *role-plays* and *simulations*), **games, discussions,** and debates, as well as informal classroom chat.

task

methodology

A task is a classroom activity the focus of which is on communicating meaning. The objective of a task may be to reach some consensus on an issue, to solve a problem, to draft a plan, to design something, or to persuade someone to do something. In contrast, practicing a preselected item of language (such as the present perfect) for its own sake would not be a valid task objective. In the performance of the task, learners are expected to make use of their own language resources. In theory, tasks may be receptive or productive, and may be done individually, or in pairs or small groups. However, in practice, most activities that are labelled "tasks" in course books involve production (either speaking or writing, or both) and require learners to interact with one another.

Tasks are the organizing principle in **task-based learning.** In order to devise a syllabus of tasks, it is necessary both to classify tasks, and to identify the factors that make one task more difficult than another. Different criteria for classifying tasks have been suggested. For example, tasks can be *open-ended* or *closed.* An open-ended task is one in which learners know there is no predetermined solution. It might be planning an excursion, or debating a topical issue. A closed task, on the other hand, requires learners to discover the solution to a problem, such as identifying the differences in a spot-the-difference task (→ **communicative activity**). Tasks can also be classified according to the kinds of operations they involve, such as *ranking, selecting, sorting, comparing, surveying,* and *problem-solving.*

Factors which influence the degree of difficulty of the task, and hence which affect the grading of tasks, include:

- *linguistic factors*: How complex is the language that learners will need to draw on, in order to do the task? How much help, either before or during the task, will they get with their language needs?
- *cognitive factors*: Does the task require the processing of complex data? Is the task type familiar to learners?
- *performance factors*: Do the learners have to interact in real time in order to do the task? Do they have time to rehearse? Do they have to "go public?"

The term *task* is now widely accepted as a useful way of labeling certain types of classroom activity, including many which have a thinly disguised grammar agenda. But the concept of task is not without its critics. Some writers feel that the association of task with "work" undervalues the more playful—and possibly less authentic or communicative—types of classroom activity, such as games, songs, and drama.

vocabulary teaching

methodology

Vocabulary describes that area of language learning that is concerned with word knowledge. Vocabulary learning is a major goal in most teaching programs. It hasn't always been so. In methods such as **audiolingualism**, vocabulary was subordinated to the teaching of grammar structures. Words were simply there to fill the slots in the sentence patterns. The move towards *semantic* (i.e., meaning-based) **syllabuses** in the 1970s, along with the use of **authentic** materials, saw a revival of interest in vocabulary teaching. Subsequently, developments in **corpus** linguistics and **discourse analysis** started to blur the distinction between vocabulary and grammar. In the 1990s, the **lexical approach** ushered in a major re-think regarding the role of vocabulary. This concerned both the *selection* of items (**frequency** being a deciding factor) and the type of items: **formulaic language** (or lexical chunks) was recognized as being essential for both **fluency** and **idiomaticity**. These developments have influenced the design of teaching materials. Most contemporary course books incorporate a lexical syllabus alongside the grammar one. Recent developments in lexicography have complemented this trend. There is now a wide range of **dictionaries** available for learners, many of which come with sophisticated software for accessing databases of examples and collocations.

It is now generally agreed that, in terms of goals, learners need a receptive vocabulary of around 3,000 high-frequency words (or, better, **word families**) in order to achieve independent user status. This will give them around ninety per cent coverage of normal text. For a productive vocabulary, especially for speaking, they may only need half this number.

Classroom approaches to achieving these goals include dedicated vocabulary lessons. Typically these take the form of teaching lexical sets of words (i.e., groups of thematically linked words) using a variety of means, including visual aids, demonstration, situations, texts, and dictionary work. As well as the **meaning** of the items, **the form**, both spoken (i.e., **pronunciation**) and written (i.e., **spelling**), needs to be dealt with, especially if the words are being taught for productive use. Other aspects of word knowledge that may need to be highlighted include **connotation** and **style**, **collocation**, derived forms, and grammatical features, such as the word's **word class**. Vocabulary is also taught as preparation for listening or reading (*pre-teaching vocabulary*) or as a byproduct of these skills.

It would be impossible, in class, to teach all the words that learners need. Learners therefore need opportunities for *incidental* learning, e.g. through *extensive reading*. They may also benefit from training in how to make the most of these opportunities, e.g. by means of dictionary use, note-keeping, etc. Some strategies for deducing the meaning of unfamiliar words will also help.

Amassing a fully functioning vocabulary is essentially a **memory** task, and techniques to help in the memorizing of words can be usefully taught, too. It also helps to provide learners with repeated encounters with new words, e.g. through the re-reading of texts, or by reading several texts about the same topic. Constant recycling of newly learned words is essential. One simple way of doing this is to have a *word box* (or word bag) in the classroom. New words are written on to small cards and added to the word box. At the beginning of the next lesson, these words can be used as the basis for a review activity. For example, the teacher can take words out of the box and ask learners to define them, provide a translation, or put them into a sentence. The words can also form the basis for peer-testing activities, in which learners take a number of word cards and test each other in pairs or small groups.

writing

methodology

Like speaking, writing is a productive skill, and, like other skills, writing involves a hierarchy of sub-skills. These range from the most mechanical (such as handwriting or typing legibly) through to the ability to organize the written text and lay it out according to the conventions of the particular text type. Along the way, writers also need to be able to:

- produce grammatically accurate sentences
- connect and punctuate these sentences
- select and maintain an appropriate style
- signal the direction that the message is taking
- anticipate the reader's likely questions so as to be able to structure the message accordingly

In order to enable these skills, writers need an extensive knowledge base, not only at the level of vocabulary and grammar, but at the level of connected discourse. This includes familiarity with a range of different text types, such as informal letters, instructions, product descriptions, etc. It follows that if classroom writing is mainly spelling—or grammar-focused—many of the sub-skills of writing will be neglected.

Nevertheless, the teaching of writing has tended to focus on the "lower-level" features of the skill, such as being able to write sentences that are both accurate and complex, that demonstrate internal cohesion, and that are connected to the sentences next to them. This language-based approach is justified on the grounds that stricter standards of accuracy are usually required in writing than in speaking. Also, writing demands a greater degree of explicitness than speaking, since writers and their readers are separated in time and space. They therefore can't rely on immediate feedback in order to clear up misunderstandings.

By contrast, a text-based approach to teaching writing takes a more "top-down" view. This approach finds support in **discourse analysis**, which shows that a **text** is more than a series of sentences, however neatly linked. Instead, texts are organized according to larger *macrostructures*, such as problem-solution, or definition examples. Hence, learners need explicit guidance in how texts are structured. This typically involves analyzing and imitating models of particular text types. For example, a business letter might be analyzed in terms of its overall layout, the purpose of each of its paragraphs, the grammatical and lexical choices within each paragraph, and the punctuation. Each of these features is then practiced in isolation. They are then recombined in tasks aimed first at reproducing the original text and then at producing similar texts incorporating different content.

This approach is called a *product approach* to the teaching of writing, since the focus is exclusively on producing a text (the product) that reproduces the model. By contrast, a *process approach* argues that writers do not in fact start with a clear idea of the finished product. Rather, the text emerges out of a creative process. This process includes: *planning* (*generating ideas*, *goal setting*, and *organizing*), *drafting* and *re-drafting*; *reviewing*, including *editing* and *proofreading*, and, finally, "*publishing*." Advocates of a process approach argue for a more organic sequence of classroom activities, beginning with the brainstorming of ideas, writing preliminary drafts, comparing drafts, re-drafting, and *conferencing*, that is, talking through their draft with the teacher, in order to fine-tune their ideas.

The process approach to writing has a lot in common with the **communicative approach** to language teaching, and each has drawn support from the other. The communicative approach views writing as an act of communication in which the writer interacts with a reader or readers for a particular purpose. The purpose might be to ask for information about a language course, to relay personal news, to complain about being overcharged at a hotel, or simply to entertain and amuse. Thus, advocates of a communicative approach argue that classroom writing tasks should be motivated by a clear purpose and that writers should have their reader(s) in mind at all stages of the writing process. Such principles are now reflected in the design of writing tasks in public examinations, such as this one, from the Cambridge ESOL First Certificate in English (FCE) paper:

> The school where you learn English has decided to buy some videos in English. You have been asked to write a report to the Principal, suggesting what kinds of videos the school should buy. In your report you should also explain why students at the school will like these videos. Write your report.

The social purposes of writing are also foregrounded by proponents of a *genre-based approach*. **Genre** analysis attempts to show how the structure of particular text types are shaped by the purposes they serve in specific social and cultural contexts. Put simply, a business letter is the way it is because of what it does. Advocates of genre-based teaching reject a process approach to teaching writing. They argue that to emphasize self-expression at the expense of teaching the generic structures of texts may in fact disempower learners. Many learners, especially those who are learning English as a second language, need a command of those genres—such as writing a résumé, or requesting a bank loan—that permit access to the host community. A genre approach to teaching writing is not unlike a product approach, therefore. It starts with model texts that are subjected to analysis and replication. The difference is that these models are closely associated with their contexts of use, and they are analyzed in functional terms as much as in linguistic ones. The genre approach has been particularly influential in the teaching of academic writing.

In reality, none of these approaches is entirely incompatible with any other. Resourceful teachers tend to blend elements of each. For example, they may encourage learners to "discover" what they want to write, using a process approach. They may then give them a model text, both as a source of useful language items, and as a template for the final product. They may also provide exercises in specific sub-skills, such as linking sentences, or using a formal style.

Life Skills

What are Life Skills?

Life Skills are the skills students need to deal effectively with the challenges in everyday life, whether at school, at work, or in their personal lives. Students who are able to understand and use these skills, along with their educational qualifications, will be better placed to take advantage of educational and employment opportunities. In a constantly changing environment, having life skills is an essential part of being able to meet the challenges of everyday life.

The dramatic changes in global economies over the past five years have been matched by the transformation in technology and these are all impacting on education, the workplace, and our home life. To cope with the increasing pace and change of modern life, students need new life skills such as the ability to deal with stress and frustration. Today's students will have many new jobs over the course of their lives, with associated pressures and the need for flexibility. As medical science advances, home life and the community will place additional demands on future generations.

Topics:

Social Skills

People Management

Critical Thinking

Time Management

Cultural Awareness

Networking

Career and Work

Study Skills

Creativity

Self-awareness

Getting Organized

www.macmillanenglish.com/life-skills/classroom-resources/

How do we approach Life Skills in this book?

In every unit of *American Inside Out Evolution*, one of these topics will be discussed, according to the theme of the unit, and students will have the opportunity to reflect and discuss based on simple activities.

The Common European Framework of Reference for Language Learning

Introduction

The Common European Framework of Reference (CEFR) is a widely used standard created by the Council of Europe. In the classroom, familiarity with the CEFR can be of great help to any teacher in identifying students' actual progress and helping them to set their learning priorities.

Students can use the descriptors (description of competences) at any point to get a detailed, articulated, and personal picture of their own individual progress. This is important, as no two language learners progress in the same way, and consequently it is always rather artificial to apply a "framework level" to a class as a whole, or to a course or course book.

The European Language Portfolio is another Council of Europe project, designed to give every learner a structure for keeping a record of their language learning experiences and their progress as described in the CEFR. Up-to-date information about developments with the CEFR and Portfolio can be found on www.coe.int/portfolio.

The Swiss-based Eurocentres Foundation played a major role in the development of the levels and the descriptors for the CEFR and the prototype Portfolio. The CEFR descriptors, developed in a Swiss National Research Foundation project, were presented in clearer, simpler, self-assessment form in the prototype (Swiss) Portfolio. There are now dozens of different national versions of the Portfolio for different educational sectors, but the only version for adults is that developed from the Swiss version[1] by EAQUALS[2] (European Association for Quality Language Services) in collaboration with ALTE[3] (Association of Language Testers in Europe). The descriptors used in this guide are taken from the EAQUALS/ALTE Portfolio. An electronic version which can be completed online can be downloaded in English or French from www.eelp.org. The EAQUALS/ALTE Portfolio descriptors have been used in this guide, as they are more concrete and practical than the original CEFR descriptors.

American Inside Out Evolution CEFR Checklists

American Inside Out Evolution Upper Intermediate is appropriate for students who can already use basic English in a limited range of situations and are now facing the daunting task of expanding their language abilities towards more general competence. By the end of *American Inside Out Evolution Upper Intermediate*, if the students have had access to English outside the classroom, and have had the opportunity to practice, they should feel able to accomplish the things described at the B1 level with a good degree of confidence.

In order to help the teacher and student assess their progress, we've provided a list of B1 descriptors for each unit of *American Inside Out Evolution Upper Intermediate*. A good ability with the A2 descriptors is presupposed at the start of the book, and most students who have reached that level will already be able to make a fair attempt at some of the things described at B1. The intermediate level is about building confidence and expanding the range of situations in which the student can operate comfortably in English. The descriptors allow the teacher to see a typical pattern of language acquisition. It's important to remember that every student learns differently, and that the various abilities will be acquired in a different sequence and at a different pace by each individual.

At intermediate level students have reached a stage at which it's difficult to direct their learning effectively. Up to now there's been a clear set of basic grammar rules and essential vocabulary to learn, but now students begin to realize that there's a vast amount more information about the language that they need in order to use it well, and that that information is much more difficult to codify and organize. They can gain a real sense of achievement, however, from understanding the slightly technical descriptors and applying them to their own experience.

Suggested targets for the checklist are provided for each unit. They allow the teacher to see how a typical student's confidence might be building, to identify the key skills focused on in each unit, and so to select supplementary materials or change the emphasis as necessary. At the same time, they give the students a yardstick to measure themselves against, so that they can easily identify their own weak areas and take responsibility for their own learning. It's a good idea to include the students in the ongoing planning of the course at this level: they can now express their needs and preferences in English and so if they feel consulted about the course, it's possible to establish very productive feedback.

1 Schneider, Gunther, & North, Brian (2000): "Fremdsprachen können – was heisst das?" Zürich, Ruegger; North, Brian (2000): "The Development of a Com mon Framework Scale of Language Proficiency", New York, Peter Lang.

2 EAQUALS is a pan-European language school accreditation body with over 100 full members.

3 ALTE is an association dedicated to raising standards in language testing and encompasses the major European examination providers. Eurocentres provides high-quality language teaching in countries where the language concerned is spoken. EAQUALS, ALTE, and Eurocentres are the three NGO advisers for language learning to the Council of Europe and all three implement the CEFR.

CEFR Student Checklists

Unit 1

Complete the checklist.

1 = I can do this with a lot of help from my teacher.

2 = I can do this with a little help.

3 = I can do this fairly well.

4 = I can do this really well.

5 = I can do this almost perfectly.

Competences	Page	Your score
I can understand most recorded material delivered in standard language and can identify speaker viewpoints and attitudes as well as the information content.	9, 10, 14, 16	1 2 3 4 5
I can read and understand articles and reports on current problems in which the writers express specific attitudes and points of view.	12, 13	1 2 3 4 5
I can produce stretches of language with a fairly even tempo; although I can be hesitant as I search for expressions, there are few noticeably long pauses.	8, 9, 11, 16	1 2 3 4 5
I can use a good range of vocabulary for matters connected to my field and on most general topics.	10, 12, 15, 16	1 2 3 4 5
I can write emails conveying degrees of emotion and highlighting the personal significance of events and experiences and commenting on the correspondent's news and views.	17	1 2 3 4 5

Unit 2

Complete the checklist.

1 = I can do this with a lot of help from my teacher.

2 = I can do this with a little help.

3 = I can do this fairly well.

4 = I can do this really well.

5 = I can do this almost perfectly.

Competences	Page	Your score
I can understand in detail what is said to me in standard spoken language even in a noisy environment.	22, 23, 24, 25, 26	1 2 3 4 5
I can help a discussion along on familiar ground, confirming comprehension, inviting others in, etc.	18, 22, 23, 26	1 2 3 4 5
I can explain a viewpoint on a topical issue, giving the advantages and disadvantages of various options.	22, 23, 24	1 2 3 4 5
I can scan quickly through long and complex texts, locating relevant details.	18, 19, 20	1 2 3 4 5
I can pass on detailed information reliably.	25	1 2 3 4 5

Unit 3

Complete the checklist.

1 = I can do this with a lot of help from my teacher.

2 = I can do this with a little help.

3 = I can do this fairly well.

4 = I can do this really well.

5 = I can do this almost perfectly.

Competences	Page	Your score
I can quickly identify the content and relevance of news items, articles, and reports on a wide range of topics, and decide if closer study is worthwhile.	31, 34	1 2 3 4 5
I can initiate, maintain, and end discourse naturally with effective turn-taking.	30, 32, 33, 35, 36	1 2 3 4 5
I can speculate about causes, consequences, and hypothetical situations.	33	1 2 3 4 5
I can write clear, detailed descriptions of real or imaginary events and experiences.	33	1 2 3 4 5
I can use a variety of strategies to achieve comprehension, including listening for main points and checking comprehension by using contextual clues.	29, 32, 35, 36	1 2 3 4 5

Unit 4

Complete the checklist.

1 = I can do this with a lot of help from my teacher

2 = I can do this with a little help

3 = I can do this fairly well

4 = I can do this really well

5 = I can do this almost perfectly

Competences	Page	Your score
I can with some effort catch much of what is said around me in a discussion with native speakers.	42, 45	1 2 3 4 5
I can read many kinds of texts quite easily at different speeds and in different ways according to my purpose in reading and the type of text.	40, 41, 44, 46	1 2 3 4 5
I can convey degrees of emotion and highlight the personal significance of events and experiences.	48	1 2 3 4 5
I have sufficient vocabulary to express myself on matters connected to my field and on most general topics.	40, 42, 44, 47, 49	1 2 3 4 5
I show a relatively high degree of grammatical control and I do not make mistakes which lead to misunderstanding.	43, 45, 47	1 2 3 4 5

Unit 5

Complete the checklist.

1 = I can do this with a lot of help from my teacher

2 = I can do this with a little help

3 = I can do this fairly well

4 = I can do this really well

5 = I can do this almost perfectly

Competences	Page	Your score
I can understand in detail what is said to me in standard spoken language even in a noisy environment.	52, 55, 57, 58	1 2 3 4 5
I can exchange considerable quantities of detailed factual information on matters within my field of interest.	52, 53, 55	1 2 3 4 5
My vocabulary accuracy is generally high, though some confusion and incorrect word choice does occur without hindering communication.	50, 54, 55	1 2 3 4 5
I show a relatively high degree of grammatical control and I do not make mistakes which lead to misunderstanding.	53, 57, 58	1 2 3 4 5
I can write an essay or report which develops an argument systematically with appropriate highlighting of significant points and relevant supporting detail.	59	1 2 3 4 5

Unit 6

Complete the checklist.

1 = I can do this with a lot of help from my teacher

2 = I can do this with a little help

3 = I can do this fairly well

4 = I can do this really well

5 = I can do this almost perfectly

Competences	Page	Your score
I can understand most TV news and current affairs programmes such as documentaries, live interviews, talk shows, plays, and the majority of films in standard language.	62, 68	1 2 3 4 5
I can use a variety of strategies to achieve comprehension, including reading for main points and checking comprehension by using contextual clues.	60, 61, 64, 68	1 2 3 4 5
I can scan quickly through long and complex texts, locating relevant details.	64, 65, 66, 67	1 2 3 4 5
I can engage and participate in extended conversation on most general topics.	60, 62, 64, 68	1 2 3 4 5
I have sufficient vocabulary to express myself on matters connected to my field and on most general topics.	61, 62, 64, 67, 68, 69	1 2 3 4 5

Unit 7

Complete the checklist.

1 = I can do this with a lot of help from my teacher

2 = I can do this with a little help

3 = I can do this fairly well

4 = I can do this really well

5 = I can do this almost perfectly

Competences	Page	Your score
I can understand standard spoken language, live or recorded, on both familiar and unfamiliar topics normally encountered in personal, academic, or professional life.	75, 78, 80	1 2 3 4 5
I can read many kinds of texts quite easily at different speeds and in different ways according to my purpose in reading and the type of text.	72, 73, 74, 75, 78	1 2 3 4 5
I can use a limited number of cohesive devices to make what I say clear and coherent.	78, 81	1 2 3 4 5
I show a relatively high degree of grammatical control and I do not make mistakes which lead to misunderstanding.	74, 75, 79	1 2 3 4 5
I can write clear, detailed text on a wide range of subjects related to my interests. I can write clear, detailed texts (compositions, reports, or texts of presentations) on various topics related to my field of interest.	81	1 2 3 4 5

Unit 8

Complete the checklist.

1 = I can do this with a lot of help from my teacher

2 = I can do this with a little help

3 = I can do this fairly well

4 = I can do this really well

5 = I can do this almost perfectly

Competences	Page	Your score
I can understand most TV news and current affairs programs such as documentaries, live interviews, talk shows, plays, and the majority of films in standard language.	82, 84, 88, 90	1 2 3 4 5
I can read and understand articles and reports on current problems in which the writers express specific attitudes and points of view.	82, 83, 85, 86	1 2 3 4 5
I can give clear, detailed descriptions on a wide range of subjects related to my field of interest.	82, 84, 85, 88, 89, 91	1 2 3 4 5
I show a relatively high degree of grammatical control and I do not make mistakes which lead to misunderstanding.	84, 85, 89	1 2 3 4 5
I can vary my vocabulary to avoid frequent repetition, but gaps in my vocabulary can still cause hesitation.	82, 84, 86, 90, 91	1 2 3 4 5

Unit 9

Complete the checklist.

1 = I can do this with a lot of help from my teacher

2 = I can do this with a little help

3 = I can do this fairly well

4 = I can do this really well

5 = I can do this almost perfectly

Competences	Page	Your score
I can understand the main ideas of complex speech on both concrete and abstract topics delivered in standard language.	94, 96, 98	1 2 3 4 5
I can understand articles and reports concerned with contemporary problems in which the writers adopt particular stances or viewpoints.	92, 93, 97	1 2 3 4 5
I can develop a clear description or narrative, expanding and supporting my main points with relevant supporting detail and examples.	101	1 2 3 4 5
I can understand and summarize orally short extracts from news items, interviews, or documentaries containing opinions, argument, and discussion.	92, 97, 98	1 2 3 4 5
I can speculate about causes, consequences, and hypothetical situations.	95, 97, 98	1 2 3 4 5

Unit 10

Complete the checklist.

1 = I can do this with a lot of help from my teacher

2 = I can do this with a little help

3 = I can do this fairly well

4 = I can do this really well

5 = I can do this almost perfectly

Competences	Page	Your score
I can read and understand articles and reports on current problems in which the writers express specific attitudes and points of view.	106, 107, 110, 111	1 2 3 4 5
I can explain a viewpoint on a topical issue giving the advantages and disadvantages of various options.	105, 108, 109, 111, 112	1 2 3 4 5
I can use a good range of vocabulary for matters connected to my field and on most general topics.	104, 106, 107, 110, 112, 113	1 2 3 4 5
I can follow the essentials of lectures, talks and reports, and other forms of presentation which use complex ideas and language.	105, 108, 112	1 2 3 4 5
I can engage and participate in extended conversation on most general topics.	104, 106, 108, 109, 111	1 2 3 4 5

Unit 11

Complete the checklist.

1 = I can do this with a lot of help from my teacher

2 = I can do this with a little help

3 = I can do this fairly well

4 = I can do this really well

5 = I can do this almost perfectly

Competences	Page	Your score
I can carry out an effective, fluent interview, following up on interesting replies.	118, 122	1 2 3 4 5
I can give clear, detailed descriptions on a wide range of subjects related to my field of interest.	114, 116, 117, 121	1 2 3 4 5
I can write clear, detailed texts on a variety of subjects related to my field of interest, using information from different sources.	123	1 2 3 4 5
I have a broad reading vocabulary, but I sometimes experience difficulty with less common words and phrases.	114, 117, 119, 121	1 2 3 4 5
I show a relatively high degree of grammatical control and I do not make mistakes which lead to misunderstanding.	117, 118	1 2 3 4 5

Unit 12

Complete the checklist.

1 = I can do this with a lot of help from my teacher

2 = I can do this with a little help

3 = I can do this fairly well

4 = I can do this really well

5 = I can do this almost perfectly

Competences	Page	Your score
I can read many kinds of texts quite easily at different speeds and in different ways according to my purpose in reading and the type of text.	126, 127, 130, 131	1 2 3 4 5
I can use a variety of strategies to achieve comprehension, including listening for main points and checking comprehension by using contextual clues.	128, 130, 132	1 2 3 4 5
I can initiate, maintain, and end discourse naturally with effective turn-taking.	128, 129, 130	1 2 3 4 5
I can speculate about causes, consequences, and hypothetical situations.	128, 130, 132	1 2 3 4 5
My vocabulary accuracy is generally high, though some confusion and incorrect word choice does occur without hindering communication.	124, 128, 130, 133	1 2 3 4 5

CEFR Student Checklists: Suggested targets

Unit 1

Competences	Page	Your score
I can understand most recorded material delivered in standard language and can identify speaker viewpoints and attitudes as well as the information content.	9, 10, 14, 16	1 2 (3) 4 5
I can read and understand articles and reports on current problems in which the writers express specific attitudes and points of view.	12, 13	1 (2) 3 4 5
I can produce stretches of language with a fairly even tempo; although I can be hesitant as I search for expressions, there are few noticeably long pauses.	8, 9, 11, 16	1 (2) 3 4 5
I can use a good range of vocabulary for matters connected to my field and on most general topics.	10, 12, 15, 16	(1) 2 3 4 5
I can write emails conveying degrees of emotion and highlighting the personal significance of events and experiences and commenting on the correspondent's news and views.	17	1 2 (3) 4 5

Unit 2

Competences	Page	Your score
I can understand in detail what is said to me in standard spoken language even in a noisy environment.	22, 23, 24, 25, 26	1 (2) 3 4 5
I can help a discussion along on familiar ground, confirming comprehension, inviting others in, etc.	18, 22, 23, 26	1 2 (3) 4 5
I can explain a viewpoint on a topical issue, giving the advantages and disadvantages of various options.	22, 23, 24	1 2 (3) 4 5
I can scan quickly through long and complex texts, locating relevant details.	18, 19, 20	1 (2) 3 4 5
I can pass on detailed information reliably.	25	1 2 (3) 4 5

Unit 3

Competences	Page	Your score
I can quickly identify the content and relevance of news items, articles, and reports on a wide range of topics, and decide if closer study is worthwhile.	31, 34	1 (2) 3 4 5
I can understand specialized articles outside my own field if I can occasionally check a dictionary.	28, 30	1 (2) 3 4 5
I can initiate, maintain, and end discourse naturally with effective turn-taking.	30, 32, 33, 35, 36	1 (2) 3 4 5
I can speculate about causes, consequences, and hypothetical situations.	33	(1) 2 3 4 5
I can write clear, detailed descriptions of real or imaginary events and experiences.	33	1 2 (3) 4 5
I can use a variety of strategies to achieve comprehension, including listening for main points and checking comprehension by using contextual clues.	29, 32, 35, 36	1 2 (3) 4 5

Unit 4

Competences	Page	Your score
I can with some effort catch much of what is said around me in a discussion with native speakers.	42, 45	1 ② 3 4 5
I can read many kinds of texts quite easily at different speeds and in different ways according to my purpose in reading and the type of text.	40, 41, 44, 46	1 ② 3 4 5
I can convey degrees of emotion and highlight the personal significance of events and experiences.	48	1 ② 3 4 5
I have sufficient vocabulary to express myself on matters connected to my field and on most general topics.	40, 42, 44, 47, 49	1 ② 3 4 5
I show a relatively high degree of grammatical control and I do not make mistakes which lead to misunderstanding.	43, 45, 47	① 2 3 4 5

Unit 5

Competences	Page	Your score
I can understand in detail what is said to me in standard spoken language even in a noisy environment.	52, 55, 57, 58	1 2 3 ④ 5
I can exchange considerable quantities of detailed factual information on matters within my field of interest.	52, 53, 55	1 2 ③ 4 5
My vocabulary accuracy is generally high, though some confusion and incorrect word choice does occur without hindering communication.	50, 54, 55	1 2 ③ 4 5
I show a relatively high degree of grammatical control and I do not make mistakes which lead to misunderstanding.	53, 57, 58	1 ② 3 4 5
I can write an essay or report which develops an argument systematically with appropriate highlighting of significant points and relevant supporting detail.	59	1 2 ③ 4 5

Unit 6

Competences	Page	Your score
I can understand most TV news and current affairs programmes such as documentaries, live interviews, talk shows, plays, and the majority of films in standard language.	62, 68	1 ② 3 4 5
I can use a variety of strategies to achieve comprehension, including reading for main points and checking comprehension by using contextual clues.	60, 61, 64, 68	1 2 ③ 4 5
I can scan quickly through long and complex texts, locating relevant details.	64, 65, 66, 67	1 2 ③ 4 5
I can engage and participate in extended conversation on most general topics.	60, 62, 64, 68	1 ② 3 4 5
I have sufficient vocabulary to express myself on matters connected to my field and on most general topics.	61, 62, 64, 67, 68, 69	1 2 3 ④ 5

Unit 7

Competences	Page	Your score
I can understand standard spoken language, live or recorded, on both familiar and unfamiliar topics normally encountered in personal, academic, or professional life.	75, 78, 80	1 2 ③ 4 5
I can read many kinds of texts quite easily at different speeds and in different ways according to my purpose in reading and the type of text.	72, 73, 74, 75, 78	1 2 ③ 4 5
I can use a limited number of cohesive devices to make what I say clear and coherent.	78, 81	1 2 ③ 4 5
I show a relatively high degree of grammatical control and I do not make mistakes which lead to misunderstanding.	74, 75, 79	1 2 ③ 4 5
I can write clear, detailed text on a wide range of subjects related to my interests.	81	1 2 ③ 4 5

Unit 8

Competences	Page	Your score
I can understand most TV news and current affairs programmes such as documentaries, live interviews, talk shows, plays, and the majority of films in standard language.	82, 84, 88, 90	1 2 3 ④ 5
I can read and understand articles and reports on current problems in which the writers express specific attitudes and points of view.	82, 83, 85, 86	1 2 3 ④ 5
I can give clear, detailed descriptions on a wide range of subjects related to my field of interest.	82, 84, 85, 88, 89, 91	1 ② 3 4 5
I show a relatively high degree of grammatical control and I do not make mistakes which lead to misunderstanding.	84, 85, 89	1 2 ③ 4 5
I can vary my vocabulary to avoid frequent repetition, but gaps in my vocabulary can still cause hesitation.	82, 84, 86, 90, 91	1 2 3 ④ 5

Unit 9

Competences	Page	Your score
I can understand the main ideas of complex speech on both concrete and abstract topics delivered in standard language.	94, 96, 98	1 2 ③ 4 5
I can rapidly grasp the content and the significance of news, articles, and reports on topics connected with my interests or my job, and decide if a closer reading is worthwhile.	92, 93, 97	1 2 3 ④ 5
I can develop a clear description or narrative, expanding and supporting my main points with relevant supporting detail and examples.	101	1 2 3 ④ 5
I can understand and summarize orally short extracts from news items, interviews, or documentaries containing opinions, argument, and discussion.	92, 97, 98	1 2 ③ 4 5
I can speculate about causes, consequences, and hypothetical situations.	95, 97, 98	1 2 ③ 4 5

Unit 10

Competences	Page	Your score
I can read and understand articles and reports on current problems in which the writers express specific attitudes and points of view.	106, 107, 110, 111	1 2 ③ 4 5
I can explain a viewpoint on a topical issue giving the advantages and disadvantages of various options.	105, 108, 109, 111, 112	1 2 3 ④ 5
I can use a good range of vocabulary for matters connected to my field and on most general topics.	104, 106, 107, 110, 112, 113	1 2 3 ④ 5
I can follow the essentials of lectures, talks and reports, and other forms of presentation which use complex ideas and language.	105, 108, 112	1 2 3 ④ 5
I can engage and participate in extended conversation on most general topics.	104, 106, 108, 109, 111	1 2 3 ④ 5

Unit 11

Competences	Page	Your score
I can carry out an effective, fluent interview, following up on interesting replies.	118, 122	1 2 3 ④ 5
I can give clear, detailed descriptions on a wide range of subjects related to my field of interest.	114, 116, 117, 121	1 2 3 ④ 5
I can write clear, detailed texts on a variety of subjects related to my field of interest, using information from different sources.	123	1 2 3 ④ 5
I have a broad reading vocabulary, but I sometimes experience difficulty with less common words and phrases.	114, 117, 119, 121	1 2 3 ④ 5
I show a relatively high degree of grammatical control and I do not make mistakes which lead to misunderstanding.	117, 118	1 2 3 ④ 5

Unit 12

Competences	Page	Your score
I can read many kinds of texts quite easily at different speeds and in different ways according to my purpose in reading and the type of text.	126, 127, 130, 131	1 2 3 4 ⑤
I can use a variety of strategies to achieve comprehension, including listening for main points and checking comprehension by using contextual clues.	128, 130, 132	1 2 3 4 ⑤
I can initiate, maintain, and end discourse naturally with effective turn-taking.	128, 129, 130	1 2 3 ④ 5
I can speculate about causes, consequences, and hypothetical situations.	128, 130, 132	1 2 3 4 ⑤
My vocabulary accuracy is generally high, though some confusion and incorrect word choice does occur without hindering communication.	124, 128, 130, 133	1 2 3 ④ 5

1 Impressions Overview

Section	Aims	What the students are doing
Speaking SB page 8	Fluency work	Matching pictures with events and putting them in chronological order. Writing notes about the events and then discussing them.
Listening & Reading SB page 9	Listening for detail Reading for detail	Matching speakers with pictures. Completing what people say about events. Writing about memorable events and asking questions about them.
Grammar SB page 9	Verb structures	Underlining appropriate verb structures in sentences. Changing sentences so they are true for them.
Vocabulary SB page 10	Collocation	Talking about first impressions of people. Forming collocations for personal characteristics.
Listening SB page 10	Listening for gist and detail	Listening to a conversation and identifying the context. Completing a table with information from the conversation.
Grammar SB page 11	Auxiliaries (1)	Making sentences with *and so*, *and neither*, or *but* ... Writing sentences about themselves and a partner to play a game.
Grammar & Pronunciation SB page 11	Auxiliaries (2)	Studying tag questions. Choosing the correct question tags and practicing intonation.
Speaking: anecdote SB page 11	Fluency practice	Talking about a person who made a big impression on them.
Reading SB page 12	Reading for gist and detail	Completing a summary of an article about Adam Levine. Writing questions and correcting false statements.
Vocabulary SB page 12	Word formation	Studying words that can take the prefix *re*. Writing example sentences with words that take *re*.
Listening SB page 14	Listening for gist and detail	Looking at pictures of men and talking about the image they convey. Listening to the men describing their style, noting down the order they speak, and choosing adjectives to describe the journalist's attitude. Answering questions about the men. Then talking about men they know.
Grammar & Speaking SB page 15	Indirect questions	Studying the differences between direct and indirect questions. Completing indirect questions and asking a partner.
Vocabulary SB page 15	Items of clothing	Matching items of clothing to accessories. Choosing alternatives to complete idiomatic expressions.
Language for Life SB page 16	Talking about people's appearance	Listening to conversations and answering questions. Matching useful phrases to functions and expressions to speakers. Completing sentences with useful phrases.
Life Skills SB page 16	Making a good first impression	Discussing first impressions. Ranking tips for making a good first impression.
Writing Extra SB page 17	Introduction emails	Rewriting informal expressions with more suitable formal ones. Writing a formal introduction email.
Writing WB page 7		Writing a short biography.

1 Impressions *Teacher's notes*

Warm up

Ask the students what they think is the most memorable image from television, newspapers, advertising, or movies that they've ever seen. Get them to describe the event this image depicts and talk about why the image made such an impression on them. You might like to start them off by choosing your own memorable image and describing it to the class.

Speaking (SB page 8)

1

- Pairwork. Focus the students' attention on the four pictures and give them time to discuss in pairs what they can see and to match them with the events in the box.
- Check answers with the class before asking the students to decide in their pairs the chronological order of the events.

ANSWERS:
a Rio de Janeiro Olympics
b "The Great American Eclipse"
c Climbing Mount Everest
d Invention of the iPhone
Order: **c** 1953, **d** 2007, **a** 2016, **b** 2017

2

- Pairwork. Go through the headings with the class and ask the students for some information about the events pictured in Exercise 1 that could go under these headings.
- Give the pairs a time limit to write as much information as they can about the events under the headings. Emphasize that no piece of information is too small.
- Either conduct feedback with the class or put the students into groups to share their information and discuss the impression the events made on them.

Cultural notes

Rio de Janeiro Olympics /riːəʊ də dʒəˈnɪərəʊ əˈlɪmpɪks/
The 2016 summer Olympics, also known as *Rio 2016*, were held from August 5-21, 2016 in 6 different cities in Brazil. Over 11,000 athletes from around the world competed, and the host nation won seven gold medals. Before the start of the games, there was controversy due to economic issues in Brazil and safety concerns over the Zika virus.
"The Great American Eclipse" /ðə greɪt əˈmerɪkən ɪˈklɪps/
"The Great American Eclipse" was the name given by the media to the total solar eclipse on August 21, 2017. This eclipse was special as it was visible throughout mainland USA, as well as parts of Canada, South America, Europe, Africa, and Asia. The last such eclipse occurred in 1918, nearly one hundred years earlier.
Climbing Mount Everest /ˈklaɪmɪŋ ˌmaʊnt ˈev(ə)rəst/
On May 29, 1953, New Zealander Edmund Hillary and Nepalese Tenzing Norgay were the first people to reach the summit of Mount Everest, the tallest mountain in the world at over 29,000 feet. They were part of a British expedition led by John Hunt. Many people still argue over who really reached the top first, Hillary, Tenzing, or other climbers from earlier expeditions.
Invention of the iPhone /ɪnˈvenʃ(ə)n əv ði aɪfoʊn/
The iPhone was first unveiled in a conference by CEO Steve Jobs on January 9, 2007. It was the first 'smartphone' as we know them today. Six months after the unveiling, the iPhone went on sale, and there was immediately a huge demand. It was named the invention of the year by *Time* magazine.

Listening & Reading (SB page 9)

1 ▶ 1.02–1.05

Focus attention on the four pictures and explain that these people are journalists (TV and newspaper), and that they are going to talk about the four events shown on page 8. Ask them to listen and match the people to the events.

ANSWERS:
Chris: **b** Margot: **d** Ritu: **c** Rafael: **a**

▶ 1.02
Rafael
As a television reporter, this was maybe the most exciting time of my career. The whole country was filled with visitors and the international media, and there was just so much going on every single day for those two weeks. I would get up at dawn and stay out until late at night – I think I am still recovering from it! The highlight for me was reporting live from the beach volleyball tournament where our men's team took home the gold. Interviewing Alison and Bruno afterwards, I knew the whole country was cheering them on.
▶ 1.03
Chris
Unlike some other stories, we knew in advance when it was going to happen, so we were really prepared that day. I remember people were going

crazy, trying to find special glasses and a good place to see it, and everyone was happy to talk to us. As a journalist, I'm always reporting on negative events, and I have been doing this a long time, so this was a nice change for me. When it actually happened, it was truly spectacular and there was no need to say anything – we just watched and filmed, amazed like everyone else.

1.04

Ritu

This was a long time ago, and I'd only been reporting the news for a couple of months at that point. But already, I had seen a lot of people come to try to do the impossible. So, even though I knew it could happen, I was still shocked when they actually made it to the peak. I knew everyone would want all the details, so I made sure to ask everyone involved as many questions as I could, especially our new local national hero! Many people have reached the summit since, but it used to be more difficult back then, and plus, it's always more special the first time.

1.05

Margot

I had come all the way from Europe to San Francisco just to go to this event, so I definitely had a feeling that something important was going to be revealed. I had already been coming to these kinds of things for a few years now, but when Steve Jobs gave us his presentation, we were all blown away – the camera, the internet, we had never seen anything quite like it! Even so, I would never have guessed just how much that little handheld device would change all of our lives! Nowadays, we take them for granted, but back then, it was way ahead of its time.

2

- Go through the instructions with the class and direct their attention to the example in the text by Chris. Ask the students to complete the remaining texts. Allow them to work in pairs if they wish.
- Go around, monitoring and giving help. Check answers with the class, accepting alternative answers that are grammatically correct, and then ask four students to read aloud the completed texts so that they hear the verbs in context. Then play the recording again for a final check.

ANSWERS:

Chris	**Ritu**
1 was going	**6** had seen
2 have been doing	**7** have reached
	8 used to be
Margot	**Rafael**
3 had	**9** would get
4 had already been coming	**10** am still recovering
5 take	

3

- Go through the instructions with the class and ask the students to work individually to choose their three memorable events for each category. Ask them to think about the words they'd need to describe these events and the effect they had on them.
- Put the students into pairs and ask them to take turns talking to each other about the events they chose. Encourage them to ask follow-up questions to find out as much detail as possible about all the events.
- Ask the students to report back to the class on the information they discussed about the events.

Grammar (SB page 9)

Verb structures

1

Do this exercise with the whole class and make sure the students understand the difference between the different structures and their uses. Point out the verbal clues that can help determine which tense to choose, for example, the various time expressions, the use of *for* and *since*, etc.

ANSWERS:

a I've known	**e** I've been learning
b I had	**f** I've gone
c I was talking	**g** I'd already met
d I like	**h** I used to have

Language note

Grammar: verb structures (present and past)
(See Student's Book page 140.)

2

- Go through the instructions with the class and ask the students to work individually to choose their five sentences and change the names. Remind them that the completed sentences must be true.
- Put the students into pairs and ask them to read each other's sentences and to ask follow-up questions to find out more about the people named in them.
- Encourage the students to report back to the class on what they learned about their partners.

3 Grammar Extra 1, Part 1

Ask the students to turn to Grammar Extra 1, Part 1 on page 140 of the Student's Book. Here they'll find an explanation of the grammar they've been studying and a further exercise to practice it.

ANSWERS:

1

a remember; heard	**e** used to; have changed
b 've seen	**f** affected
c watched	**g** 'd never enjoyed; saw
d think; was	

Vocabulary (SB page 10)

1

- Focus the students' attention on the picture and caption. Elicit or explain that a *first impression* is the reaction people have to you the first time they meet you. The saying *You never get a second chance to make a first impression* emphasizes the importance of creating a good impression when you meet people for the first time, as it's often only their first impression of you that they remember. If this first impression is bad, then you'll have difficulty making them think more highly of you in the future.
- Go through the ideas in the box with the class. Then put the students into pairs and ask them to discuss which of these things they notice most about people when they meet them for the first time. In a class feedback session, put them in order of importance.

2

- Go through the information about collocations with the class and remind them that a good dictionary will help them with the common collocations of a word.

ANSWERS:

a ~~brand~~	**b** ~~shiny~~	**c** ~~circular~~	**d** ~~pointy~~
e ~~strong~~	**f** ~~fair~~	**g** ~~heated~~	**h** ~~profound~~

Language note

Vocabulary: collocation

The examples of collocation in this unit are adjective + noun collocations and focus on ways of describing people's appearance. Although *pointy* and *spiky* mean the same, you'd say someone has *a pointy chin* and *spiky hair* but not ~~*pointy hair*~~ and ~~*a spiky chin*~~.

3

- Focus the students' attention on the example. Point out that each set of adjectives can only be matched with one word from the list in Exercise 1, though individual adjectives from each set might also collocate with other words.
- Ask them to match the remaining sets of adjectives with the words in Exercise 1. Allow them to use dictionaries if necessary, and then check answers with the class.
- Encourage the students to make sentences using the collocations so that they can hear them in context. For example, you might ask them to use them in sentences describing people they know.
- Finally, put the students into pairs and ask them to discuss which of the characteristics they'd find appealing or unappealing. Encourage them to report back to the class on their thoughts.

ANSWERS:

a handshake	**b** face	**c** smile	**d** eyes
e hair	**f** voice	**g** clothes	**h** manner

Listening (SB page 10)

1 1.06

- Go through the instructions and the questions with the class so that they understand the context of the situation and know what information to listen for.
- Play the recording and ask the students to answer the questions.

ANSWERS:

a New York (Brooklyn)
b Working
c The conversation stops because the man says something uncomplimentary about Ms. Rivera – the woman's mother.

1.06 **(W = Woman; M = Man)**

W: Excuse me, is it OK if I sit here?
M: Sure, go ahead.
W: Thanks. ... Sorry, but you're American, aren't you?
M: Yes. How did you know?
W: Oh, I heard your accent. ... It isn't very busy here today, is it?
M: No, it isn't.
W: Are you on vacation?
M: No, I'm working here for a few months.
W: Oh, really? So am I. What do you do?
M: I work for the American Central Bank.
W: Oh. And do you like it here?
M: Yeah, I love it. But I can't stand the weather. It was so hot yesterday, wasn't it?
W: Oh yeah, you're right: the heat's terrible. But, you know, I love it here too.
M: How long have you been here?
W: Oh, not long – a few weeks. How about you?
M: The same. What are you doing here?
W: I'm an artist, and I was asked to bring over some of my work to a small gallery just near here. I just had my first exhibition there.
M: Wow – that is impressive.
W: Thanks. So where are you from?
M: I'm from New York, Brooklyn, actually.
W: Really? So am I! Don't tell me you went to Brooklyn High School?
M: Yes, I did – but I wasn't a very good student.
W: Me either. What year did you graduate?
M: 2006.
W: That's weird – me, too. Do you remember Ms. Rivera?
M: The Math teacher? Yeah. She was really awful, wasn't she?
W: She's my mom.
M: Oh. ... Gee, I'm sorry. ... I didn't mean to ...

2

- Encourage the students to complete as much of the table as they can from memory.
- Play the recording for them to check their answers and fill in any blanks. Then check answers with the class.

ANSWERS:
a ✔✔ b ✘✘ c ✔✔ d ✔✘ e ✔✔
f ✘✘ g ✘✔ h ✔✔ i ✘✘ j ✔✔

3

- Make sure the students understand the expression *to put your foot in your mouth*, which means to accidentally say something embarrassing or that upsets or annoys someone.
- Put the students into pairs to discuss whether they or anyone they know has ever put their foot in their mouth. You could start them off with an example of your own.
- Encourage them to report back to the class on any interesting stories.

Grammar (SB page 11)

Auxiliaries (1): *so / neither*

1

- Go through the information in the margin with the class. (See Language notes.) Point out that the ✔s and ✘s indicate whether the response is agreement or disagreement.
- Pairwork. Put the students into pairs and explain what they have to do. Go through the example with them, pointing out that the second part of the sentence compares the woman with the man, and it establishes that the information about the man being American is also true of the woman. As a result, you use *so* + an affirmative verb. Write up on the board *The man isn't Mexican* and ask the students about the woman, eliciting *and neither is the woman*. If necessary, do one more example using *but ...*, like *The man works for a bank but the woman doesn't*, before asking them to work in their pairs and complete the exercise.

ANSWERS:

a The man is American and so is the woman.
b The man isn't on vacation and neither is the woman.
c The man is working in Mexico City and so is the woman.
d The man works for a bank but the woman doesn't.
e The woman likes Mexico City and so does the man.
f The man hasn't been in Mexico City a long time and neither has the woman.
g The woman is an artist but the man isn't.
h The man is from New York and so is the woman.
i The man wasn't a good student and neither was the woman.
j The man graduated from high school in 2006 and so did the woman.

Language notes

Grammar: auxiliaries - *so / neither*

- When you agree or disagree with someone, you use *so* or *neither*, depending on whether the first person used an affirmative or negative verb. The word *so* is used to agree with an affirmative verb and provides the affirmative idea in the response *So did I*. The word *neither* is used to agree with a negative verb and provides the negative idea in the response *Neither have I* - the verb *have* remains in the affirmative. Note the use of *did* in the responses to the first sentence, in which there's no auxiliary verb, and the use of the auxiliary *have* in the responses to the second sentence, which contains the auxiliary *have*.
- For more information see Student's Book page 140.

2

- Establish who is going to work with whom in the pairwork stage of this exercise. Then go through the sentence beginnings with the class and ask them to work individually to write sentences they believe are true for both themselves and their partner. Don't let them confer.
- Go around, monitoring and giving help where needed. Make sure everyone has nine completed sentences.

3

- Ask the students to get into their pairs and to turn to page 136 and follow the instructions there to produce their Bingo cards. Remind them that *so* and *neither* are used to express agreement, and the choice depends on whether the verb used by the original speaker was affirmative or negative. They also need to remember to use *do/did* in their reponse if the statement does not have an auxiliary verb, but if the statement does have an auxiliary verb to use the same one in their responses.
- As the students play the game, go around checking to see that they're matching the responses to the statements correctly. In a class feedback session, ask several pairs of students to read aloud their statements and responses.

Grammar & Pronunciation (SB page 11)

Auxiliaries (2): Tag questions

1

- Focus the students' attention on the information in the margin. Point out that the auxiliary used in a tag question matches that used in the original statement, but that a positive statement has a negative tag question and vice versa.

- Pairwork. Draw the students' attention to the fact that these sentences come from the conversation between the man and the woman in the Listening section on page 10. Point out the intonation arrows on the two example sentences (see Language note below.) Encourage the students to read the examples aloud using the intonation patterns marked so that they can hear the difference. Then ask them in their pairs to match the information in A and B.

ANSWERS:

A	B
positive statement	asking a real question
negative statement	negative tag question
rising intonation	asking for agreement
falling intonation	positive tag question

Language note

Pronunciation: rising and falling tone on tag questions

If you use a tag question to ask for agreement, you use a falling tone on the tag question. If you use a tag question to ask a real question, you use a rising tone. This distinction is one that students have trouble with, and it's always worth giving them as much opportunity to practice as possible.

2 1.07

- Suggest that the students tackle this in two stages: first identifying the correct tag question and then thinking about the intonation.
- As they work, go around making sure that everyone has chosen the correct tag questions. Then ask them to decide which of the questions are asking for information and which are asking for agreement. When they've decided, encourage them to say the questions aloud using the appropriate intonation so that they get a feel for what sounds right.
- Play the recording for the students to check their answers. Play it a second time for them to listen and repeat. When they've done this chorally, ask for individual repetition of the questions and insist on correct pronunciation.

ANSWERS:

a isn't it? (falling)
b aren't I? (falling)
c wasn't it? (falling)
d have you? (rising – but possibly falling)
e are they? (rising – but possibly falling)
f do you? (rising)

3 Grammar Extra 1, Part 2

Ask the students to turn to Grammar Extra 1, Part 2 on page 140 of the Student's Book. Here they'll find an explanation of the grammar they've been studying and further exercises to practice it.

ANSWERS:

2

a So have I. / I haven't.
b So am I. / I'm not.
c Neither do I. / I do.
d So was I. / I wasn't.
e Neither have I. / I have.
f So did I. / I didn't.
g Neither can I. / I can.
h Neither would I. / I would.

3

a	aren't you	**e**	mustn't he
b	isn't it	**f**	have they
c	can she	**g**	shall we
d	do we	**h**	will you

Speaking: anecdote (SB page 11)

Anecdotes are features that occur regularly in this series. They are extended speaking tasks, where the students tackle a longer piece of discourse on a personal topic. There are questions to guide them. For more information about how to set up, monitor, and repeat anecdotes, see pages xix to xx in the Introduction.

- Go through the instructions and the questions with the class. Give the students a minute or two to decide who they're going to talk about. Then ask them to look at the questions and think about their answers to them. Allow them to make notes of what they're going to say and how they're going to say it, but discourage them from writing a paragraph that they can simply read aloud. Go around, monitoring and giving help where necessary.
- Pairwork. Put the students in pairs and ask them to take turns telling their partner about the person who made a big impression on them. Encourage them to ask each other follow-up questions to get further information.
- Ask some pairs to report back to the class on what they found out.

Reading (SB page 12)

1

- Focus the students' attention on the pictures of Adam Levine on pages 12 and 13. Ask them to work in pairs and to answer the questions.
- Ask them to report back to the class and see how much information the class can pool. Write their ideas on the board. There are no right or wrong answers for this task. Remind them that thinking in advance about the things they already know about a subject will help them when they come to read a text about it.

2

- Ask the students to read the article on page 13 and to complete the article summary by filling in the gaps with the words in the box. Also ask them to identify how much of the information they discussed in Exercise 1 was actually in the text.
- Go through the summary with the class and elicit the correct answers. Ask students to give reasons to justify their answers. Go through the summary with the class and elicit the correct answers. Ask students to give reasons to justify their answers.

ANSWERS:

1 popular	**3** himself	**5** honesty
2 success	**4** family	**6** aware

Cultural notes

Los Angeles /lɒs ˈæŋgələs/
Los Angeles is the largest city in the US state of California. It has a population of just under four million. Los Angeles, often known by its initials, L.A., is the center of the US entertainment industry, especially Hollywood, where many movies and TV shows are made.

Grammy Awards /ˈgræmi əˈwɔː(r)dz/
A Grammy Award (typically known as a Grammy) is a prize given in the US each year to the best performers and writers of music. The Grammys began in 1959 and the awards show takes place in Los Angeles. The awards show is televised and many well-known artists and celebrities attend and perform.

The Voice /ðə vɔɪs/
The Voice is a popular reality television singing completion in the USA as well as in other countries. Four coaches choose their teams without seeing (only hearing) the contestants, and then every week the contestants compete against each other. The audience at home votes to decide the winner.

USA Today /jʊweseɪ təˈdeɪ/
USA Today is an American newspaper which is printed and distributed across the USA as well as countries abroad. Its stories often focus on popular culture and it is well known for its use of colorful images and graphics.

***People* magazine** /ˈpiːp(ə)l ˌmægəˈziːn/
People is an American magazine which focuses on celebrity and human interest stories. It is the most popular magazine in the United States and is well known for its special issues such as 'Best and Worst Dressed' and 'Sexiest Man Alive'.

3

Ask the students to read the article again and to write the questions for the given answers. Do the first one as an example with the class. Explain any unknown vocabulary and direct their attention to the glossary.

SUGGESTED ANSWERS (WORDING MAY VARY)

a When did Maroon 5 release their first album?
b What was the name of his first band?
c What kind of music does Maroon 5 play?
d What was his nickname?
e What activity does he practice daily?
f What are some of Adam's business ventures?
g What is his job/role on *The Voice*?
h Who named him 'sexiest man alive'?

4

Ask the students to work individually to decide if the statements are true or false. If the statements are false, students should re-write them so that they are correct. Have students check their answers in pairs before checking as a class.

SUGGESTED ANSWERS (WORDING MAY VARY)

a False. Adam's public image has never been better.
b False. Adam's first band was not successful.
c True
d False. Adam does not want to leave his band.
e True
f False. Adam is self-aware of his public image.

5

Ask the students to work in pairs and to discuss what advice they would give to someone who wanted to be famous. Encourage them to give as much advice as possible and, if necessary, give some general areas (talent, image, marketing, etc.). Then, have a class feedback session in which pairs present their ideas and similarities and differences between groups are discussed.

Vocabulary (SB page 12)

Word formation

1

Go through the information in the margin and make sure the students understand that the implication of the prefix *re* is that something is being done again. Then go through the instructions and ask them to choose the word in each line that cannot form a new verb with *re*. Strong students could try to do this without looking up the answers in the list of verbs in the margin.

ANSWERS:

a ~~change~~	**b** ~~prepare~~	**c** ~~erect~~
d ~~contemplate~~	**e** ~~copy~~	**f** ~~find~~

2

Give the students time to look in their dictionaries and find words that they know or can understand easily that have the prefix *re*. Encourage them to list words that take a particular prefix in a special section of their vocabulary notebooks. Go around and check to see that they're using their chosen words correctly in example sentences, and get several students to read aloud their sentences to the class.

Listening (SB page 14)

1

- Focus the students' attention on the pictures and ask them to think about their answers to the questions.
- In a class feedback session, find out how much agreement there is.

> **POSSIBLE ANSWERS:**
> **a** Charles: business-like, cool, fashionable
> Rick: casual, trendy
> Adam: trendy, fashionable
> Matt: casual, cool, trendy

2 1.08–1.11

- Explain that the students are going to hear a journalist interviewing the four men about their self-image. Ask them to listen and decide in what order she speaks to them. If possible, get them to say what clues in the things the men say led them to make their choices. For example, Matt talks about his sneakers; Charles mentions that he's wearing a suit.
- Play the recording again and ask the students to choose the words that best describe the journalist's attitude towards the men.

> **ANSWERS:**
> **1** Rick **2** Matt **3** Charles **4** Adam
> The journalist's attitude towards the four men is friendly, polite, and respectful.

1.08 **(J = Journalist; R= Rick)**

1

J: Excuse me.
R: Me?
J: Yes, hi there! I'm working on a feature for *DUDES* magazine about men's personal style. Do you mind if I ask you some questions?
R: No, I guess not.
J: Could you tell me what image you're trying to achieve?
R: Image? I don't really have an image. I wear clothes I feel comfortable in – I guess you'd call it a casual look.
J: Do you think that you're aware of fashion?
R: Er, probably not, no. My style hasn't changed for years.

1.09 **(J = Journalist; M = Matt)**

2

J: Hello! I'm doing some research for an article about the way men dress. Can I ask you some questions?
M: Yeah, no problem.
J: Do you mind telling me what you wear to go out at night?
M: At night? You mean clubs and that kind of thing?
J: Yes, when you go clubbing.
M: I dress exactly like this.
J: You don't dress up then?
M: Well, put it this way – I never put a suit on. The clubs I go to don't let men in if they're wearing suits.
J: Really?! How strange. OK, one more question. I'd just like to know if there's an item of clothing you couldn't live without.
M: Sneakers. Definitely couldn't live without them. I've got about twenty-five pairs.

1.10 **(J = Journalist; C = Charles)**

3

J: Excuse me! Hello.
C: Hello.
J: I work for *DUDES* magazine, and we're doing a survey about men's self-image. Do you mind if I ask you a couple of questions?
C: Oh. No, no; go ahead. What do you want to know?
J: Well, I'd like to know what your clothes say about you.
C: What do my clothes say about me? Gee – I guess they say that I'm meeting a client this afternoon, and that means I have to make the right impression. So I have to wear a suit.
J: Would you say that you care about your image?
C: Oh yes, I think I do. I like to look nice, even when I'm not working. Even when I wear jeans and a T-shirt, I like them to be neat and clean, and I think this says that I care about myself. It says that I have high self-esteem.

1.11 **(J = Journalist; A = Adam)**

4

J: Excuse me, sir. Is it OK if I ask you a couple of questions for an article I'm doing for *DUDES* magazine?
A: Yes, that's fine. Are you going to take pictures?
J: Yes, if you don't mind. But first I'd like to know whether your appearance affects your life in any way.
A: Oh yes, totally. The way I dress is my life. It hasn't really affected my career so far, but I'm hoping it will. Basically, I want to be noticed, and the reason I want to be noticed is that I want to be on TV.
J: Ah. And do you know what the last thing you bought was?
A: Oh yes, I love shopping. That would be a pink shirt I bought yesterday – oh, and a pink and black tie.

3

- Pairwork. Ask the students to discuss the questions in pairs and to make notes of their answers. Allow them to compare notes with other pairs before you play the recording again for them to check.
- Ask the students to work individually to answer the same questions with the names of men they know. Then ask them to take turns asking and answering

the questions with their partners using the new information. Encourage them to ask follow-up questions to find out more details.

ANSWERS:

a Matt	**b** Matt	**c** Adam	**d** Adam
e Rick	**f** Rick	**g** Charles	**h** Charles

Grammar & Speaking (SB page 15)

Direct questions / Indirect questions

1 1.12

- Focus the students' attention on the table. Point out that *What image are you trying to achieve?* and *Could you tell me what image you're trying to achieve?* are both correct. They're different ways of asking the same question. (See Language notes below.)
- Ask the students to complete the indirect questions in the right-hand column. Encourage them to do this first without looking up the answers in the recording script.
- Play the recording for them to check their answers. Then play it again for them to listen and repeat. When they've done this chorally, ask for individual repetition of the indirect questions. Encourage them to use a softer tone for these questions than they might for their direct equivalents.

ANSWERS:

a Could you tell me what image you're trying to achieve?
b Do you think that you are aware of fashion?
c Do you mind telling me what you wear to go out at night?
d I'd like to know what your clothes say about you.
e Would you say that you care about your image?
f I'd like to know whether your appearance affects your life.
g Do you know what the last thing you bought was?

Language notes

Grammar: indirect questions

- Indirect questions are often used as a way of putting a little (polite) distance between the person who is asking the questions and the person they're asking.
- In indirect questions, you don't put an auxiliary before the subject. The word order (subject + verb) is the same as affirmative sentences.
Direct question: *When did they meet?*
Indirect question: *Do you have any idea when they met?*
- In direct questions, the auxiliary verb *do* usually comes before the subject. Verbs like *can*, *have*, and *be* come before the subject.
Direct question: *What is your favorite color?*
Indirect question: *Could you tell me what your favorite color is?*
- *Yes/No* questions use *if* or *whether* in indirect questions.
Direct question: *Are they happy?*
Indirect question: *Can you tell me if they are happy?*

2

Ask the students to work in pairs and to discuss the main differences between the two styles of question. Ask them to make notes on the four factors listed. Then check answers with the class.

ANSWERS:

a Word order: changes from (auxiliary) verb + subject to subject + verb (the same as affirmative statements)
b *do/does/did*: not used in indirect questions
c *if/whether*: used in indirect *yes/no* questions.
d Formality: indirect questions are more polite.

3

- Ask the students to work individually to complete the questions. Go around, giving extra help where needed, and check answers with the class before moving on to the next stage of the exercise.
- Ask the students to work in pairs and to take turns asking and answering the questions.
- When they've finished, ask them to write three more questions each and then to take turns asking and answering these.

ANSWERS:

a Do you know where the cheapest clothing store in town is?
b Do you think cheap clothes are good value for the money?
c Where do you think the best place to buy jeans is?
d I'd like to know if/whether you've ever sewn a button on a shirt.
e Do you mind telling me how much money you would spend on a leather jacket?
f Could you tell me how many pairs of sneakers you have?
g Would you say (that) clothes and fashion matter to you?

Vocabulary (SB page 15)

1

Put the students into pairs and ask them to look at the list of parts and accessories and note down as many items of clothing as they can think of that have these. Allow them to use dictionaries if necessary.

ANSWERS:

a a belt: pants, a skirt, a dress, etc.
b a buckle: shoes, a skirt, a dress, etc.
c buttons: a shirt, a blouse, an overcoat, pants, a jacket, etc.
d a collar: a shirt, a jacket, etc.
e cuffs: a shirt, a jacket, etc.
f a hem: a skirt, a dress, pants, etc.
g sleeves: a shirt, a sweater, an overcoat, etc.
h a zipper: pants, a skirt, etc.

2

- Ask the students first to work individually to decide what the correct idioms are. Then ask them to discuss their answers in pairs. Tell them to use a dictionary if necessary to check and to find out the meaning of any they don't know.
- Check answers with the class and then ask the pairs to discuss whether they have any similar expressions in their language(s).
- Ask them to take turns saying whether any of the expressions could be used to describe people they know. Encourage them to report back to the class on what they found out.

ANSWERS:

a off-the-cuff
b buckle down
c as bright as a button
d tighten his belt
e on her sleeve

Extra activity

Ask the students to think about either the best-dressed or the worst-dressed person they know. Tell them to make notes about who this person is and what they wear. Then put them into pairs and ask them to take turns describing the person they chose.

Language note

Vocabulary: idiomatic expressions with clothes
There are many expressions connected with clothes. Clothes are used in similes (*as bright as a button*), in metaphors (*tighten your belt*), as well as in countless more idioms. For example, *the shoe is on the other foot* (the person who had the least power now has the most); *lose your shirt* (to lose a lot of money that you have invested or bet); *wear many different hats* (to do lots of different jobs).

Language for Life (SB page 16)

1 1.13

Focus the students' attention on the illustrations. Go through the questions with the class and tell them to listen to the conversation and find the answers.

ANSWERS:

a At a concert (or nightclub).
b Rosa and Ian are probably a couple. Mike is a friend of theirs.
c Mike's ex-girlfriend.

1.13 **(R = Rosa; I = Ian; M = Mike)**

R: Do you have the tickets?
I: No, I thought you had them.
R: Ian, honestly, I can't trust you to do anything.
I: Calm down – they're here.
R: Oh! You're so annoying.
I: You get worked up so easily. Hey, look at that woman over there.
R: The one in the green dress?
I: Yeah.
R: What about her?
I: Don't you think she's the spitting image of Gwyneth Paltrow?
R: No, she doesn't look anything like Gwyneth Paltrow.
I: Yes, she does. She has the same hair.
R: What – long and blond?
I: Not just that – I'd recognize that smile anywhere.
R: How often has Gwyneth Paltrow smiled at you?
I: I've seen enough movies with her in them. She has a very distinctive smile.
R: It can't be her – she wouldn't come here to this club. And actually, that woman bears absolutely no resemblance to Gwyneth Paltrow.
I: Oh.
...
R: Hey, there's Mike. Hi, Mike – how's it going?
M: Good – you'll never guess who I've been talking to.
I: Not Gwyneth Paltrow!
M: Gwyneth Paltrow?
R: Oh, ignore him – he's obsessed.
I: Sorry. You were saying?
M: Well, I was just at the bar, and I saw this amazing-looking woman walking towards me. I didn't recognize her until she was right in front of me. She's changed so much!
R: Who was it?
M: Sally – you know, my ex-girlfriend? Anyway, we ...

2

- Focus attention on the two columns and point out that in column 1 there are some useful phrases from the conversation. Column 2 has a list of their meanings. Ask the students to match the items in the columns.
- Ask the students to try to decide who said each of the expressions without listening to the recording.

Then play the recording for them to check their answers.

ANSWERS:	
a 2 - Ian	**d** 5 - Rose
b 3 - Rose	**e** 1 - Mike
c 6 - Ian	**f** 4 - Ian

3

Put the students into pairs and ask them to complete the useful phrases from the conversation, using the words in the box.

ANSWERS:	
a that woman	**f** that smile
b in the	**g** a very
c spitting image	**h** no resemblance
d look anything	**i** looking woman
e the same	**j** changed so

4

- Ask the students to work individually to complete the sentences. Allow them to compare in pairs before checking answers with the class.
- Ask the students to change the sentences to make them true for themselves and their parents. They should then compare them in pairs and discuss their sentences.

ANSWERS:

a the spitting image of him.
b got the same eyes.
c a very distinctive way of walking.
d anything like her/my mother.
e absolutely no resemblance to the rest of the family.
f was an amazing-looking woman when she was younger.

Life Skills (SB page 16)

Introduce the topic of *first impressions* by eliciting situations where it is important to make a good first impression, e.g. at a job interview, meeting a boy/girlfriend's parents for the first time, etc. If necessary, clarify the meaning of *first impression* (the effect or influence that someone has on a person's thoughts or feelings when they meet for the first time).

1

Pairwork. Ask students to read the quotation and to decide what it means to them. Check answers with the class and elicit whether they agree or disagree with this statement and why.

2

- Individually, students read the tips for making a good first impression and put them in order from most to least important. This task aims to get students to consider the different elements of making a first impression, and there are no right or wrong answers.
- In groups, students compare their answers and try to come to a consensus. You may wish to refer students back to relevant vocabulary from SB page 10. Check answers as a class, discussing differences between groups, and elicit further tips to add to the list.

Writing Extra (SB page 17)

Introduction emails

1

Ask the students to work in pairs and discuss the questions.

2

Ask the students to read the email. Give them time to absorb what they read and decide whether the language is appropriate or not.

ANSWER:

A lot of the language isn't appropriate as it's a formal email that contains a lot of informal email features.

3

- Ask the students to read the email again and to replace the underlined words and expressions with their more formal equivalents. When checking answers, encourage the students to read the email aloud so that they get a feel for what sounds right.
- Have a class discussion on anything else they would change in the email. If you need to give them a hint, ask them to look at features of the email other than the language.

ANSWERS:

1 j	**2** f	**3** b	**4** e	**5** a	**6** l
7 g	**8** k	**9** i	**10** c	**11** d	**12** h

Other things to change to make the email more appropriate:
use a more professional email address and email signature, be more specific in the subject line, use one font and font size throughout, check for spelling mistakes (*excelent, intrested, busines*) and consistent spacing

You may wish to provide students with the corrected version of the email from the previous tasks to use as a model in their own writing.

To	info@fitnesstime.com
From	fatima@econsultants.com
Subject	Potential business partnership

Dear Dmitri,
My name is Fatima Raheem and I am a social media consultant at E-Consultants, a company specializing in online consultancy. I believe you know my colleague, Michael Beatty, who is a member of your gym and speaks very highly of your business.
I am writing to you today to see whether you might be interested in working together. Although your gym already has an excellent location, website, and facilities, we have conducted research and discovered that your business has very little online presence. Your name does not appear in searches for local gyms, and you do not seem to have any active company Facebook or Twitter accounts.
I believe that with my assistance as an expert in social media, we would be able to significantly increase traffic to your website and location, ensuring that the local community is aware of the fantastic services you provide. Because we realize how busy you must be as a business owner, we are interested in a partnership in which we would take care of 100% of your ongoing social media activity.
If you are interested in learning more, I would be pleased to provide further details about our work, experience, and what we can offer you. I would also be very happy to visit you at your business in order to meet face-to-face to discuss this opportunity.
Please do not hesitate to contact me, and I look forward to hearing from you.

Kind regards,
Fatima
Social Media Consultant
E-Consultants
fatima@econsultants.com
phone: 555-5555

4

- The writing could be done at home for homework. Alternatively, set aside class time and go around monitoring and giving help where needed. Point out that when they've written their emails, they'll be exchanging them with another student and replying to the email they receive.
- The writing could be written by hand. However, if possible, for more authentic email writing, have students write their emails on a computer and send them electronically.

5

Set up the exchange of emails and ask the students to reply to the one they've received. If they do this in class, go around offering help where necessary. The finished pairs of emails could be displayed in the classroom.

Writing

Workbook page 7
Writing a short biography
Sentence structure and paragraph organization
Spelling

Further practice material

Need more classroom practice activities?

Photocopiable resource materials in the Teacher's Presentation Kit / Extra Resources

Need more tests?

Test Generator
Teacher's Presentation Kit / Extra Resources / Tests

Need more on important teaching concepts?

Key concepts in *American Inside Out Evolution* pages xxi-xxxvi

Need student self-study practice?

Workbook pages 4-7

Need more information and ideas?

American Inside Out Evolution website www.macmillan.com.br/americaninsideoutevolution

Need to check what your students can do by the end of this unit?

Self-evaluation checklists on pages xxxix-xlvi

2 Generations *Overview*

Section	Aims	What the students are doing
Reading & Vocabulary SB page 18	Reading for detail	Matching ages to stages in life. Reading an article about learning a foreign language through a pen friend, and answering questions. Categorizing words and using them to complete comprehension questions. Discussing the advantages of international exchanges and study trips.
Reading SB page 20	Reading for gist and detail	Reading two personal profiles of a mother and a daughter and answering questions.
Grammar & Vocabulary SB page 21	Verb patterns (1)	Categorizing verbs from an article according to their patterns. Completing sentences using various verb patterns. Matching sentence halves to make advice for parents with teenagers.
Pronunciation & Vocabulary SB page 22	Single vowel sounds	Listening to and repeating single vowel sounds. Matching sayings with their meanings.
Speaking & Listening SB page 22	Fluency practice Listening for detail	Discussing what employers look for in prospective employees. Listening to managers talking about an upcoming second interview with a prospective employee. Choosing verbs to complete sentences.
Listening SB page 23	Listening for detail	Listening to a prospective employee explaining how he feels about going for his second inteview for a new job.
Grammar & Vocabulary SB page 23	Adjective structures	Choosing the correct prepositions to follow adjectives. Completing sentences with appropriate prepositions. Talking about feelings.
Reading & Listening SB page 24	Reading for detail	Choosing expressions to complete conversations. Discussing advice for attending job interviews.
Listening & Speaking SB page 25	Listening for gist Fluency practice	Listening to someone talking about a school exchange and identifying the gist of what she says. Putting an account of a visit in the correct order. Writing and discussing true sentences with verb + preposition structures.
Speaking: anecdote SB page 25	Fluency practice	Talking about staying in someone's home.
Language for Life SB page 26	Useful conversational phrases for showing someone around your house	Listening to someone showing a new au pair around their home and answering questions. Numbering rooms in the order they're mentioned. Matching the two halves of useful phrases.
Life Skills SB page 26	Intergenerational Communication	Discussing intergenerational communication. Suggesting solutions for intergenerational communication conflicts.
Vocabulary Extra SB page 27	Learning about words	Reading a text about word frequency and answering questions. Answering questions on the dictionary entry for *word*. Discussing the meaning of common phrases with *word*.

2 Generations *Teacher's notes*

Warm up

- Ask the students to write the names of members of their own family on pieces of paper and ask and answer questions in groups. For example:
  Who is Annie?
  She's my sister.
  Is she older than you or younger than you?
  She's older than me.
  And who's Bill?
  He's my brother-in-law. He's married to Annie.
- Ask the students which members of their family they consider come from a different generation from themselves. Find out if this is always a question of age or whether they think attitudes play a role in how they define different generations.

Reading & Vocabulary (SB page 18)

1

- Focus attention on the two pictures and ask the students to say how old they think the baby and the man are.
- Put the students into pairs and ask them to decide what ages correspond to the stages in the chart and to fill them in. Then discuss their answers as a class. Answers may vary, but find out how much consensus there is. Check to see that the students understand *international exchanges* (see Language note).
- Keep the students in the same pairs and ask them to discuss the remaining tasks. Again, answers will vary (see suggestions below), but see how much consensus there is across the class.

SUGGESTED ANSWERS:
0–3 – infancy: probably associated with first words
4–12 – childhood: probably associated with learning to swim and school trips or international exchanges
13–17 – adolescence: probably associated with school trips or international exchanges
(You could also talk about "youth," which might be from adolescence to 40s depending on your vantage point.)
18 and up – adulthood: probably associated with buying a car, changing a baby's diaper, leaving home
45/50–about 60/65 – middle age: probably associated with retiring, senior discounts given at places like museums and hotels in the US
70+ – old age (getting older all the time!): perhaps get the students to suggest events that they associate with old age

2

Focus the students' attention on the article on page 19. Point out that it was written by a young man named Antonio about his experience with a pen pal. Go through the questions with the class to make sure that they know what information to look for when they read the article for the first time.

ANSWERS:
a Hannah. From the United States.
b Yes. His English was getting better every day but he needed to improve his fluency, so he did video calls with Hannah. He spoke English with Hannah and her family for three whole days. His English improved immensely in the month he spent with Hannah and her family. He achieved his lifelong dream of learning a foreign language.
c He remained friends with Hannah. He visited her again in the United States and Hannah visited his hometown Óbidos again during her gap year.

Language note

Pen pal
A pen pal is a friend from another city or country that you write letters or emails to. This kind of friendship or relationship was common in the past among children and teenagers. Nowadays, young people prefer to communicate via text message or online video chat as they are much faster than email. It is very rare for young people to send letters through the post. Pen pals helped young people to learn a foreign language and/or learn about different cultures and places, and to improve their literacy.

3

Ask the students to look at the highlighted words in the article and put them in the table under the correct headings.

ANSWERS:

Language learning	Relationships	Describing people
pen pal	doted on	sporty
fluency	soured	cool
aptitude	grew apart	hip
immersion	barely speaking	urban
rusty	in touch	

4

- Do the first question with the class as an example and then ask them to complete the remaining questions with words from Exercise 3.
- Make sure all the students have completed the questions correctly before getting them to answer them.

> **ANSWERS:**
> **a** aptitude
> **b** pen pal
> **c** hip and urban
> **d** sporty
> **e** dote on
> **f** in touch
> **g** rusty
>
> **a** Antonio's teachers encouraged him to find internet pen pals to practice his English language skills.
> **b** To practice his new found language skills.
> **c** Because they wore fashionable clothes and used all the latest slang.
> **d** Basketball.
> **e** So that he wouldn't feel homesick.
> **f** Yes. They write each other at birthdays and special occasions.
> **g** Antonio continued to practice his English so he would never become rusty.

5

Put the students into small groups to discuss the questions. Encourage them to report back to the class on what they found out.

Reading (SB page 20)

1

- Pairwork. Focus the students' attention on the two pictures and ask them to discuss the two questions with a partner.
- Ask the students to read the article. Then ask them to discuss as a class which generation each woman belongs to.

> **ANSWERS:**
> **a** The woman on the left is a Generation Xer. The woman on the right is a Millennial.
> **b** Students are free to make suggestions. Listen to their ideas and have them read the text below to confirm their ideas. Discuss this question further after reading.

Cultural notes

The term 'generation' refers to a group of people in a society who are born and live around the same time. Even though there are general descriptions of each generational group or cohort, the characteristics of each generation may differ from country to country, depending on the culture, politics, and economy of each place. The following table has some information on the six generational cohorts alive today.

GENERATION	YEARS	CHARACTERISTICS
G.I. Generation	1901 - 1926	Young people from this generation fought in WWI and WWII
The Silent Generation	1927 - 1945	Post-war euphoria, with peace, jobs, and access to housing.
Baby Boomers	1946 - 1964	Marked by free-love and social movements in the 1960s
Generation X	1965 - 1980	Entrepreneurial and individualistic. Transition generation between analog and digital technologies.
Millennials	1981 - 2000	Computer literate, this generation has high expectations of themselves. They are good at team work. They do not live to work and prefer a more laid-back work atmosphere.
Generation Z	2001 onwards	Very tech and media savvy. Very well informed about the world.

2

- Go through the questions with the class. Make sure that everyone understands them. Then ask them to work individually to re-read the article and find the answers.

> **ANSWERS:**
> **a** Martha spent a lot of time outdoors playing with friends but her children didn't. Martha believes that her children missed out on the kind of childhood she had because they spent more time indoors reading and playing video games.
> **b** So she could help them with anything they need.
> **c** Because she had all the latest games.
> **d** Tiffany.
> **e** No.

Grammar & Vocabulary (SB page 21)

Verb patterns (1)

1

- Go through the advice on verb patterns with the class. Make sure everyone understands the abbreviations: *sb* = somebody; *sth* = something.
- Focus attention on the verb patterns in the boxes and ask the students to look back at the underlined words in the article and Exercise 2 on page 20. Ask them to record these verb patterns in the correct boxes.

ANSWERS:
- **a verb + *to*-infinitive:** get to do sth, love to do sth, try to do sth, manage to do sth, attempt to do sth
- **b verb + object + *to*-infinitive:** want sb to do sth, force sb to do sth
- **c verb + gerund:** love doing sth, can't stand doing sth, enjoy doing sth, hate doing sth
- **d verb + object + gerund:** dread sb doing sth
- **e verb + object + infinitive without *to*:** made sb do sth

Language note
Grammar: verb patterns
(See Student's Book page 140.)

2
- Go through the instructions with the class. Do one or two as an example. Then put the students into pairs and ask them to categorize the remaining verbs and verb phrases in the box. Allow them to use dictionaries if they wish.
- Check answers with the class. Ask the students if they can make example sentences using these verb patterns.

ANSWERS:
- **a verb + *to*-infinitive:** aim, arrange, ask, can't afford, decide, expect, help, hope, offer
- **b verb + object + *to*-infinitive:** allow, ask, expect, encourage, help, teach, tell, urge, warn (not)
- **c verb + gerund:** avoid, finish, not mind, spend time
- **d verb + object + gerund:** avoid, not mind
- **e verb + object + infinitive without *to*:** let

3
- Ask the students to complete the sentences with the correct form of the verb in parentheses. When checking the answers, get the students to read aloud the whole sentence so that they hear each word in context.
- Put the students into pairs and ask them to discuss which of the sentences are true for them.

ANSWERS:
- **a** talking
- **b** to save
- **c** lending
- **d** to drive
- **e** stay out
- **f** studying
- **g** sitting; watching
- **h** to start

4
- Pairwork. Ask the students to work in pairs to match up the sentence halves. Remind them that the advice should be sensible.
- When you've checked the answers, ask the pairs to discuss what advice their parents gave them when they were teenagers. Encourage them to report back to the class on what they found out.

EXPECTED ANSWERS:
- **a** You should help them do well at school.
- **b** You shouldn't let them smoke.
- **c** You should make them keep their rooms clean.
- **d** You should tell them not to believe everything they hear.
- **e** You should warn them not to take drugs.
- **f** You should encourage them to stay healthy.
- **g** You should ask them not to play their music too loud.
- **h** You should expect them to respect their elders.

Extra activity
Put the students into small groups. Ask them to prepare a list of eight children's rules for parents. These could be general rules or rules aimed at limiting the embarrassment they cause their children.

5 Grammar Extra 2
Ask the students to turn to Grammar Extra 2 on page 140 of the Student's Book. Here they'll find an explanation of the grammar they've been studying and further exercises to practice it.

ANSWERS:

1
- **1** to get
- **2** to rush
- **3** to go
- **4** to buy
- **5** taking
- **6** coming
- **7** to do
- **8** make

2
- **a** to cook
- **b** living; to move
- **c** going
- **d** to have
- **e** obey; do; getting

Pronunciation & Vocabulary (SB page 22)
Single vowel sounds

1 1.14
Focus the students' attention on the phonetic symbols and example words in the margin. Play the recording

and ask the students to listen and repeat. Point out the different spellings that can represent the vowel sounds.

2 1.15

- Play the recording and ask the students to listen and repeat.
- They should then write the phonetic symbol that represents the vowel sound in each underlined syllable.

> **ANSWERS:**
> **a** /æ/, /ɪ/
> **b** /ʌ/, /ɔ/
> **c** /ɑ/
> **d** /e/, /ɑ/
> **e** /u/, /i/
> **f** /ʊ/, /ə/

3

Point out that all the sentences in Exercise 2 are sayings in English. Go through the meanings with the class and ask them to match them to the sayings.

> **ANSWERS:**
> 1 **f**
> 2 **d**
> 3 **a**
> 4 **e**
> 5 **c**
> 6 **b**

4

- Put the students into pairs to discuss which of the sayings they like best and whether there are any similar sayings in their own language(s). Encourage them to report back to the class.
- Point out that although there are many sayings and proverbs like these in the English language, they are very seldom used and are probably best avoided by non-native speakers in conversation. These sayings most often occur in writing and are often alluded to in part rather than used in their entirety.

Speaking & Listening (SB page 22)

1

- Groupwork. Go through the points with the class and make sure that everyone understands them. Then ask the groups to discuss which they think parents would consider important or not important.
- In a class feedback session, find out whether there is general agreement across the groups. Then discuss as a class whether it makes a difference if the child is a son or a daughter.

2 1.16

- Go through the instructions and the statements with the class. Then play the recording and ask the students to mark the statements true or false.
- Check answers and ask the students to correct the false statements.

> **ANSWERS:**
> **a** False. They have interviewed him before.
> **b** True
> **c** True
> **d** False. He has the right qualifications. In fact, he went to one of the best universities in the country.
> **e** False. If he passes this second interview stage, he will sit our internal exam.
> **f** True

> 1.16 **(HR=Human Resources; EM=Employing Manager)**
> **HR:** Thanks for meeting with me about this next round of interviews.
> **EM:** No problem. I'm really looking forward to meeting Andy again.
> **HR:** Yes, he really stood out from the others. Of the three who passed to the next round, he is perhaps the most promising.
> **EM:** Yes, I agree, but I am bit worried, because he has changed jobs quite a lot since he graduated from university.
> **HR:** I see what you mean. It's difficult to know with the younger generation really, but it is quite common nowadays. Younger people rarely stay in a job for more than two or three years.
> **EM:** Do you see that as a problem?
> **HR:** No. In fact, it might even be a positive thing because it is essential for the company to find an employee with right kind of experience for the job.
> **EM:** That's a good point. And he will bring with him a lot of knowledge of the industry.
> **HR:** Yes. It's important for us to find someone with the right balance of experience and qualifications.
> **EM:** From what I saw on his résumé, he has the right qualifications. In fact, he went to one of the best universities in the country. I was impressed with that.
> **HR:** Yes, but remember that if he passes this second interview stage, he will sit our internal exam, which will test his knowledge of the area.
> **EM:** Will it provide us with enough information to make a decision?
> **HR:** Almost. If he does well in the test, then we ask for three recommendations from former employers. These should tell us something about his personality and work ethic, which is more difficult to test.
> **EM:** True. A strong work ethic is important. And he needs to be a strong character to deal with the kind of clients we have.

HR: If it works out and we offer him an attractive package, he is likely to stay with us for three to five years. Let's see how he performs in this new interview.
EM: (laughing) ... Yes, let's. Shall we call him in and get started?

3

- Ask the students to work individually to choose the correct verb forms to complete the sentences. Remind them of the work they've done on verb patterns.
- Allow the students to compare their sentences in pairs before playing the recording for them to check their answers.

ANSWERS:
a meeting
b know
c have
d find
e be
f stay

Listening (SB page 23)

1 1.17

- Remind the students that in the last section they heard two managers discussing an upcoming interview with a prospective employee, Andy. Now, they're going to listen to Andy explaining how he feels about the interview.
- Play the recording and ask students to say what reasons Andy gives for looking for a new job.

ANSWER:
He's looking for a new job because he is interested in facing new challenges. He has been in his present job for two and a half years, which is good by today's standards - not too long and not too short. He thinks it is important to change companies occasionally as this is the best way to learn about his industry and to keep growing as a professional.

1.17 **(I = Interviewer; A = Andy)**
I: And, how do you feel about this second interview?
A: I am a little nervous about being interviewed a second time, but I think it's normal in any hiring process to be a little nervous. I decided to apply for a job in a new company because I'm interested in facing new challenges. Besides, I have already been in my present job for two and a half years, which is good by today's standards - not so long that I become stuck in the same company, not too short that I seem unstable or unreliable to future employers. I think it is important to change companies occasionally as this is the best way to learn about my industry and to keep growing as a professional. On the other hand, some managers, especially more traditional ones, might see this as moving around too much and might think that I will not be reliable or stay long in their company so I'm afraid of being taken as irresponsible. Another thing that I worry about doing in this interview is freezing because of my shyness. I'm terrible at talking to people, and this can come across as unfriendly or stand-offish. However, I know that I have great industry experience and a suitable educational background, so I'm optimistic about meeting the requirements of the job.

2

- Go through the items in the box and ask students to underline the ones that Andy says might make a bad impression on the interviewers.
- Play the recording for them to check their answers, then ask what Andy is thinking will make a good impression on the interviewers.

ANSWERS:
His shyness and his conversation skills.
Because this can come across as unfriendly or stand-offish.

By his great industry experience and his suitable educational background.

Grammar & Vocabulary (SB page 23)

Adjective structures

1

- Focus the students' attention on the information on the three adjective structures and the example sentences in the margin.
- Ask them to read the three extracts from the conversation between the two managers and the interview with Andy, and underline the correct prepositions.

- When you check their answers, get them to identify who says each of these extracts.

> **ANSWERS:**
> **a** with (Employing Manager)
> **b** of (Human Resources Manager)
> **c** for (Andy)

Language notes

Grammar: adjective structures
Adjective + *to*-infinitive
This is a very common structure when using adjectives describing degrees of difficulty (*It's **easy to do** / I find it **hard to imagine***) or feelings (*It's so **irritating to do** what she wants all the time*).
Adjective + *for* + object + *to*-infinitive
An extension of the previous structure allows the speaker to apply the phrase to a third party (*It's **easy for you to do** / It's **hard for her to imagine***).
Adjective + preposition
Other adjectives commonly followed by prepositions are: *embarrassed about, proud of, good at, worried about, satisfied with, excited about, scared of.*

2

- Ask the students to work individually to complete the sentences. As they work, go around giving extra help if necessary.
- Check answers with the class, and then put the students into pairs to take turns asking and answering the questions.

> **ANSWERS:**
> **a** at
> **b** for
> **c** about
> **d** of
> **e** to
> **f** in
> **g** with
> **h** about

3

Ask the students to look at the table. Point out that the two example sentences have been formed by taking different elements from the table. Ask the students to write three facts about their feelings on a piece of paper. Point out that they can form these from the elements of the table or they can use their own ideas.

4

- Collect all the pieces of paper from the students, and then go through the instructions with the class. Use the question structure to elicit further examples of possible questions.
- Shuffle the pieces of paper and distribute them at random. Make sure that no one has received their own piece of paper. Then ask the students to mingle and ask questions to find out who wrote the sentences on the piece of paper they've received.

Reading & Listening (SB page 24)

1 1.18–1.19

- Focus attention on the two conversations. Point out that they are similar in that both involved people arriving somewhere. Ask the students to say what is the difference between them. If they are unsure, ask them what the relationships are between the people in each conversation, and how well they know each other. Get the students to predict that the conversation at the interview is likely to be more formal because it is a workplace setting and Andy needs to make a good impression to get the job.
- Ask the students to work individually to choose the most appropriate options to complete the two conversations.
- Allow them to compare their answers in pairs before playing the recording.

> **ANSWERS:**
> **Conversation 1**
> 1 **a** The door's open
> 2 **c** That's great
> 3 **b** how's it going
> 4 **a** beat
> 5 **a** What've you been up to
> 6 **c** chill out
> 7 **a** Do you want
> 8 **b** Whatever
> 9 **c** No idea
> 10 **b** on my last legs
>
> **Conversation 2**
> 1 **b** Come in
> 2 **a** Thank you
> 3 **a** How have you been
> 4 **b** Fine
> 5 **b** What have you been doing
> 6 **b** relax
> 7 **b** Would you prefer
> 8 **c** I don't mind
> 9 **b** I don't really know
> 10 **a** a little old-fashioned

1.18

Conversation 1

(S = Sarah; A = Andy)

S: Hello!

A: Hi. The door's open!

S: Here, I remembered to bring you the book.

A: OK, that's great!

S: So, how's it going?

A: All right, but I'm beat.

S: Why? What've you been up to?

A: Nothing – it's just that I worked late last night.

S: Oh. Well, you'd better just chill out this evening. Do you want to watch TV, or watch something online?

A: Whatever.

S: Do you know what's on TV tonight?

A: No idea. Trash as usual.

S: Oh, you're in a bad mood. You're not nervous about the interview this week, are you?

A: No, just tired. I feel like I'm on my last legs.

S: Get some rest and don't worry. I'll make you a cup of coffee.

1.19

Conversation 2

(HR=Human Resources; EM=Employing Manager; A=Andy)

EM: Hello. Please, come in!

HR: Welcome, Andy, nice to see you again.

A: Good afternoon. Thank you for calling me back for a second interview.

EM: Shall we begin? Please have a seat here, Andy.

HR: How have you been since our last interview?

A: Fine. Thanks for asking.

EM: What have you been doing?

A: Well, I have been working a lot lately, but that is normal at this time of the year, isn't it?

HR: Well, we hope you have found time to relax too.

A: Thanks.

EM: Just a reminder ... we'll be having a short written test after the interview. Would you prefer paper or computer?

A: I don't mind doing it on the computer.

HR: Good. Let's get started. Andy, we are interested in your knowledge about the industry. What do you know about our Corporation?

A: Well, all I know is what is public knowledge, what appears in the media and on your website. I have studied it, but I don't really know much more than this.

EM: Okay. I do know that you have worked at XYZ Ltd. What can you tell us about your time there?

A: I really enjoyed my time working there. I had several opportunities to grow which is always great because it prevents us from becoming a little old-fashioned.

HR: I see. Last time you spoke about ...

Language notes

Vocabulary: social register

This section deals with the different ways you talk to people depending on how well you know them. In many languages, there's a formal and an informal way of addressing people. The same applies in English, although it's the choice of phrase rather than a formal/informal way of saying "you" that makes the difference. Colloquial language like *chill out* is acceptable when speaking to friends, but in more formal circumstances *relax* would be the appropriate choice. On the other hand, it would sound strange if you said to a friend *May I take your coat?* as this is a formal way of trying to put someone at ease in your home. *You can put your coat on the bed* is a more likely way of speaking to a friend.

2

Groupwork. Go through the situation with the class, and then ask the students to discuss in their groups the kind of advice they might give and to make a list.

Listening & Speaking (SB page 25)

1

- Pairwork. Ask the students to discuss the question in pairs and to make a list of the things they'd expect.
- In a class feedback session, get each pair to present their list to the class.

2 1.20

- Focus attention on the picture and explain that it shows Rosa, a young woman from Colombia who lived with an American family for a while. Go through the statements with the class.
- Play the recording and ask the students to mark the statements true or false. Correct the false statements.

ANSWERS:

a True
b False. She was excited about trying out new things.
c False. She hates warm winters.
d False. They were happy to talk about Rosa's family and her boyfriend.
e True

1.20

I knew there were a lot of things I would have to get used to when I decided to go to the USA and stay with a family. But I was looking forward to experiencing a new culture. I am not difficult when it comes to food, so I was excited about trying new things. Also, I hate warm winters, so I was dreaming of the typical gray days in Seattle, where the family lived. I was a little worried about making new friends, and whether my host family would object to having my friends in their home. But they insisted on treating me like a member of the family. When I met them for the first time, they gave me a big hug and then asked me about my family, my work, and even my boyfriend. The other surprise was the weather – I think global warming has succeeded in turning Seattle into a tropical city! I had problems with the language at first – I couldn't understand anything! But the family made me feel at home, and it was definitely the best way to improve my English. In a family situation, you have to sink or swim. It's as simple as that.

3

- Ask the students to put the sentences in order. Then have them compare in pairs before checking with the class.
- Point out the use of verb + preposition structures in Rosa's account of her stay in the USA.

ANSWER:

Correct order: 1, 8, 4, 2, 5, 11, 6, 12, 10, 3, 7, 9

4

- Go through the sentences with the class and make sure everyone understands them. Point to the example sentence and elicit from the students that if a verb follows a preposition, its structure is verb + *ing*. Then ask them to work individually to complete the sentences so that they are true for them.
- Tell the students to discuss their sentences in pairs, asking follow-up questions to find out more details.

Speaking: anecdote (SB page 25)

For more information about how to set up, monitor, and repeat anecdotes, see pages xix to xx in the Introduction.

- Go through the instructions and the questions with the class. Give the students a minute or two to decide what they're going to talk about. Then ask them to look at the questions and think about their answers to them. Allow them to make notes of what they're going to say and how they're going to say it, but discourage them from writing a paragraph that they can simply read aloud. Go around, monitoring and giving help where necessary.
- Pairwork. Put the students in pairs and ask them to take turns telling their partner about the time they stayed in somebody's home. Encourage them to ask each other follow-up questions to get further information. Then ask some pairs to report back to the class about what they found out.

Language for Life (SB page 26)

1 1.21

- Focus the students' attention on the picture and ask them to say what they think is happening.
- Go through the instructions and the questions with the class and ask them to listen to the recording and note down their answers.

ANSWERS:

a Two.
b The kitchen.
c Pink.

1.21 **(J = Jennifer; M = Maria; B = Ben; K = Katy)**

J: Hello, Maria, come in. Did you have a pleasant flight?
M: Pleasant flight?
J: A good trip?
M: Oh yes, thank you. Very good.
J: Well, welcome to our home. I hope you'll be happy here. It's not very big, but I think you'll have everything you need.
M: Yes, thank you. It's very nice.
J: Oh good, I'm glad you like it. Let me introduce you to the rest of the family, and then I'll show you around.
M: OK, thank you, Mrs. Brown.
J: Oh, please, call me Jennifer. Now, this is Ben – he's thirteen.

B: Hello.
M: Hello, Ben.
J: And this is Katy - she's eleven.
M: Hello, Katy.
K: Hello.
J: And this is Max - he's a baby so he can get a little excited. ... Down, Max. Sorry. I hope you don't mind dogs.
M: No, I love dogs.
J: Oh good. So this is the kitchen - we usually eat breakfast in here. Help yourself to coffee. The refrigerator is here, look - and the cups and saucers are in this cabinet. I'm afraid the microwave is broken, but we seem to manage without it.
M: It's a nice kitchen.
J: Yes, it's my favorite room. Now, this is the living room - excuse the mess, but Ben and Katy have a lot of friends over. This is the dining room - Max isn't allowed in here, are you, Max? ... Down, boy! ... Now, if you'd like to leave your bags here for a minute, I'll show you the upstairs.
M: Thank you.
J: Here's the bathroom. Sorry about the pink walls - that was Katy's idea.
M: Oh, I like pink. My bedroom walls are pink.
J: Really? How funny. OK, this is Katy's room - we're not allowed to go into Ben's room, but it's probably just as well. And this is your room. It's quiet in here because the window looks out on the backyard.
M: Oh, it's great - thank you.
J: Now, you make yourself at home, and if there's anything you need, just holler, OK?
M: OK.
J: Oh, by the way, Ben's a vegetarian, so we don't usually eat meat because he gets upset. Is that OK with you?
M: Yes, I like vegetables.

2

- Go through the rooms in the box and make sure everyone understands them. Play the recording again. Ask the students to number the rooms in the order that Jennifer shows them to Maria.
- Check their answers and ask them to identify the three rooms that Jennifer doesn't show her.

ANSWERS:
1 the kitchen
2 the living room
3 the dining room
4 the bathroom
5 Katy's room
6 Maria's room

She doesn't show Maria her own room (Jennifer's room), Ben's room, or the study.

3 1.22

- Ask the students to work individually to match the two halves of the useful phrases. Then allow them to compare in pairs.
- Play the recording for the students to check their answers. Play it a second time for them to listen and repeat. When they've done this chorally, ask for individual repetition of the useful phrases.

ANSWERS:
a 4
b 3
c 7
d 2
e 8
f 5
g 6
h 1

1.22
a Did you have a pleasant flight?
b Welcome to our home.
c Let me introduce you to the rest of the family.
d Then I'll show you around.
e Please call me Jennifer.
f Help yourself to coffee.
g Make yourself at home.
h If there's anything you need, just holler.

Life Skills (SB page 26)
Intergenerational Communication

As you can see from the Culture Notes on page 15, each generation has different characteristics and influences, which affects their world view and communication styles. These differences can lead to conflict in relationships, families, and in the workplace. The exercise presented shows the kinds of conflicts that could occur.

To prepare students for this exercise, use the information from the Culture Notes to discuss the different characteristics of each generation.
Have students work in pairs or small groups to discuss the different communication problems in the table and to come up with possible solutions. The solutions presented below are suggestions, but students can also have their own ideas.

1

- In the workplace, have very clear rules about workplace communications and what is expected, allowed, and prohibited.
- With friends or family members, discuss and come to an agreement on the best way to communicate with each other. A text to your friends or siblings may be okay but it may not be the best way to communicate with your grandparents.

2

- In the workplace, it is always best to have a discussion between supervisor and subordinate on what the objectives and deliverables are. Expectations must be made clear. Subordinates need to make it clear to supervisors that the work is being done, even on a flexible time schedule. Constant communication will avoid conflict and misunderstanding.
- With family members of different generations, be flexible and try to understand their needs. Older generations may want to spend more time with family members or need more attention. Younger people can consider scheduling more time for family who need/want their attention.

3

- In the workplace younger generations could request a clear written outline of what the expectations are so that they do not require constant verbal feedback on their work. They could use the written parameters to verify their work and learn to work more independently. They can also request regularly scheduled feedback sessions with supervisors.

Vocabulary Extra (SB page 27)

Learning about words

1

Pairwork. Ask the students to discuss the questions quickly in pairs. Have a quick class feedback session to find out their answers.

2

Ask the students to read the information about word frequency, look at the graph, and discuss the questions.

> **ANSWERS:**
> **a** *the*
> **b** Around 45%.
> **c** 80%.
> **d** 7,500.

3

Ask the students to look at the dictionary extract for *word* and to answer the questions.

> **ANSWERS:**
> **a** Five.
> **b** News or information about someone or something.
> **c** News or information about someone or something.
> **d** 27 (some phrases have two possibilities).
> **e** Students' own answers.

4

Pairwork. Put the students into pairs and ask them to discuss the situations or contexts in which they might hear the sentences. Ask them to compare their ideas in small groups before having a class feedback session.

> **POSSIBLE ANSWERS:**
> **a** When they are asking a witness to a crime or accident for information.
> **b** When someone can't remember the lyrics to a song.
> **c** When someone is about to give a speech.
> **d** When someone, particularly in a work situation, would like to have a confidential chat with a co-worker.
> **e** When someone is asking the other person to keep information secret.

5

- Ask the students to make their choices without referring to the dictionary extract if they can. When they've finished, allow them to check their answers and the meaning of the phrases in the extract.
- Check answers with the class and see if the students can use the phrases in mini-conversations.

ANSWERS:
a say
b keep
c hear
d put
e Take
f fail

6

- Ask the students to look at their own dictionaries and compare the way they present the entry for *word* with the extract on the Student's Book page. Then ask them to report back to the class on what they found.
- Ask the students to choose five useful phrases to learn that include *word*. Encourage them to record the phrases in their vocabulary notebooks in example sentences.

Further practice material

Need more classroom practice activities?

Photocopiable resource materials in the Teacher's Presentation Kit / Extra Resources

Need more tests?

Test Generator Teacher's Presentation Kit / Extra Resources / Tests

Need more on important teaching concepts?

Key concepts in *American Inside Out Evolution* pages xxi-xxxvi

Need student self-study practice?

Workbook pages 8-11

Need more information and ideas?

American Inside Out Evolution website www.macmillan.com.br/americaninsideoutevolution

Need to check what your students can do by the end of this unit?

Self-evaluation checklists on pages xxxiv-xlvi

3 Gold Overview

Section	Aims	What the students are doing
Reading SB page 28	Describing people	Reading a text about the California gold rush.
Listening SB page 29	Listening for specific information	Connecting items in a picture with the story of a gold rush millionaire. Completing sentences to retell the story they've heard.
Vocabulary SB page 29	Collocations with *have*, *make*, and *take*	Completing collocations from the reading text. Completing more collocations with *have*, *make*, and *take*. Completing sentences with nouns and writing example sentences.
Vocabulary SB page 30	Metaphor Reading for detail	Studying the use of metaphors involving movement. Completing extracts from the reading text with metaphors. Reading a conversation and completing metaphors. Completing a table with metaphors.
Reading & Grammar SB page 31	Reading for gist Reported speech	Reading about a teenager who skipped class to go shopping. Rewriting reported speech as direct speech. Identifying how to change direct speech into reported speech.
Pronunciation SB page 32	The schwa sound	Completing a paragraph about the schwa sound. Underlining vowel sounds pronounced using a schwa.
Listening & Vocabulary SB page 32	Listening for gist Money expressions	Discussing questions about money. Listening to people talking about their attitudes towards money. Identifying expressions connected with money.
Grammar SB page 33	Unreal conditionals	Matching clauses to make conditional sentences. Discussing the structure and meaning of conditional sentences. Discussing hypothetical situations. Completing conditional sentences.
Reading & Vocabulary SB page 34	Reading for gist	Reading about shopping from the comfort of your home. Identifying true and false sentences. Matching words and meanings.
Listening SB page 35	Listening for gist	Matching possessions with notes on the stories about them. Reconstructing the stories from notes.
Speaking: anecdote SB page 35	Fluency practice	Talking about their most treasured possession.
Language for Life SB page 36	Shopping – money expressions; explaining what you want	Listening to a conversation about shopping and answering questions. Matching useful phrases to meanings. Rewriting requests in less direct language.
Life Skills SB page 36	Negotiating	Negotiating using key expressions for buying or selling a car.
Writing Extra SB page 37	Description	Completing a text about an imaginary perfect day with linking words. Adding their own details to the text. Writing an account of their own perfect day.
Writing WB page 15		Writing a story from pictures.

3 Gold Teacher's notes

Warm up

Ask the class if they know why the population of California increased dramatically around 160 years ago. If anyone mentions the gold rush, find out what they know about it.

Reading (SB page 28)

1

Focus the students' attention on the picture that goes with the text and ask them what they think the text will be about. Then go through the two items below with the class, and ask them to read the article and find what the links are between the items in each list.

ANSWERS:
- California is known as the Golden State and the idea of gold is closely associated with the state because of the Gold Rush, the Golden Gate Bridge, and the golden colored poppies which grow in the spring.
- James Marshall was working at Sutter's Mill in Coloma when he discovered gold in the river.

Cultural notes

San Francisco /ˈsæn frænˈsɪskoʊ/

San Francisco was founded in 1776 by Spanish settlers. It experienced rapid growth during the California gold rush in 1848. In 1906 an earthquake devastated the city, but it was quickly rebuilt, and it has become a popular tourist destination, as well as being home to 750,000 residents.

President James Polk /ˈprezɪdənt dʒeɪmz ˈpoʊk/ (1795–1849)

James Polk was the 11th president of the United States. He served from 1845 to 1849.

2

- Go through the words in the box with the class and make sure that everyone understands them. Explain that *dreamer* and *visionary* are similar in meaning, although *dreamer* tends to have negative connotations and *visionary* positive ones. Similarly, someone who might be praised by some people as an *entrepreneur* might be criticized by others as an *opportunist*.
- Ask the students to work in pairs and decide which words they'd use to describe the Forty-Niners. Then ask them to discuss whether they could use any of the words to describe people they know.

POSSIBLE ANSWER:
dreamer, risk-taker, opportunist

Listening (SB page 29)

1 1.23

- Focus the students' attention on the picture of Sam Brannan and tell them that he was the first person to become a millionaire in the California gold rush. Ask them to look at the picture of the Forty-Niner and identify the objects mentioned in the caption. Tell them that there's a connection between these items and Sam Brannan's fortune and that they're going to listen to the recording and find out what that connection is. With strong classes, ask the students to speculate on this connection before they listen.
- You may need to play the recording more than once. Encourage them to write brief notes as they listen.

ANSWERS:
During the Gold Rush, Sam Brannan made his fortune by selling these items and others to the gold diggers. He had the only store between San Francisco (Yerba Buena) and the gold fields. He bought up all the mining tools he could find and then he sold them to the Forty-Niners and made a lot of money. In the end he lost his fortune because of drink (liquor).

1.23
During the Gold Rush, Sam Brannan became one of the most successful businessmen in California. He arrived in California in 1846, when San Francisco (then called Yerba Buena) was just a small community of a few hundred people. When gold was discovered on John Sutter's land in 1848, Sam Brannan was running the only store between San Francisco and the gold fields. Quickly recognizing a gap in the market, he bought up all the picks, shovels, and pans he could find, and then ran up and down the

streets of San Francisco shouting, "Gold, gold on the American River!"
He had no intention of digging for gold! No, he was planning to sell shovels. And having cornered the market, he ended up with a lot more gold than the person who had to dig for it. This was a man who really understood the laws of supply and demand. A metal pan that sold for twenty cents a few days earlier was now available from Brannan for fifteen dollars. In just nine weeks, he made $36,000. Within a few years, he had become the first gold rush millionaire.
In the end, though, Sam Brannan lost his fortune and his health, as did many of those who first benefited from the Gold Rush. Alcoholism finally led to his downfall, and California's first millionaire died an unnoticed death.

2

- Pairwork. Go through the instructions with the class, and then ask the students to work in pairs to complete the sentences. Encourage them to try to do this without looking at the sentence endings.
- Play the recording again for them to check their answers.

ANSWERS:
a 3
b 6
c 8
d 1
e 10
f 4
g 2
h 9
i 5
j 7

Vocabulary (SB page 29)

1

Ask the students to look through the article on page 28 and find the extracts and the words that complete them.

ANSWERS:
a took
b make
c had

Language note

Vocabulary: collocations
Many words in English exist as part of a group of words that commonly occur together in a certain order. Verbs like *have*, *make*, and *take* are all commonly used in collocations. *Have breakfast* is much more natural than *eat breakfast*; you *make a mistake*, you don't *do a mistake*; you *take a picture*, you don't *make a picture*.

2

- Focus the students' attention on the table. Ask them to complete it by adding *have*, *make*, and *take*.
- Put the students into pairs and ask them to check the collocations in the list that they already know. In a class feedback session, encourage the students to teach the collocations that they know to students who don't know them.

ANSWERS:
a make
b take
c have

3

- Ask the students to complete the sentences and to think about which ones are true for them.
- When you've checked and discussed their answers, ask them each to choose five collocations from Exercise 2 that they think will be useful for them and to write example sentences. As they do this, go around monitoring and helping where necessary. Encourage the students to read aloud their sentences to the class.

ANSWERS:
a mess
b sense
c office
d difficulty
e sugar
f right

Vocabulary (SB page 30)

Metaphor

1

Focus the students' attention on the dictionary definitions. Read them aloud or get a student to read them. Ask for suggestions on what the words have in common. Explain that these are all metaphors and that a metaphor is a way of describing something by comparing it to something else that has similar qualities. (See Language notes on page 28.)

ANSWER:
They all have something to do with both water and movement.

Language notes

Vocabulary: metaphor

- A metaphor is a word or phrase that means one thing and is used for referring to another thing in order to emphasize their similar qualities.
- In this unit, movement (of people, mainly) is compared to water through metaphor. A *trickle* is a small flow of water, whereas *flood* and *deluge* refer to much larger flows. Using metaphor in this way gives the text a more literary sense.

2

- Pairwork. Put the students into pairs and ask them to use words from the dictionary definitions to complete the extracts. Encourage them to do this first without looking back at the article on page 28.
- Go around, giving help and encouragement. Then allow them to check their answers in the article on page 28.

ANSWERS:
a trickle, flood, deluge
b drifted
c streamed

3 1.24

- Go through the instructions with the class and allow the students plenty of time to read the conversation. Ask them what the difference is between Martha's and her dad's attitudes towards Martha's idea (Martha is enthusiastic, her father dismissive), and how her dad's attitude changes towards the end of the conversation (he begins to see that the idea is a good one). This will help them with the meaning of the metaphors they have to complete.
- Play the recording for the students to check their answers.

ANSWERS:
1 spare
2 precious
3 worth
4 wasting
5 profitably
6 half-baked
7 chewing
8 food
9 digest
10 running out
11 spend

1.24 **(M = Martha; D = Dad)**

M: Morning!
D: You're in a good mood today. Any particular reason?
M: Yes, there is. I've decided to become a millionaire.
D: You've decided to become a millionaire. I see. And how exactly do you propose to do that?
M: Well, if you can spare a couple of minutes, I'll tell you.
D: Martha, you know how precious my time is ...
M: Dad, I promise you it will be worth your while.
D: Oh, OK – but just five minutes or I'll be late for work.
M: OK. I've got this idea for a website ...
D: Oh come on, you're wasting your time if you think you can make money out of the internet. All the best ideas have been used up. You should be using your time more profitably, getting a real job ...
M: I promise you it's not some half-baked idea. It's something I've been chewing over for the last few weeks. Please just have a look at these plans, then tell me what you think.
D: Hm, yes, interesting. There's certainly food for thought here. How are you going to find the money to do it?
M: Well, I was hoping you might help me. Will you?
D: Well, I can't tell you until I've had time to digest all this information. But you certainly have a good idea. Very original.
M: But we're running out of time. If we don't do it very soon, somebody else will.
D: Yes, you could be right. Look, I've got to go now, but as soon as I get back from work I'll spend the rest of the evening looking at it. Have you told anybody else your idea?
M: No, not yet.
D: Well, don't ... I think you've really got something here.

4

- Ask the students to put the metaphors from the conversation in Exercise 3 into the table. Allow them to compare their answers in pairs.
- Check answers and make sure everyone understands all the metaphors. Then ask them to discuss whether they have similar metaphors in their own language(s).

ANSWERS:
Time = money
to spare a couple of minutes
to know how precious sb's time is
to be worth sb's while
to waste sb's time
to use sb's time profitably
to run out of time
to spend time
Ideas = food
a half-baked idea
to chew sth over
to be food for thought
to digest all the information

5

- Ask the students to complete the sentences.
- Check answers and then put the students into pairs to discuss whether they agree or disagree with them.

> **ANSWERS:**
> **a** chew
> **b** run
> **c** waste
> **d** food
> **e** spend

Reading & Grammar (SB page 31)

Reported speech

1

- Pairwork. Ask the students to discuss the questions in pairs. You may need to explain *extravagant* (spending a lot of money on something that isn't really necessary).
- Ask the pairs to report back to the class on what they found out about each other.

2

- Go through the instructions with the class and ask them why, in their opinion, the girl had to do community service.

> **POSSIBLE ANSWER:**
> The girl had to do community service as a form of punishment for the irresponsible act of skipping school, putting herself at risk, and having spent money that was not hers.

3

- Focus attention on the sentences in the margin. Point out that these are examples of reported speech, i.e. when you say what one person said to another without using their actual words.
- Ask the students to look through the newspaper again and to underline any examples of reported speech. Then check their answers.
- Go through the example with the class. Point out that there are differences between direct speech and indirect speech. Ask them to think about what the actual words are most likely to have been.

> **ANSWERS:**
> **a** am planning
> **b** did ... get
> **c** gave
> **d** are going
> **e** have punished
> **f** needed ... have been studying

Language note

Grammar: reported speech

(See Student's Book page 142.)

4

Go through the list of changes that occur when speech is reported with the class. Then ask the students to work in pairs and to find examples of each in the article. You could also ask them to look back at the sentences in the margin and to say what the actual words were in direct speech.

> **ANSWERS:**
> **a** Tense changes, e.g. was planning → had been planning; did → get → got; gave → had given; have punished → had punished
> needed/have been studying → had needed/had been studying
> **b** Word order changes, e.g. where did you get the money → where she got the money
> **c** Pronoun changes, e.g. you → she; I → she; my → her
> **d** Time reference changes, e.g. are going → were going

5 Grammar Extra 3, Part 1

Ask the students to turn to Grammar Extra 3, Part 1 on page 142 of the Student's Book. Here they'll find an explanation of the grammar they've been studying and a further exercise to practice it.

> **ANSWERS:**
> **1**
> **a** He said that he was just thinking about me.
> **b** She told us that they'd been to Paris a few days previously.
> **c** He said that when he got his bonus, he was going to spend it wisely.
> **d** He asked us how we managed to live on so little money.
> **e** She asked him what would happen to them the following day.
> **f** My manager told me that he thought my work was excellent.
> **g** I asked her if we could afford a vacation that year.

Pronunciation (SB page 32)

1

- Ask the students to read the explanation and underline the correct words to complete it.
- Then ask a student to read the explanation aloud, making sure that they're pronouncing the short words correctly.

> **ANSWERS:**
> **1** vowel
> **2** unstressed
> **3** never

Language note

Pronunciation: the schwa

The schwa /ə/ is a neutral, unstressed single vowel sound. It is the most common vowel sound in English. Getting the schwa sound right is a good way for your students to make their pronunciation sound natural. Students should always focus on the (phonetic) pronunciation of a word rather the way it's spelled. For example, in these words the schwa sound is: the *a* in *about* /əˈbaʊt/, the *e* in *fiftieth* /ˈfɪftiəθ/, the *i* in *identity* /aɪˈdentəti/, the *o* in *melody* /ˈmelədi/, and the *u* in *survive* /sərˈvaɪv/.

2 1.25

- Encourage the students to read the sayings aloud so they can hear which vowel sounds are pronounced using a schwa sound. They could do this in pairs, taking turns reading aloud a saying and identifying the schwa sounds.
- Play the recording for them to check their answers, then play it again for them to listen and repeat. When they've done this chorally, ask for individual repetition of the sayings and make sure they're pronouncing the schwa correctly.

ANSWERS:
a Money makes the world go around.
b There's no such thing as a free lunch.
c Put your money where your mouth is.
d The love of money is the root of all evil.

3

- Ask the students to discuss the sayings with a partner. Get them to report back to the class on which, if any, they like and whether similar sayings exist in their own language(s). (See Language notes below.)
- As with those in Unit 2 (Student's Book page 22), it would be wise to warn the students that these sayings are not often used in everyday life and that they are probably best avoided by non-native speakers, certainly in conversation.

Language notes

Vocabulary: money expressions

a *Money makes the world go around.* = Money is powerful and the world relies on it.
b *There's no such thing as a free lunch.* = Be suspicious of people who give you something free, as they'll probably expect something in return.
c *Put your money where your mouth is.* = Make your actions match your words.
d *The love of money is the root of all evil.* = People do evil things to get rich.

There are a lot of expressions where money is compared metaphorically to food: *bring home the bacon* (earn the money), *chicken feed* (small money), *breadwinner* (money earner); money is related metaphorically to clothes (see page 15): *tighten your belt, lose your shirt, live on a shoestring*; and money is related to the ocean: *splash out, push the boat out* (see Student's Book page 36).

Listening & Vocabulary (SB page 32)

1

- Groupwork. Go through the questions with the class and ask them to think about their answers.
- Put them into small groups and ask them to discuss their answers. Encourage each group to appoint a spokesperson to report back to the class.

2 1.26

- Tell the students that they're going to listen to three people talking about their answers to the questions in Exercise 1. Go through the list of items and ask them to listen and identify who talks about each one.
- Play the recording. You may need to pause after each speaker to allow the students to note down the speaker's initial next to the relevant items.

ANSWERS:
a Patti
b Lewis
c Lewis
d Patti
e Eric
f Eric

1.26 **(I = Interviewer; P = Patti; E = Eric; L = Lewis)**

I: It's impossible to have too much money – do you agree with that, Patti?
P: Yes. If you have dreams, money makes them possible. Personally, I can't imagine having too much money. I'm always broke. Anyway, if I ever felt I had too much money, I'd give it away to charity.
I: And Patti, would you prefer fame or fortune?
P: Being practical, I'd say fortune, but if I were single with no kids and no responsibilities, I'd go for fame.
I: Eric, were you given or did you earn an allowance as a child?
E: I was given a quarter a week by my father, but on the condition that I behaved myself. If I didn't behave well, I didn't receive it. Parents were much stricter in those days.
I: And Eric, what was the first thing you saved up for and bought yourself?
E: A set of toy soldiers. Not the plastic ones you get nowadays, but little metal ones, beautifully hand-painted. It took me almost a year to save up for them. If I'd known

that they would become valuable antiques, I would've kept them. They'd probably be worth a fortune now.

I: Tell me, Lewis, if you could buy yourself a skill or a talent, what would it be?

L: Well, there are lots of things I'd like to be better at, but if I had to choose one, it would have to be soccer – I'd like to be a great soccer player!

I: And finally, Lewis, what can't money buy?

L: Happiness. I tend to think that once I have enough money to buy some new clothes or get a better car, then I'll be happy. But it never works out like that.

3 1.27

- Go through the instructions with the class and make sure they understand that they first have to choose the correct alternative to make common money expressions, and then decide who gave each answer.
- Play the recording for the students to check their answers, and then focus on the money expressions and make sure everyone understands them (see Language notes below).
- Finally, put the students into pairs and ask them to discuss what their own answers to the two questions would be. Encourage them to report back to the class.

ANSWERS:
Question 1
a living – Eric
b breadwinner; loaded – Lewis
c Patti
Question 2
a rainy; debt; out – Patti
b blow – Lewis
c peanuts – Eric

Language notes

Vocabulary

- *Loaded* is a slang expression for *rich*.
- *To save something for a rainy day* is to save some money so that you can use it at a time when you don't have much.
- *Splash out* means to buy something expensive.
- *To blow money on* means to spend all your money on something.
- *Peanuts* is a slang expression for a small amount of money.

1.27 **(I = Interviewer; P = Patti; E = Eric; L = Lewis)**

Question 1

I: Does it matter if a wife earns more than her husband? How would you handle it?

P: It wouldn't matter to me, but it might matter to my husband. It shouldn't matter, but human nature being what it is, it probably would.

E: I would feel like a failure if my wife earned more than I did. It's a man's job to earn a living, and a woman's place is in the home.

L: It wouldn't worry me. I know lots of couples where the woman is the main breadwinner. In fact, it would be really good to have a wife who was loaded.

Question 2

I: If you were given $1,000 to save, spend, or invest, what would you do?

P: Uh, the sensible thing to do would be to save it for a rainy day or pay off my debt, but I think I'd rather splash out on a family vacation.

E: I think I'd be tempted to get a new computer. Mine's getting a little slow. You can get them for peanuts these days, you know ...

L: Well, I certainly wouldn't save or invest it – I'd probably blow it on a new music system and some massive speakers.

Grammar (SB page 33)

Unreal conditionals

1

- Focus the students' attention on the example in the margin. Read it aloud and ask them if the speaker used his or her credit card to buy the thing (no). Ask if he or she is still paying for it now (no). Point out that in this sentence you're using an unreal conditional to talk about the likely results of some action that in fact never happened.
- Ask the students to match the two halves of the other conditional sentences. Check answers with the class before putting the students into pairs to analyze the sentences and answer questions ***a*** to ***d***.

ANSWERS:
a 5 **b** 3 **c** 1 **d** 4 **e** 2
a Two. Yes.
b Real situations: a, c.
c Hypothetical situations: b, d, e.
d *would*

Language note

Grammar: unreal conditionals
(See Student's Book page 142.)

2

- Focus the students' attention on the picture and the caption. Point out that the caption underneath the picture is the beginning of an unreal or hypothetical conditional sentence. The man is talking about what his life would be like if his circumstances were different.
- Ask the students to look at the table and read the real situations and the hypothetical ones. Ask them to say what happens to the verb form when you move from a real situation to a hypothetical one.
- Go through the list of *if*-clauses and ask the students which one isn't acceptable in modern English.

> **ANSWERS:**
> The verb moves one step back into the past. (It backshifts.)
> Clause **e** is considered incorrect. It should be *If I were you, ...*

3

Groupwork. Go through the instructions and ask the students to discuss the questions in small groups. As they work, go around making sure they're using unreal conditionals correctly. Ask each group to appoint a spokesperson who can report back to the class on the decisions they make.

4

- Ask the students to work individually to complete the sentences so that they are true for them. Go around, offering help with vocabulary where necessary.
- Put the students into pairs and tell them to discuss their sentences.

5 Grammar Extra 3, Part 2

Ask the students to turn to Grammar Extra 3, Part 2 on page 142 of the Student's Book. Here they'll find an explanation of the grammar they've been studying and further exercises to practice it.

> **ANSWERS:**
> **2**
> **a** If you could speak English fluently, what would you do?
> **b** If you had won the lottery, what would you have bought?
> **c** If you were rich, where would you go?
> **d** If you could afford an expensive car, what would you choose?
> **e** If you hadn't arrived on time this morning, what would have happened?
> **f** If you were the president of your country, what would you change?
> **g** If it hadn't rained yesterday, what would you have done?
> **h** If you hadn't had to work last weekend, where would you have gone?
>
> **3**
> **a** If I could speak English fluently, I'd become a teacher.
> **b** If I had won the lottery, I'd have bought ...
> **c** If I was/were rich, I'd go ...
> **d** If I could afford an expensive car, I'd choose ...
> **e** If I hadn't arrived on time this morning, ...
> **f** If I was/were president of my country, I'd ...
> **g** If it hadn't rained yesterday, I'd have ...
> **h** If I hadn't had to work last weekend, I'd have gone ...

Reading & Vocabulary (SB page 34)

1

- Go through the questions with the class and make sure they understand them.
- Ask students to read the article and compare their own answers with the information given in the text. Ask them if they are surprised that catalogs date back to 1498.

> **ANSWERS:**
> **a** Personal answer.
> **b** Catalogs are said to date back to 1498 Venice, Italy.
> **c** The most notable approach in recent years is the creation of special days on which consumers are heavily encouraged to part with their hard-earned money to buy gifts or take advantage of special discounts and offers.

Language notes

mail order
a way of buying goods in which you order them by post, telephone, or the Internet and they are posted to you

mail order catalog
a book with a list of all the goods that you can buy from a shop or website and which can be sent to you

TV shopping channel
television specialty channels targeted at home shoppers that broadcast product demonstrations or explanations

e-commerce
the activity of buying and selling goods on the Internet

2

- Ask the students to mark the sentences true or false, checking the article if necessary. Ask them to correct the false sentences. Then check answers with the class before moving on.
- Focus the students' attention on the underlined words in the sentences. Ask them to look back at the article to find words or phrases with the same meaning.

> **ANSWERS:**
> **a** True
> **b** True
> **c** True
> **d** True
> **e** False
> **f** False
> **g** True

Listening (SB page 35)

1 1.28–1.30

Focus the students' attention on the pictures, the list of items, and the notes, and explain that they're going to hear these three people talking about their most treasured possessions. Play the recording and ask them to match the notes to the possessions.

> **ANSWERS:**
> **a** 2
> **b** 1
> **c** 3

> 1.28
> **1 Chris**
> I suppose you'd call it a vintage camera now. It's a Zeiss Contaflex, and I bought it in South Africa 50 years ago. It cost $50, which was a lot of money for me then, but it was still a lot less than I would have paid back home. So I was delighted – it was the best camera you could get at the time and it was a bargain. Unfortunately, I had to pay nearly $40 in tax at customs when I arrived back in the USA, so in the end it was less of a bargain. But I've certainly had my money's worth out of it. It's been everywhere with me and all our family photographs were taken on this camera. Last year, for my 70th birthday, my children bought me a wonderful, and very modern, digital camera. It takes much better pictures than my old Zeiss, but I can't use it. I'm afraid I'm too old-fashioned.

> 1.29
> **2 Katie**
> I know it sounds stupid, but this is the thing I would least like to lose. It's not because it's worth anything, although it is an expensive one because it's got GPS – you know, satellite navigation – on it, too. But the main thing is that if I lost this, I'd lose the addresses and numbers of practically everybody I know. It contains the details of about three hundred people.

> 1.30
> **3 Heather**
> This is my most precious possession because it saved my life when I got caught in an avalanche in Johnson Pass in Alaska's Chugach Mountain Range. It had been snowing for four days, and the temperature rose that morning – perfect avalanche conditions. When the first person in our group of snowboarders leaped off the cornice, the rest of us decided to follow his tracks – no traversing and no hard turns, so as to not disturb the snow. When it was my turn, I made it down the first pitch safely and thought I was out of danger. But the person behind me started before I was at a safe distance and nervously made a hard right turn. I heard a loud crack, and then WHOMPH! The snow hit me really fast in the back of the neck. I pulled my neck-warmer over my face, which kept the snow out of my mouth and nose, allowing me to breathe as the avalanche swept me up. I began frantically swimming and tried to stay aware of which way was up. When the snow finally settled, I had managed to get part of my glove up through the surface. It took the others a few minutes to find me, but I knew they would. Luckily, my neck-warmer allowed me the extra air to wait out those few minutes.

2

- Put the students into pairs and ask them to use the notes to try to reconstruct the stories. Ask several pairs to tell their stories to the class.
- Play the recording again for the students to check.

> **SUGGESTED ANSWERS:**
> **a** Chris's camera is a vintage Zeiss Contaflex that he bought in South Africa 50 years ago. It was a bargain compared with the price in the USA, but in the end he had to pay nearly $40 in tax at customs. All his family pictures were taken on this camera. For his 70th birthday, his children bought him a digital camera, but he prefers his old camera.
> **b** Katie's cell phone is an expensive one because it has GPS on it. But the main reason Katie doesn't want to lose it is that she'd lose the addresses and numbers of the people she knows. Her cell phone contains the details of about three hundred people.

c Heather's neck-warmer saved her life when she got caught in an avalanche. She pulled the neck-warmer over her face, which kept the snow out of her mouth and her nose. This allowed her to breathe until she was rescued.

Extra activity

Ask the students to think of two possessions they would save if their house was on fire. What would they choose and why?

Speaking: anecdote (SB page 35)

For more information about how to set up, monitor, and repeat anecdotes, see pages xix to xx in the Introduction.

- Go through the instructions and the questions with the class. Give the students a minute or two to decide what they're going to talk about. Then ask them to look at the questions and think about their answers to them. Allow them to make notes of what they're going to say and how they're going to say it, but discourage them from writing a paragraph that they can simply read aloud. Go around, monitoring and giving help where necessary.
- Pairwork. Put the students in pairs and ask them to take turns telling their partner about their most treasured possession. Encourage them to ask each other follow-up questions to get further information. Ask some pairs to report back to the class about what they found out.

Language for Life (SB page 36)

1 1.31

- Focus the students' attention on the picture and ask them to describe the situation (a man is buying an engagement ring for his fiancée in a jewelry store. Tell them that they're going to listen to conversations between the man, a female friend that is helping him, and two sales clerks.
- Go through the questions with the class before you play the recording so that they know what information to listen for.

ANSWERS:
a Julia is John's fiancée.
b Three or four hundred dollars.
c $950.

1.31 **(J = John; C = Cara; SC1 = Sales Clerk 1; SC2 = Sales Clerk 2)**

J: Thanks for doing this. I really don't know where to start.
C: OK, first you need to tell me what you're looking for. Do you have any ideas?
J: Well, diamonds are always good.
SC2: That one's $1,400.
J: OK. I guess I was thinking of something a little less pricey.
SC2: What's your budget?
J: I suppose I could stretch to $1,000.
SC2: OK. This one costs $950.
J: What do you think?
C: I think it's beautiful, and I think Julia would love it.
J: I should certainly hope so. This is definitely the last time I'm doing this.

2

- Ask the students to match the pairs of useful phrases to their meanings.
- Check answers before playing the recording again and asking the students to number the phrases in the order in which they hear them.

ANSWERS:
a and **b**: 4 | **e** and **f**: 2
c and **d**: 1 | **g** and **h**: 3
1 **a** 2 **c** 3 **b** 4 **e** 5 **g** 6 **d** 7 **f** 8 **h**

3 1.32

- Do the first part with the whole class and explain that in English you often use *a little* when you mean *a lot*. This sort of indirect expression is used for reasons of politeness and to soften a hard fact – in this case, that the rings are much too expensive for John.
- Focus attention on the other statements where John uses less direct language and ask the students to put the words in order.
- Play the recording for them to check their answers.

ANSWERS:
a They're much too expensive.
(See answers for 1 and 2, which are underlined in the audioscript below.)

1.32
1 I was hoping for <u>something a little more sparkly</u>.
2 I guess I was thinking of <u>something a little less pricey</u>.

4 1.33

- Do the first one as an example with the class and then ask the students to rewrite the remaining requests in less direct language.
- Play the recording for them to check their answers. Then play it again for the students to listen and repeat. When they've done this chorally, ask for individual repetition of the requests.

(See answers in audioscript below.)

1.33

a I was looking for something a little less tight.
b I'd prefer something a little more comfortable.
c I'm looking for something a little more fashionable.
d I'd like something a little more formal.
e I was looking for something a little more stylish.
f I was wondering if you might have something a little less colorful.

Life Skills: Social Skills (SB page 36)

Negotiating

1

Go through the key expressions with students. Make sure that students understand when and how to use each expression. Focus on pronunciation and intonation.

2

Get students to work in pairs. They will negotiate a used car. One student will take the role of a buyer (A) and one will take the role of a seller (B). Explain to students that they should use as many expressions as they can when negotiating to get the best deal possible.

Writing Extra (SB page 37)

Description

Extra activity

Ask the students to look at the picture of the woman. Get them to describe her and predict how she would spend a typical day.

1

Focus the students' attention on the text and picture and tell them it's an account of an imaginary day in this woman's life. Ask them to complete it using the linking words and expressions in the box. Tell them that they can only use each word or expression once, but some can go in more than one place. As they work, go around giving help where necessary and making sure everyone understands the meaning and function of the linking words.

ANSWERS:
1 when / as soon as
2 Then
3 while
4 After
5 As / Just as
6 until
7 During
8 As soon as / When
9 By the time
10 Just as / As

2

- Ask the students to decide where in the text to insert the adjectives. Remind them that they should appear in the same order as in the box.
- Ask them to compare their answers with a partner. Then check with the class. There may be more than one way to do this, so accept any other answers that make sense.

POSSIBLE ANSWERS:

breathtaking view; vigorous exercise; luxurious shower; extremely efficient personal assistant; huge package; a light lunch; close friend; latest movie; absolutely famished

3

- Go through the instructions with the class, and then ask the students to work individually to decide what details to add to the account. They will need plenty of time to think of ideas, and you could ask them to write out the whole text including their new details.
- When they've finished, put them into pairs and ask them to take turns reading their accounts to each other. As they work, go around monitoring and taking note of any particularly good versions that could be repeated later for the class.

4

This writing exercise could be done for homework. Remind the students that they should use linking words to make their texts flow well and should include adverbs and adjectives to make them more interesting.

5

You could ask the students to exchange their accounts in pairs or small groups and read each other's. Alternatively, the finished accounts could be displayed in the classroom for everyone to read. This would make it easier to take a class vote on which is the best.

Writing

Workbook page 15
Writing a story from pictures
Time expressions
Using adverbs

Further practice material

Need more classroom practice activities?

Photocopiable resource materials in the Teacher's Presentation Kit / Extra Resources

Need more tests?

Test Generator
Teacher's Presentation Kit / Extra Resources / Tests

Need more on important teaching concepts?

Key concepts in *American Inside Out Evolution* pages xxi-xxxvi

Need student self-study practice?

Workbook pages 12-15

Need more information and ideas?

American Inside Out Evolution website www.macmillan.com.br/americaninsideoutevolution

Need to check what your students can do by the end of this unit?

Self-evaluation checklists on pages xxxix-xlvi

Review A *Teacher's notes*

These exercises act as a check of the grammar and vocabulary that the students have learned in the first three units. Use them to find any problems that students are having, or anything that they haven't understood and that will need further work.

Grammar (SB page 38)

Remind the students of the grammar explanations they read and the exercises they did in the Grammar Extra on pages 140 to 143.

1

This exercise reviews verb structures from Unit 1. Remind the students to look for time expressions and other clues that will help them decide which verb form is needed.

ANSWERS:

1 've had	7 was expecting
2 've been working	8 had been
3 've met	9 were
4 have traveled	10 were
5 was	11 had to
6 were living	12 had never seen

2

This exercise reviews responses with *so* and *neither* from Unit 1. Remind the students that they need to look at whether the verb in the initial sentence is in the affirmative or the negative as this will determine whether the agreement response requires *so* or *neither*. Check answers with the class before putting the students into pairs to compare their own responses to the questions.

ANSWERS:
a 2 **b** 6 **c** 5 **d** 4 **e** 1 **f** 3
a Neither am I. / I am.
b So can I. / I can't.
c So did I. / I didn't.
d Neither have I. / I have.
e So have I. / I haven't.
f So would I. / I wouldn't.

Cultural note

James Bond /ˈdʒeɪmz ˈbɒnd/
James Bond is a fictional British spy, code named 007. The first Bond novel, *Casino Royale*, was written by Ian Fleming in 1953. The first Bond movie, *Dr. No*, was shown in 1962. Bond has been played by six actors including Sean Connery, Roger Moore, Pierce Brosnan, and Daniel Craig.

3

This exercise reviews tag questions from Unit 1. Remind the students that positive statements take negative tag questions and vice versa. Check answers before asking the students to give their own true responses to the questions.

ANSWERS:
a isn't (Yes, it is. / No, it isn't.)
b don't (Yes, I do. / No, I don't.)
c aren't (Yes, I am. / No, I'm not.)
d do (Yes, I do. / No, I don't.)

4

This exercise reviews indirect questions from Unit 1.

ANSWERS:
a Could you tell me what time it is?
b Do you know where the station is?
c Do you think it's going to rain today?

5

This exercise reviews verb patterns with gerunds and infinitives with *to* from Unit 2.

ANSWERS:

1 helping	6 to lend
2 to go	7 to buy
3 to take	8 lending
4 to spend	9 to pay
5 working	

6

This exercise reviews reported speech from Unit 3. Remind students that they may need to make changes to tenses, word order, pronouns, and time expressions when changing direct speech to reported speech.

ANSWERS:
a he had an idea to make some money.
b he'd been thinking about it for a long time.
c he wanted to open a store.

7

This exercise reviews conditional sentences from Unit 3.

> **ANSWERS:**
> **a** were; 'd buy
> **b** borrow; 'll be
> **c** won; wouldn't keep; 'd give
> **d** didn't have; wouldn't buy
> **e** had known; wouldn't have married

Vocabulary (SB page 39)

1

This exercise reviews adjective and noun collocations from Unit 1.

> **ANSWERS:**
> **a** 6 **b** 2 **c** 5 **d** 3 **e** 4 **f** 1

2

This exercise reviews clothing vocabulary from Unit 1.

> **ANSWERS:**
> **a** collar **b** button **c** sleeve **d** cuff
> **e** belt **f** buckle **g** zipper **h** hem

3

This exercise reviews verbs that can take the prefix *re* from Unit 1.

> **ANSWERS:**
> **a** rearrange **b** reconsider **c** reword
> **d** reconstruct **e** relocate

4

This exercise reviews collocations with *have*, *make*, and *take* from Unit 3.

> **ANSWERS:**
> 1 having 2 making 3 making 4 take
> 5 taking 6 take 7 took 8 is making

Pronunciation (SB page 39)

1

Explain to the students that the boxes show the syllables of a word and the large boxes indicate the stressed syllables. Here they're being asked to classify words according to how many syllables they have and where the main stress falls. Encourage them to say each word aloud to get a feeling for what sounds right.

> ### Language note
> **Pronunciation: word stress**
> You can check the stress of any word by looking in your dictionary. Dictionaries usually mark the stress of a word as well as giving the phonetic script, e.g. *ambitious* /æmˈbɪʃəs/. In *American Inside Out Evolution* you will find the stressed syllable underlined in pronunciation exercises.

2 1.34

Ask the students to underline the stressed syllables in the words in the table. Then play the recording for them to check their answers. Play it a second time for them to listen and repeat.

ANSWERS:
1 and 2

A: □☐□	B: ☐□□	C: □☐□□
appearance	aptitude	advantages
decision	businessman	embarrassing
designer	everything	relationship
impression	talented	spectacular

> ### Further practice material
> **Need more classroom practice activities?**
> Photocopiable resource materials in the Teacher's Presentation Kit / Extra Resources
>
> **Need more tests?**
> Test Generator
> Teacher's Presentation Kit / Extra Resources / Tests
>
> **Need more on important teaching concepts?**
> Key concepts in *American Inside Out Evolution* pages xxi-xxxvi
>
> **Need more information and ideas?**
> *American Inside Out Evolution* website www.macmillan.com.br/americaninsideoutevolution

4 Challenge *Overview*

Section	Aims	What the students are doing
Reading & Vocabulary SB page 40	Reading for detail	Speculating on the trip of two teenaged travelers. Matching missing sentences to the appropriate places in an article. Marking statements true or false. Studying the prefix *self-* and suffixes *able/ible*.
Listening & Vocabulary SB page 42	Listening for detail Collocations	Identifying true and false facts about Canada. Answering questions about an account of an incident during the trip. Identifying tenses used in the story. Completing collocations from the story.
Grammar SB page 43	Narrative tenses	Matching sentence endings with meanings and naming tenses.
Speaking: anecdote SB page 43	Fluency practice	Talking about doing something challenging.
Reading SB page 44	Reading for gist	Matching headings to sections of an article. Choosing correct collocations and answering the questions. Talking about raising money for good causes.
Grammar SB page 45	Future progressive and future perfect	Completing a table with future forms from the reading text. Writing sentences in the future progressive and in the future perfect. Making questions using *How many ...?* and *How much ...?*
Listening & Vocabulary SB page 45	Listening for detail	Discussing excuses for not getting exercise. Listening to people talking about why they don't exercise. Finding out about classmates' exercise habits.
Reading SB page 46	Reading for detail	Talking about becoming a vegetarian or vegan. Reading an article and identifying the writer's views.
Vocabulary SB page 47	Phrasal verbs	Reading information and advice about phrasal verbs. Replacing phrases with phrasal verbs in sentences. Completing sentences by putting object pronouns in the correct position.
Speaking SB page 47	Fluency practice	Talking about health using phrasal verbs.
Language for Life & Pronunciation SB page 48	Common ailments; showing sympathy; recommendations	Listening to conversations and matching them to ailments. Completing conversations with advice. Identifying whether speakers are sympathetic or unsympathetic, and practicing the stress and intonation of the useful phrases. Describing problems, reacting to them, and giving advice.
Life Skills SB page 48	Advice on dealing with challenges	Interpreting proverbs and quotations on dealing with challenges.
Vocabulary Extra SB page 49	Phrasal verbs	Studying phrasal verbs and writing definitions for them. Completing phrasal verbs with verbs and particles. Matching phrasal verbs with their definitions. Replacing words and phrases with phrasal verbs in sentences.

4 Challenge *Teacher's notes*

Warm up

Ask the students to say what they understand by the word *challenge*. What kinds of things do they think are challenging? Do they see challenges simply in terms of things like extreme sports or do they think the word can be applied to everyday events and personal relationships?

Reading & Vocabulary (SB page 40)

1

- Focus attention on the pictures on page 41 and ask students what kind of people they think Julia and Anthony Giles are and what words they might expect people to use to describe them. Go through the questions with the class and then ask them to discuss them in pairs.
- Ask the class for their ideas before asking the students to read the article on page 41. Check answers and find out how accurate their guesses were. Get their reactions to the text. Would any of them think about doing something like this?

ANSWERS:
a Camping trip.
b Not finding anywhere to camp at night; getting tired; not eating well; exposure to the bad weather.
c How to live with few resources.

Cultural note

In 2017 Canada celebrated 150 years of the Canadian Confederation, when different parts of North America under British rule came together to form a confederation known as the Dominion of Canada. The original territories in the confederation were Ontario, Quebec, Nova Scotia, and New Brunswick. Since then, the country's borders have changed and expanded, and Canada is now comprised of ten provinces and three territories.

2

Go through the sentences with the class and make sure everyone understands them. Explain that these sentences have been removed from the article on page 41. Ask the students to match them to the appropriate places in the article. Check answers with the class.

ANSWERS:
a 5
b 3
c 2
d 1
e 4

3

- Ask the students to read the sentences and decide if they are true or false.
- Check answers before asking the students to identify the words and phrases in the article that have the same meaning as those underlined in the sentences.

ANSWERS:
a F; itinerary
b F; budget
c T; TV media/Local newspaper
d T; kindness and generosity
e F; hitchhiked
f T; siblings
g F; lanscape
h T; unbearable

4

- Go through the instructions and read aloud the information in the margin to the class. Ask them to complete the sentences using words from the margin.
- Check answers before asking the students to say whether any of the sentences are true for them.

ANSWERS:
a self-conscious
b self-employed
c self-esteem
d reasonable
e enjoyable
f unbearable

Language notes

Vocabulary: word formation

- The prefix *self-* relates to yourself. Other examples include: *self-indulgent*, *self-righteous*, *self-assured*, *self-confessed,* and *self-destructive*. It's usually paired with words of English or Latin origin. The prefix *auto-* also relates to yourself, but pairs with other words, usually of Greek origin, to make new words. In many cases the words are not hyphenated, e.g. *autograph*, *autobiography*, *autonomy*, etc.
- The suffixes *-able* and *-ible* can be used with adjectives to indicate something that can be done. *-able* is more common than *-ible*, but there's no magic formula for deciding which suffix to use.

5

- Ask the students to use their dictionaries to look up the words that take the prefix *self-*. They should check the ones they already know or can understand easily.
- Ask them to choose three more to learn and to write example sentences for these. As they work, go around monitoring and helping where necessary.

Listening & Vocabulary (SB page 42)

1 1.35

- Put the students into pairs and ask them to read the list of statements about Canada and decide whether or not they think they are true.
- Play the recording and ask them to check their answers according to what Anthony and Julia say.

ANSWERS:

a False
b True
c False
d True
e False

1.35 **(I = Interviewer)**

I: Before I introduce my next guests, Julia and Anthony Giles, I thought it might be interesting for our listeners around the world who may not know much about Canada to have some background information on the country. This will bring the amazing adventure that Jules and Tony, as they are called by family and friends, into perspective. As we said at the top of the program, Julia and Anthony are a brother and sister who traveled across Canada together this summer. This is no small feat, as Canada is the second largest country in the world, with ten provinces and three territories. It is a multi-cultural, multi-lingual country, with English and French as its official languages. Canada is famous for its very harsh winters in the east and milder winters in the west. Despite this weather, Canada is famous for its thriving agricultural industry. Crossing such a vast country with such varied cultures must not have been easy. Today we have a brother and sister duo to tell us about how they did it.

2 1.36

Pairwork. Ask the students to discuss the questions based on what they can remember. Then play the recording again for them to check their answers.

ANSWERS:

a Europe, India, and South Africa.
b **1** to not burden their parents with more expenses and **2** to be more self-sufficient and resourceful.
c Anthony.
d The day on the farm when Anthony drove the combine.
e One week.
f Just short of the barn.
g Travel with at least one other person.

1.36 **(I = Interviewer; J = Julia; A = Anthony)**

I: It is a pleasure to have you here today. Julia and Anthony, welcome.
J: Thanks for having us.
A: It's a pleasure to be here.
I: So tell us how you came up with this idea.
A: Well, we had always planned to do a gap year traveling around. We had thought about different places like Europe, India, and South Africa. Then we saw stories of other young people who had made trips across Canada and we thought it would be interesting to do the same once we graduated. It was a way to kick off our gap year. We are not the first to do this kind of trip. We were inspired by others who did the same.
I: And why on such a small budget?
J: Once we had decided to make this trip as our personal way of commemorating Canada's 150th anniversary, we thought it would be important to make the trip on a very low budget – for two reasons. One, we didn't want to ask our parents for the money. They have enough on their plate and pretty soon we would be going to university, which is expensive, especially when you are supporting two kids at the same time, so we didn't want to burden them even further. Secondly, we thought that doing it on a very low budget would force us to be more self-sufficient and resourceful. It certainly forced us to interact more with people than we would have if we had taken a more comfortable route.

A: Yes, for sure. Julia's point about being resourceful is very true. We each have unique skills, so we each were in charge of different tasks during the trip. I think that was one of the reasons we were able to get through such a challenging trip successfully. Julia was in charge of navigation and transportation and I was in charge of food and shelter. We make a great team.
J: (laughing) Maybe because as twins we have always had to work together.
A: (laughing) True ... Another thing to note is that although this was a cross country trip, we knew from the onset that it would be impossible to travel through all 10 provinces and three territories of Canada. It is probably impossible to travel across the second largest country in the world in two months with only $200. So, if anyone wants to repeat our feat, and we do encourage people to get out there and get to know the country, they should keep that in mind.
J: And we did it in summer. It would have probably been impossible to do this kind of trip in our very cold Canadian winter.
A: As you showed in an earlier report, our parents, especially our mother, were very concerned for our safety.
J: Yes, she was. To help her feel better about our trip, we put some safety measures into place. We each had a cell phone with us at all times and we sent her two messages a day - one first thing in the morning and one before going to bed. She definitely felt more at ease knowing that we were a phone call away. Another thing we promised to do was to ask her to wire us money if we ever really needed it. Luckily, we never did, but it was good to have that as a back-up plan.
I: What was the highlight of your trip?
A: Hmmm (thinking) For me, I'd have to say it was the two days we spent with a family in Quebec and getting to know the French Canadian culture.
J: Really? For me the highlight was that day on the farm ... remember?
A: Oh, yes! That was quite exciting ... and scary!
J: Well, we had been working on the farm for a week, so we were quite familiar with the routine. On this day we wake up really early and head down to the fields to continue the harvest, which is done with a big machine called a combine. Anthony has been in training for a week, and this is the day he gets to drive the combine by himself. All is going well, when suddenly Anthony loses control, and the combine is racing off across the fields. It almost crashes into one of the barns, but luckily it stops just short of the barn and disaster is averted. Can you imagine what would have happened if he was not able to stop?
I: Wow! What a scare.
A: Umm hmm!
I: What advice would you give to other young people who might be thinking of doing a similar trip?
A: Well, it depends on a lot of things - what kind of trip the person wants to do, what time of the year they intend to travel, how much money they have to spend, and so on. So, all of these things need to be taken into account. Based on these factors, they can then decide on what kind of experience they want to have. The most important thing is to travel with at least one other person for safety and company and to have a plan. After that, everything else will fall into place.
I: Julia and Anthony, thank you.
J, A: Thank you.

3

Play the recording again and ask the students to read the extract as they listen and note the tenses used. Discuss as a class why these tenses are used.

ANSWERS:
On this day, we **wake** up really early and **head down** to the fields to continue the harvest, ... this is the day he **gets** to drive the combine by himself. All **is going** well, when suddenly Anthony **loses** control and the combine **is racing off** across the fields. It almost **crashes** into one of the barns, but luckily it **stops** just short of the barn and disaster **is** averted.

4

- Ask the students to complete the collocations from memory, if they can.
- Ask them to check their answers in the Audioscript. Get them to choose the three most useful expressions and to write their own example sentences.

ANSWERS:
a kick
b plate
c burden
d charge
e onset
f feat
g safety measures
h ease

Grammar (SB page 43)

Narrative tenses

1

- Focus the students' attention on the information in the margin. Read aloud the example sentences or get a student to read them. Explain that these tenses are all commonly used to tell stories or describe past events.
- Read aloud the sentence beginning in the exercise and focus the students' attention on the possible endings. Point out that each ending gives the sentence a slightly different meaning. Ask them to match the endings to their meanings.
- Ask the students to name the tenses and to write the negative and question forms. Check answers before moving on to the next stage.
- Ask the students to make their own sentences about different situations when they got home yesterday, using each of the tenses. Go around, giving help where necessary. Then put the students into pairs and ask them to tell each other their sentences.

ANSWERS:
a 2 **b** 3 **c** 1 **d** 4

a Simple past: He didn't make dinner. Did he make dinner?
b Past progressive: He wasn't making dinner. Was he making dinner?
c Past perfect simple: He hadn't made dinner. Had he made dinner?
d Past perfect progressive: He hadn't been making dinner. Had he been making dinner?

Language note

Grammar: narrative tenses
(See Student's Book page 142.)

2 Grammar Extra 4, Part 1

Ask the students to turn to Grammar Extra 4, Part 1 on page 142 of the Student's Book. Here they'll find an explanation of the grammar they've been studying and a further exercise to practice it.

ANSWERS:
1
1 was climbing
2 had
3 set off
4 were following
5 had taken
6 had advised
7 was
8 wore
9 ate
10 had never experienced
11 arrived
12 had traveled
13 had been keeping
14 wrote
15 had faced

Speaking: anecdote (SB page 43)

For more information about how to set up, monitor, and repeat anecdotes, see pages xix-xx in the Introduction.

1

Pairwork. Focus the students' attention on the list of challenges and make sure they understand all of them. Ask them to discuss in pairs which ones they think are most daunting (difficult or frightening) and which, if any, they've had to face. Encourage them to report back to the class on what they discussed.

2

- Go through the instructions and the questions with the class. Give the students a minute or two to decide what they're going to talk about. Then ask them to look at the questions and think about their answers to them. Allow them to make notes of what they're going to say and how they're going to say it, but discourage them from writing a paragraph that they can simply read aloud. Go around, monitoring and giving help where necessary.
- Pairwork. Put the students in pairs (if possible, not with the same people they worked with in Exercise 1) and ask them to take turns telling their partner about a time when they did something challenging. Encourage them to ask each other follow-up questions to get further information. Then ask some pairs to report back to the class about what they found out.

Reading (SB page 44)

1

- Focus the students' attention on the picture and ask them what they think the text will be about (a woman doing a sponsored run to raise money for charity).
- Ask them to read the text and match the headings to the sections.

ANSWERS:
a Charity Night Run
b Fitness and training
c Nutrition
d Clothing
e The mind

2

- Encourage the students to try to identify the correct collocations without looking back at the text.
- When they've finished, ask them to look back at the text to check their answers. Explain any unknown vocabulary. Then ask them to answer the questions.

- Put the students into pairs and ask them to discuss whether they've ever done anything to raise money for a good cause, or if they know anybody else who has. Encourage them to report back to the class.

> **ANSWERS:**
> **a** raise **b** fitness **c** diet **d** regular
> **e** pair **f** mind
>
> **a** Cancer treatment and awareness.
> **b** Going to the gym four times a week.
> **c** With protein drinks and vitamins.
> **d** To maintain blood sugar levels.
> **e** To get the right support for her feet and ankles.
> **f** That she's doing it for a very good cause.

Grammar (SB page 45)

Future progressive and future perfect

1

- Focus the students' attention on the example sentences in the margin. Then get them to look at the headings of the table in Exercise 1 and the example in the first column. Ask them to look back at the article on page 44 and find more examples of the future progressive and the future perfect to add to the table. As they do this, go around offering help and making sure that they're putting their sentences in the correct columns.
- When you've checked answers with the class, get them to answer questions ***a*** and ***b***.

ANSWERS:

Things *she'll be doing* to prepare for the Charity Night Run	**Things *she'll be doing* during the Charity Night Run**	**Something *she'll have done* when she's completed the Charity Night Run**
She'll be working on her stamina and general fitness levels. She'll be going to the gym. She'll be supplementing her diet. She'll be investing in a good pair of sneakers.	She'll be eating energy bars, bananas, and other fruit snacks. She'll be drinking plenty of water. She'll be wearing a hat.	She'll have contributed a sum of money to a good cause.

a Future progressive.
b Future perfect.

> ### Language note
> **Grammar: future progressive and future perfect**
> (See Student's Book page 142.)

2

Go through the instructions with the class. Then ask the students to work individually to complete the sentences. Check answers by getting several students to read aloud their sentences.

3

- Go through the example with the class, and then ask the students to work individually to write sentences using the prompts. Go around, making sure that everyone is forming the future perfect correctly. Then check answers by getting several students to read their sentences to the class.
- Look at the example question under the prompts with the class and ask them for a few more examples of questions they could ask with *How many ...?* and *How much ...?* With weaker classes, get the students to write all the questions and then check that they've formed them correctly.
- Put the students into pairs and ask them to take turns asking and answering questions about the things they'll have done by the end of today.

> **ANSWERS:**
> **a** By the end of the day, how much money will you have spent?
> **b** ... how many text messages will you have sent?
> **c** ... how many people will you have spoken to?
> **d** ... how many stores will you have been into?
> **e** ... how much exercise will you have done?
> **f** ... how many kilometers will you have driven?
> **g** ... how much chocolate will you have eaten?
> **h** ... how much time will you have spent online?
> **i** ... how many times will you have said sorry?

4 Grammar Extra 4, Part 2

Ask the students to turn to Grammar Extra 4, Part 2 on page 142 of the Student's Book. Here they'll find an explanation of the grammar they've been studying and a further exercise to practice it.

> **ANSWER:**
> **2** (Students' own answers.)

Listening & Vocabulary (SB page 45)

1

- Focus the students' attention on the list of reasons people give for not getting any exercise. Explain any difficult vocabulary (e.g. *Lycra* is the stretchy fabric used to make sports and fitness clothing).

- Put the students into pairs and ask them to discuss the questions. Encourage them to report back to the class on their discussion and find out whether the class as a whole likes getting exercise or not.

2 ▶ 1.37–1.40

- Focus attention on the pictures and ask the class to speculate on whether these people enjoy getting exercise.
- Tell the students that they're going to listen to the four people in the pictures answering the questions in Exercise 1. Ask them to listen and make notes of the reasons they give for not getting any exercise.

ANSWERS:
Steve – 5: he's too tired after work.
Maria – 4: bad weather, which means she can't go running.
Sam – 8: she doesn't have time because she has three kids under five.
Tim – 7: nothing usually. He only doesn't exercise if he's pulled a muscle or something, and it hurts.

▶ 1.37 **(P = Presenter; I = Interviewer; S = Steve)**

P: A recent survey revealed that only 38% of us would be motivated to do more exercise if our life depended on it. In other words, six out of ten of us would rather die than exercise! We went out on the streets to find out how much exercise people are really doing, and if they're not doing it, what exactly is stopping them?
I: How much exercise do you do?
S: Oh, not as much as I should. I used to have an expensive gym membership, but I only went twice so I canceled it. I'm not very sporty so I don't do any team sports like baseball or anything. I do love baseball, but strictly as a spectator, not as a participant. I have noticed that it's harder to keep the weight off than when I was younger, though, so I've started riding my bike into work. That's about forty minutes of exercise every day. Better than nothing.
I: What stops you?
S: I'm just so tired after work – I get home, sit on the couch and do nothing.

▶ 1.38 **(I = Interviewer; M = Maria)**

I: How much exercise do you do?
M: I'm studying for exams right now, so I go running a lot, just to get some fresh air. There's nothing worse than being stuck inside all day. I think it helps if you have someone to go with – it's really hard to motivate yourself, but if you make plans to go running with a friend, you feel like you can't let them down, and that forces you to go.
I: What stops you?
M: The weather! If it's raining, or really cold, I can usually talk myself out of it.

▶ 1.39 **(I = Interviewer; S = Sam)**

I: How much exercise do you do?
S: I run up the stairs, and that's it. Well, on weekends I do a few hours of housework – that must burn off a few calories. I hope so, anyway, because when I've finished, I sit down with a cup of coffee and a box of doughnuts. I certainly don't go to the gym, if that's what you mean. Can you imagine me in Lycra? Ha ha.
I: Is that what stops you from going to the gym?
S: Er, not really. It's finding time to fit it in around everything else I have to do. I have three kids under five, so there's no way I have time to go to the gym or anything like that. But I figure I run a marathon every day just running around after the children!

▶ 1.40 **(I = Interviewer; T = Tim)**

I: How much exercise do you do?
T: I go swimming and I work out at the gym. I try to do some kind of aerobic exercise for about thirty minutes three times a week, and I do weights a couple of times a week. On weekends I often go for a walk in the park, and my girlfriend's trying to get me to go to salsa classes – she says it's a really good workout.
I: What stops you?
T: Nothing, really – unless I've pulled a muscle or something, and it hurts. I love it. I sit at a desk all day long, and if I don't do some physical exercise at least three or four times a week, I feel really out of shape. But it isn't just about weight loss – exercise gives me a general feeling of well-being.

3

- Pairwork. Ask the students to turn to page 136 and follow the instructions. As they work, go around giving extra help where needed. Allow them to consult the Audioscript, if necessary.
- Check answers with the class before asking the students to mingle and find out who does or has done the activities.

ANSWERS:
burns off calories by riding a bike into work
does team sports
feels out of shape
gets plenty of fresh air
goes running
goes for a brisk walk on weekends
has canceled a gym membership
is stuck inside all day
wears Lycra gear at the gym
works out at the gym

Reading (SB page 46)

1

- Find out how many people in the class are vegetarians or vegans. If there are, ask them what the process of changing their diet was like. Is there anyone who would like to change their diet but is unable to?
- Go through the items with the class and write their answers on the board.

POSSIBLE ANSWERS:

a Eating meat can be bad for your health; bad for the environment; and animals are treated cruelly.
b Because it is everywhere and in many of the foods we eat; meat is an accessible source of protein, and dairy is an accessible source of calcium; and meat and dairy are delicious.
c Their health could suffer; finding affordable substitutes; eating together with family and friends.

2

- Ask the students to read the article and note down Jessica's reasons for wanting to become a vegetarian, her current diet and the steps Richard recommends for changing her diet.
- Check their answers and answer any questions about the text. Then have a class discussion on whether they think Jessica is likely to give up eating meat and fish and to give reasons for their opinions.
- Widen the discussion on vegetarianism and veganism if the students are interested in the topic.

ANSWERS:

a Her concern for the environment.
b Steaks, hamburgers, fish and chips.
c Take it step by step. Give up one thing at a time. Consult the internet for advice and ideas.

Vocabulary (SB page 47)

Phrasal verbs

1

- Remind the students that phrasal verbs are verbs that consist of more than one word, often a verb + one or two particles. They are sometimes known as multi-word verbs.
- Put students in pairs to discuss the questions. Then check their answers as a class.
- Ask the students to underline all the phrasal verbs in the article on page 46 and discuss with their partner what type of phrasal verbs they are.

ANSWERS:

a *pick a book up* is literal, i.e. you understand the meaning from the verb and particle.
pick a language up is idiomatic, i.e. you don't necessarily understand the meaning from the verb and particle. Here *pick* means "to learn."
b *I gave up* is intransitive. It doesn't take an object. The meaning (to stop doing sth) is idiomatic.
I gave my independence up is transitive. The object is "independence." The meaning is literal.
c *I looked up it* is not possible. When a phrasal verb is separable (i.e. the particle is an adverb) and the object is a pronoun, the pronoun always goes between the verb and the particle.
d *I looked the matter into* and *I looked it into* are not possible. When a phrasal verb is not separable (i.e. the particle is a preposition), the object always comes after the particle.

Phrasal verbs from the article:
pick sth up – literal – transitive – separable
pick sth up – idiomatic (= to learn) – transitive – separable
look into sth – idiomatic (= to investigate) – transitive – non-separable
hang out – idiomatic (= to spend time with people) – intransitive – non-separable

Language notes

Vocabulary: phrasal verbs

- Like other words, each phrasal verb can have several different meanings. For example: *go off* = start making a noise (an alarm); *go off* = explode, etc.
- Sometimes the meaning is literal and you can guess it from the verb and the particle. For example, *go off* = leave; *take off* = remove, etc.
- Mostly, the meaning is abstract, and you can only guess it from the context. For example, *go off* = take place/happen; *take off* = start flying, etc.
- When your students encounter a phrasal verb in a text, tell them to try to guess the meaning from the context. This will help if they then look it up in a dictionary. A good dictionary will tell you if the verb needs an object (transitive) or doesn't (intransitive). These are often marked [T] and [I].
- There are two types of transitive phrasal verbs, separable and non-separable.
In separable phrasal verbs, the object can separate the phrasal verb or come after it: ***Throw** the banana peel **away**. / **Throw away** the banana peel.*

But if the object is a pronoun, it must separate the phrasal verb:
Throw it away.
In non-separable phrasal verbs, the object always comes after it:
*Could you **deal with** the problem? / Could you **deal with** it?*

- If a phrasal verb has two particles (*get along with*), the object always comes after it:
  *My husband **gets along with** my parents. / He **gets along with** them.*

2

Ask students to use a phrasal verb from the article to replace the underlined phrases in the sentences.

> **ANSWERS:**
> **a** she won't be able to give them up
> **b** Richard told Jessica to look into
> **c** but you pick it up as you go
> **d** find it hard to hang out with vegans
> **e** Richard advised Jessica to look it up

3

- Ask the students to look at the sentences and decide where the object pronoun, given in parentheses, should go in each one. Check answers with the class, getting the students to say the sentences aloud so that they get a feel for what sounds right.
- Have a class discussion of whether any of the sentences are true for any of the students.

> **ANSWERS:**
> **a** It really put me off.
> **b** ... I always seem to come down with it.
> **c** ... it usually takes me forever to shake it off.
> **d** It's a shame I don't take after him.
> **e** I just don't feel up to it.
> **f** ... my kids wear me out.

Speaking (SB page 47)

1

Ask the students to find and underline all the phrasal verbs in the statements. Encourage them to use dictionaries to look up the meaning of any that they don't know.

> **ANSWERS:**
> **a** keep up with sth/sb; come out
> **b** put sth off
> **c** do without sth
> **d** come up with sth
> **e** cut down on sth
> **f** take sth up; take up sth

2

- Put the students into groups and ask them to discuss which of the statements they relate to most.
- Encourage them to report back to the class on their discussion.

Language for Life & Pronunciation (SB page 48)

1

- Ask the students to go through the list of ailments in the box, making sure everyone understands them. Then ask the students to read the six conversations and match an ailment to each one.
- When you've checked their answers, give help with any difficult vocabulary or expressions (e.g. *you look like death warmed over* is a slang expression for "you look terrible"; *I didn't sleep a wink* means "I didn't sleep at all"; *it's killing me* means "it's really painful").

> **ANSWERS:**
> **a** difficulty sleeping
> **b** a twisted ankle
> **c** a sore throat
> **d** sunburn
> **e** a splitting headache
> **f** hay fever

2 ▶ 1.41

- Pairwork. Point out that the conversations all end where one of the speakers is about to give some advice. Ask the students to think about what advice they'd give in the circumstances and to note this down. As they work, go around monitoring, encouraging, and giving help where needed.
- Play the recording for the students to compare their advice with the original conversations. Then find out how close the students' advice was to the original.

> **ANSWERS:**
> (See answers underlined in the audioscript below.)

> ▶ 1.41
> **a**
> **A:** Oh, no – you look like death warmed over. Late night last night?
> **B:** No, not really. But I couldn't sleep. I don't think I slept a wink, and now I feel exhausted.
> **A:** Oh, it's horrible when that happens. You should try listening to soft music. That usually works for me.

b
C: Oh, no! What happened?
D: I did something to my ankle. It's killing me!
C: You poor thing! It looks really swollen.
D: I know, and it's getting worse.
C: If you ask me, you need to lie down and put an ice pack on it.

c
E: Ugh! I can't swallow anything.
F: Oh, yes. I know what you mean. I was the same last week. I could only eat ice cream!
E: So, what did you do?
F: Well, you could try this. Chop up some ginger and put it in boiling water with some honey and lemon. Drink it as hot as you can.
E: Does it work?
F: Well, it makes you feel better, but it's probably a good idea to take some aspirin, too.

d
G: Don't touch my back!
H: Why? What's wrong?
G: I wanted to get a tan quickly, so I didn't bother to put any sunblock on.
H: Oh well, it serves you right, then, doesn't it?
G: It really stings.
H: Have you tried putting some cream on it?
G: I can't reach my back.
H: OK, take your shirt off. I'll do it for you.

e
I: When did it start?
J: After I'd been playing computer games for a few hours. I feel as if my head's going to explode!
I: Oh well, you've only got yourself to blame.
J: I know, I know. But I've taken some aspirin, and it hasn't worked.
I: Well, you could try putting your hands over your eyes and leaving them there for about five minutes. That usually works for me.

f
K: Do you have a cold?
L: No, I'm all right - I always get a runny nose and red eyes at this time of the year.
K: That must be awful. If I were you, I'd try acupuncture. My sister used to suffer terribly, but then she had three sessions of acupuncture, and that was it.
L: Really? Can you find out who she saw?

3 1.42

- Ask the students to look at the highlighted expressions in the conversations and listen to the recording. Tell them to make a note of whether they think the speaker sounds sympathetic or unsympathetic. Point out that stress and intonation can affect the impression given by a speaker.
- Put the students into pairs and ask them to practice saying the useful phrases to each other, using the same stress and intonation as the recording.

1.42
a Oh, it's horrible when that happens.
b You poor thing!
c Oh, yes, I know what you mean.
d Oh well, it serves you right then, doesn't it?
e Oh well, you've only got yourself to blame.
f That must be awful.

ANSWERS:
a Sympathetic.
b Sympathetic.
c Sympathetic.
d Unsympathetic.
e Unsympathetic.
f Sympathetic.

Language note

Pronunciation: stress and intonation
Note how the speaker's tone is softer and the tonal range more varied when being sympathetic, whereas it's harder and more monotonous when being unsympathetic.

4

Put the students into pairs and tell them who will be Student A and who will be Student B. Ask them to turn to their respective pages and follow the instructions. As they do the exercise, go around monitoring and giving help. Take note of any errors that may need particular attention later, and also any examples of good language use that you can praise.

Life Skills (SB page 48)

Proverb	Your Interpretation
Nothing is so difficult that diligence cannot master it. Malagasy Proverb	**POSSIBLE ANSWER:** With hard work (diligence) we can achieve even the most difficult tasks.
When one is prepared, difficulties do not come. Traditional Proverb	**POSSIBLE ANSWER:** If we are prepared, nothing is difficult.
Quote	**Your Interpretation**
"The ultimate measure of a man is not where he stands in moments of comfort and convenience, but where he stands at times of challenge and controversy." Martin Luther King Jr.	**POSSIBLE ANSWER:** A person's true personality is seen when he/she faces difficulties and challenges, not when things are going well.

Vocabulary Extra (SB page 49)

Phrasal verbs

1

- Pairwork. Ask the students to look at the diagrams. Point out that the words in the center can be combined with the particles around the outside to form phrasal verbs.
- Ask them to follow the instructions. Go around as they work, offering help and encouragement. Check answers with the class.

2

Ask the students to work individually to complete the questions. Check answers with the class, and then put the students into pairs to ask and answer the questions.

ANSWERS:
a get
b take
c get
d take
e get
f get

3

Focus the students' attention on the "meaning menus" (A–F). Ask them to read each one and decide which phrasal verb is being defined in each case. Go through the example with the class first, demonstrating that *come up* has all ten meanings in menu A. Use example sentences if the students need convincing.

ANSWERS:
a come up
b get on
c go on
d put up
e set off
f take on

4

- Ask the students to replace the underlined phrases with the correct phrasal verbs. As they work, go around giving extra help where needed.
- Check answers with the class before asking the students to discuss in pairs if any of the sentences are true for them.

ANSWERS:
a going on
b set off
c come up
d got on
e take on
f put people up

5

- Do the first one as an example with the class, and then ask them to complete the remaining sentences. Allow them to use dictionaries if necessary.
- Check answers with the class before asking the students to say what the situation or context might be in which someone would say these sentences.

ANSWERS:
a with (Possible situation: boss addressing an employee; a teacher talking to a student.)
b for (Possible situation: when someone thinks their insurance needs renewing.)
c with (Possible situation: parent to child when feeling impatient.)
d at (Possible situation: teenager to parent when feeling exasperated.)
e with (Possible situation: parent to teenager when they feel angry.)
f on (Possible situation: responding to a friend's offer of help or accommodation.)

6

- Ask the students to look in their own dictionaries to find out how phrasal verbs are presented.
- Ask the students to choose five new phrasal verbs to learn. Encourage them to record them in their vocabulary notebooks in example sentences.

Further practice material

Need more classroom practice activities?

Photocopiable resource materials in the Teacher's Presentation Kit / Extra Resources

Need more tests?

Test Generator Teacher's Presentation Kit / Extra Resources / Tests

Need more on important teaching concepts?

Key concepts in *American Inside Out Evolution* pages xxi-xxxvi

Need student self-study practice?

Workbook pages 16-19

Need more information and ideas?

American Inside Out Evolution website www.macmillan.com.br/americaninsideoutevolution

Need to check what your students can do by the end of this unit?

Self-evaluation checklists on pages xxxiv-xlvi

5 Ritual *Overview*

Section	Aims	What the students are doing
Reading SB page 50	Reading for detail	Reading an article and discovering idiosyncrasies of famous people. Reading for detail: matching new vocabulary from the text to definitions by using contextual information.
Vocabulary SB page 50	Guessing from context	Looking at how the context can give clues to the meaning of a word. Completing a glossary with words and phrases from the article.
Speaking SB page 52	Fluency work	Talking about personal rituals.
Listening & Vocabulary SB page 52	Listening for detail Collocations	Listening to a woman talking about her father and identifying true and false statements. Making collocations and completing sentences with them.
Grammar SB page 53	Present and past habits	Studying verb structures for talking about habits. Writing about their own routines. Completing statements with *used to*, *will*, and *would*.
Speaking SB page 53	Fluency work	Writing sentences about their lives ten years ago compared to today. Guessing which of their partner's sentences are false.
Reading & Vocabulary SB page 54	Reading for specific information Weddings	Reading about an unusual wedding. Identifying whether statements are true or false. Matching words from the text with others with similar meanings.
Listening & Vocabulary SB page 55	Listening for specific information Weddings	Looking at various wedding rituals. Matching speakers to rituals and explaining their meaning. Studying vocabulary for talking about weddings.
Speaking: anecdote SB page 55	Fluency practice	Talking about a wedding they've been to.
Reading & Vocabulary SB page 56	Reading for gist: vacation disasters	Discussing preferences and appropriateness of activities when on honeymoon. Recognizing and producing correct verb patterns. Comparing stories about vacation disasters.
Vocabulary & Grammar SB page 57	Verb patterns (2)	Studying verb patterns with a *to*-infinitive or a gerund. Underlining the correct structures in sentences.
Listening SB page 57	Listening for gist	Listening to people talking and deciding how romantic they are. Completing sentences about being romantic and putting them in a table.
Language for Life & Pronunciation SB page 58	Talking about annoying habits	Completing descriptions with correct verb structure. Practicing the useful phrases with the correct intonation. Completing a table with more phrases and saying what annoys them.
Life Skills SB page 58	The practice of gratitude	Making a list of few happy moments. Listening to an extract to number the sentences in order.
Writing Extra SB page 59	Article: expressing an opinion	Reading an article and choosing the best title. Organizing the article into five paragraphs. Writing an article giving opinions on a given topic.
Writing WB page 23		Writing an email of complaint.

5 Ritual *Teacher's notes*

Warm up

Write the word *ritual* on the board and see if any of the students know what it means. Ask them to use dictionaries to find that there are two possible meanings: 1 a religious service or other ceremony that involves a series of actions performed in a set order; 2 a way of behaving or doing something that people or animals regularly follow when they are in a particular situation. Then ask them if they have any particular rituals that they follow.

Reading (SB page 50)

1

- Focus the students' attention on the list of factors that can be considered keys to success. In pairs, ask the students to think about each factor and put them in the order of what they consider important to achieve success, justifying their answers.
- The most important factor according to the author of the text is having good habits. In a class feedback session, get the students' reactions to the text and ask if they agree with the author of the text.

ANSWER:
According to the author, the most important factors are hard work and good habits.

Cultural notes

Serena Williams (born 1981)
American tennis player Serena Williams has won more prize money than any other female sports star. She's held the number one ranking on more than four occasions.

Michael Jordan (born 1963)
American basketball star, and arguably the greatest basketball player of all time, Jordan won 6 NBA championships with the Chicago Bulls and was 6 time NBA Finals MVP.

Benjamin Franklin (1706–1790)
Franklin was a politician, author, diplomat, inventor, and popular philosopher. He was one of the original signees of the Declaration of Independence.

Oprah Winfrey (born 1954) Winfrey grew up poor in rural Mississippi and is most famous for being a talk show host, though she has also acted and produced shows. She is now the owner of a media empire and a multi-billionaire.

Steve Jobs (1955–2011)
Steve Jobs was a college dropout who went on to found Apple and Pixar. Known for developing products such as the iPod and iPhone, he died of cancer at the age of 56.

2

- Focus the students' attention on the list of famous people. Ask the students to think about what the celebrities are famous for.
- When the students have thought about how to describe the celebrities, put them into pairs to share what they know about the celebrities. Then ask the students to read the article on page 51 to find the answers.
- Don't answer any questions about the words in the article as this would pre-empt the work the students will do in the next section. If anyone asks about these words, just say that you will be looking at their meanings later.

Vocabulary (SB page 50)

1

- Ask students to go through the article on page 51 and underline all the words and phrases they don't know. Then ask them to answer the questions.
- Ask the students if the strategies given helped them to guess the meaning of the words and expressions they didn't know.

Language note

Vocabulary: guessing from context
Always encourage your students to guess the meaning of a word by looking at the context in which it's used. If they then have to refer to a dictionary, it will cut down on searching time, as they'll have an expectation of the meaning they're looking for.

2

- Ask the students to complete the glossary with the correct words from the article. Ask them to discuss their ideas in pairs before checking with the class.
- Finally, ask the students to write glossary definitions for any other words or phrases from the article that they didn't know that haven't been covered.

ANSWERS:
1 jump to conclusions
2 countless
3 set sby/sth up
4 approach

5 chunk
6 accomplishment
7 sustainable
8 set up
9 weakness
10 strength
11 overshoot
12 vague
13 device
14 meaningful

Speaking (SB page 52)

1

Go through the list of situations with the class. Then ask the students to think of examples of personal rituals that might be performed in these situations.

2

Pairwork. Ask the students to discuss their own rituals or those of people they know.

Listening & Vocabulary (SB page 52)

1 1.43

- Explain that the students are going to hear a woman talking about her father and his car. Teach the words *obsessed with/by* and *obsession* and tell them that the woman thinks her father is obsessed with his car. Ask them what other things people can be obsessed with. Ask them if they think these people would agree that they're obsessed or whether it's just the opinion of other people who don't share their interests.
- Go through the statements with the class first. Then play the recording and ask them to say whether the statements are true or false. Encourage strong classes to correct the false statements.
- Check answers before asking whether or not Laura is sympathetic to her father's ritual.

ANSWERS:
a True
b False. (They only went out on rare occasions, and only then if the bus wasn't running.)
c False. (Their father made them wear plastic bags on their feet just in case they vandalized the seats with their shoes.)
d True
e False. (He backs out of the driveway at breakneck speed.)
f True

1.43
My dad is the most ritualistic person I know, and many of his rituals involve his car.
We've never kept domestic animals in our house, but my father's car is as close as you'll get to the family pet. In fact, the car probably gets better treatment and more affection than a pet would. Each night, the car is tucked up in its garage under a cozy blanket. Nobody – but nobody – is allowed in the garage in case they accidentally brush against "the precious one," causing who knows what damage.
When we were children, on the rare occasions when my dad would get the car out of the garage (for births, deaths, marriages, and national disasters – and then only if the buses weren't running), we would have to wear plastic bags on our feet in case we had a sudden urge to vandalize the seats with our shoes.
We would never be allowed to shut the car doors ourselves ... in case we slammed them too hard, I guess. I mean, three-, five-, and seven-year-old girls can do untold damage to a car by slamming the door shut.
Nowadays, we don't have to wear plastic bags on our feet, but the "Starting the car and setting off" ritual has never changed.
He'll start the engine and then sit there for at least five minutes with the engine on. As repulsive fumes pump out into the fresh country air, he'll take out his pipe and start tapping out his last smoke. Then he'll take a pinch of tobacco, stuff it in the bowl, and spend a minute or two patting it down. Next, he'll get out his box of matches and give it a shake. He always gives his matchbox a shake. The pipe won't light on the first try – he'll try several times, and finally, when the tobacco takes, he'll puff and puff until the car is full of smoke. With visibility dangerously reduced and a car full of choking passengers, he'll take the hand-brake off and reverse out of the driveway at breakneck speed.
It isn't pleasant being a passenger, but we've always let him get away with this strange behavior because he's the boss. None of us would dare to complain.
My father used to be a pilot in the US Air Force, and I often wonder whether he would indulge in this kind of ritual before take-off and whether his crew would let him get away with it because he was the boss. Probably.

2

- Ask the students to match the words to make collocations from the recording. Encourage them to do this from memory.
- Play the recording again for the students to check their answers. Then ask them to work in pairs to talk about the relationship between Laura's father and his car, using these collocations. As they work, go around taking note of any particularly good descriptions, which can be repeated to the class.

ANSWERS:
a domestic animals
b a cozy blanket
c a sudden urge

d slam the door
e a box of matches
f first try
g breakneck speed
h the Air Force

a He treats his car better than a domestic animal.
b He covers his car with a cozy blanket in the garage.
c He seems to think his daughters might get a sudden urge to damage the car.
d The children weren't allowed to shut the car doors in case they slammed them.
e He always gave his box of matches a shake.
f His pipe never lit on the first try.
g He would reverse out of the driveway at breakneck speed.
h He was a pilot in the US Air Force.

3

Pairwork. Ask the students to discuss anyone they know who has a strong attachment to a car or other piece of machinery or equipment. Encourage them to report back to the class on their discussion.

4

- Ask the students to use the collocations from Excercise 2 to complete the sentences.

ANSWERS:
a the Air Force
b breakneck speed
c a sudden urge
d first try

5

- Ask the students to say if any of the sentences are true for them.
- Ask the students to make new sentences using the collocations from Exercise 2. You could ask them to make sentences that are true for them. Then put the students into pairs to compare their sentences.

Grammar (SB page 53)

Present and past habits

1

- Focus the students' attention on the example sentences in the margin and explain that they are both talking about habits, the first a present habit, the second a past habit.
- Read aloud the extracts from the listening on page 52 or get a student to read them aloud. Point out that these extracts are also talking about habits. Ask the students to discuss the questions underneath in pairs.
- Check answers with the class and make sure that everyone is clear about the use of *will* + verb for present habits. Get them to look again at the examples in the margin and point out that you use *would* + verb for past habits.

ANSWERS:
a *will*
b Present habits.
c A repeated action.
d Characteristic.

2

- Read the text in its present form to the class, or get a student to read it. Explain that there's nothing wrong with the text as it stands. However, there are places where you could use *will* + verb to emphasize the habitual nature of the actions.
- Either ask the students to work individually to decide which verbs can be replaced with *will* + verb or do it as a class, taking one sentence at a time. Make sure they realize that not all the verbs can be changed. When checking answers, make sure that the students understand that you use this structure to talk about habitual actions, but not when describing states, such as *He is never late* or *She likes to take her time*.

ANSWERS:
1 'll get up
2 -
3 'll have
4 -
5 won't usually get ready
6 -
7 -
8 'll always leave
9 'll vary
10 'll usually depend

3

- Ask the students to write similar accounts of their own families' morning routines. As they work, go around giving extra help where needed and encouraging them to use *will* + verb where possible.
- Put the students into pairs. Ask them to take turns reading aloud their texts to see how their routines differ.

4

- Remind the students that you use *would* + verb to talk about past habits. Ask them to think about life when they were twelve years old and to complete the sentences in the left-hand column about their daily routines. You might like to give them an example or two of your own memories to start them off.
- Get several students to read aloud their sentences describing their daily routines.
- Focus attention on the right-hand column. Point out that this is headed "My thoughts and feelings" and get the students to identify that the structure you use to talk about past thoughts and feelings is *used*

to + verb. Before asking them to complete these sentences, give them a couple of examples from your own past.

- Check answers by getting several students to read aloud their sentences.

Language note

Grammar: present and past habits – *will, would,* and *used to*

(See Student's Book page 144.)

5

Ask the students to work individually to complete the statements. If anyone is struggling, remind them to look at the sentences they've just written and those in the earlier exercises to find the answers.

ANSWERS:
a will **b** would **c** used to

6 Grammar Extra 5, Part 1

Ask the students to turn to Grammar Extra 5, Part 1 on page 144 of the Student's Book. Here they'll find an explanation of the grammar they've been studying and a further exercise to practice it.

ANSWERS:

1

a My father will insist on smoking in the car. I hate it!
b My family and I used to live in a large house.
c During the school vacations I'd spend all my time with my friends.
d I didn't use to have dark hair when I was young.
e During the week I won't go to bed until after midnight.
f At school I'd take a lucky charm into my exams.
g My girlfriend will talk for hours on the phone. It drives me crazy!

Speaking (SB page 53)

1

- Remind the students of the structures for talking about past habits and past states, which they studied in the previous section.
- Go through the examples with the class and then ask the students to work individually to write four true sentences and one false sentence about ways in which their lives were different ten years ago. Remind them not to consult other students about their sentences. As they work, go around giving help where needed and making sure they're using *used to* + verb and *would* + verb correctly.

2

Pairwork. Put the students into pairs, preferably with people they don't know very well. Ask them to take turns reading aloud their sentences and guess which one of their partner's sentences is false. Encourage them to report back to the class about what they found out.

Extra activity

Follow up this exercise with a piece of written work for homework in which the students write an account of how life was different in the past.

Reading & Vocabulary (SB page 54)

1

- Ask the students where weddings normally take place in their country. Is it possible for people to get married in other locations, such as in their backyard, on a beach, or in an exotic location such as underwater, while parachuting, or in a helicopter?
- Put the students into pairs. Tell them to look at the picture and decide if it represents their ideal setting for a wedding. Give them plenty of time to look at the picture and discuss their answers. Then ask them to discuss what they think is the best location for a wedding and to describe it. Get the pairs to report back to the class on what they decided.

2

- Go through the questions with the class so that they know what information to look out for as they read the text. Give them plenty of time to read the text and find the answers to the questions.
- When you check their answers, encourage them to give their response to the text. Would they want a wedding like the one described?

ANSWERS:
a He proposed in the middle of a noisy family get together.
b Their wedding took place at a hotel with the Pacific Ocean in the background. They had a surprise wedding reception at Bill's parents' house.
c They decided to flip their wedding because they couldn't afford a traditional wedding.

3

- Ask the students to read the sentences, and then look back at the text to decide whether they are true or false. Tell them to ignore the underlining for the present. Ask them to rewrite any false sentences to make them true. Then check answers with the class before moving on to the next stage of the activity.
- Focus attention on the underlined expressions in the sentences. Ask the students to look through the text to find words or phrases with the same meaning. Take the opportunity to discuss any other vocabulary in the text that the students found difficult.

ANSWERS:

a True
b False. They were not invited to Hawaii; they watched over the internet.
c False. There was an endless stream of people, so it was not limited.
d True
e True
f False. There were actually 5 people at the wedding and it was the Pacific in the background.
g False. They were not worried about space; that's not why they live streamed.

a Final year = senior year
b Sudden brilliant idea = epiphany
c Parties = bashes or get togethers
d The money she had borrowed = loan
e To run away and get married = to elope
f The setting = the backdrop
g People invited = guests

Listening & Vocabulary (SB page 55)

1

Go through the rituals with the class and have a discussion on whether any of them are common in the students' country or countries. Encourage them to add any further information that they can about any of the rituals that are familiar to them and to describe any wedding rituals they know of that aren't on the list.

2 1.44-1.47

- Ask the students to look at the pictures and flags and identify where the people are from (Spain, Taiwan, Turkey, Morocco). Explain that they're going to hear these people talking about wedding rituals from their countries. Ask the students to listen and match one ritual from the list in Exercise 1 to each of the speakers. Check answers before moving on to the next stage of the activity.
- Ask the students to explain the meaning of each ritual. You may need to play the recording more than once to enable them to do this.

ANSWERS:

1 b to show that the bride and groom will share everything
2 f to protect the bride from the evil spirits (and prevent bad luck)
3 d to help set the bride and groom up with money for their new life
4 c to show that the bride and groom will be prosperous, and the bride doesn't have to do any housework until the henna wears off

1.44 **(I = Interviewer; J = Jorge)**

1

I: Tell me about weddings in your country.
J: Well, in Spain, where I'm from, there is this ritual that happens after the rings have been exchanged between the groom and the bride. It is called "*las arras*," and it consists of thirteen gold coins which the groom puts in the bride's hands. It symbolizes their intention of sharing everything: all the worldly goods they are going to receive together.

1.45 **(I = Interviewer; S = Sandra)**

2

I: Tell me about weddings in your country.
S: Well, in Taiwan we use a black umbrella to cover the bride's head, because we believe it can protect the bride from the evil spirits. So normally an elderly person will hold the umbrella when the bride leaves her house to go to the groom's house.
I: And will this bring her good luck as well?
S: Yes, it will prevent bad luck.

1.46 **(I = Interviewer; Il = Ilhan)**

3

I: Tell me about wedding traditions in Turkey.
I2: Weddings in Turkey are different from how they are in the US. There are a lot of people at the wedding. There are sometimes as many as four or five hundred guests, and one of the most interesting things, I think, about Turkish weddings is the fact that the guests at the wedding pin gold and money on the bridegroom's suit, and on the bride's dress. I think, from what I can understand, that this money and gold is used by the bride and groom to set themselves up for their new life together, living in their new house, their new home, to buy things like a fridge, and other things they might need for their future life together.

1.47 **(I = Interviewer; L = Laila)**

4

I: Tell me about wedding traditions in Morocco.
L: Oh, Moroccan weddings are elaborate affairs. Preparations take weeks, and the whole community is involved! The bride gets lots of attention in the days leading up to the wedding – a group of women, usually older than the bride, but connected to her in some way, give her a sort of milk bath, which is supposed to purify her. Then she has her hands and feet decorated in henna. This ritual symbolizes prosperity. It looks beautiful, and there's another custom which says that the bride isn't supposed to do any housework until the henna wears off.

Extra activity

Ask the students to discuss what they think the remaining rituals on the list might mean.

a This symbolizes the couple's commitment to working together through their married life.
e Rice symbolizes prosperity and fertility. It's supposed to bring the bride and groom good luck and ensure they have children.
g It's believed that the person (usually a woman) who catches the bouquet will be the next one to get married.
h Speeches from the bride's father and the groom cement the relationship between the two families. The best man thanks the bridesmaids and traditionally makes a humorous speech about the groom's past.

3

- Ask the students to read the words and phrases in the box and to work individually to complete the task. While they're doing the exercise, go around, monitoring and giving help.
- When they've finished writing their descriptions, put them into pairs and ask them to exchange their texts and read and comment on the one they've received.

ANSWERS:
b aisle, best man, bouquet of flowers, bridesmaid, church, confetti, honeymoon, photographer, priest, propose a toast, reception, rice, ring, speech, veil, vows, wedding cake, wedding presents

Speaking: anecdote (SB page 55)

For more information about how to set up, monitor, and repeat anecdotes, see pages xix to xx in the Introduction.

- Go through the instructions and the questions with the class. Give the students a minute or two to decide which wedding they're going to talk about. Then ask them to look at the questions and think about their answers to them. Allow them to make notes of what they're going to say and how they're going to say it, but discourage them from writing a paragraph that they can simply read aloud. Go around, monitoring and giving help where necessary. If any of your students have never been to a wedding, then you'll need to substitute some other ceremony. If you do this, remind the students that they'll need to change the questions to make them applicable to this event.
- Pairwork. Put the students in pairs and ask them to take turns telling their partner about a wedding they've been to. Encourage them to ask each other follow-up questions to get further information. Then ask some pairs to report back to the class about what they found out.

Reading & Vocabulary (SB page 56)

1

- Pairwork. Put the students into pairs and ask them to discuss their ideas about the perfect honeymoon. Ask them to report back to the class on the best idea.
- Ask the students to discuss what they think are the worst ideas for a honeymoon. In a class feedback session, find out how much agreement there is across the class.

2

- Pairwork. Ask the students to look at the pictures and talk about what has happened in each of the pictures. Remind any students who have forgotten of the difference in meaning between the *to*-infinitive and the gerund with some verbs, e.g. *I remembered to buy her some flowers* (= I didn't forget) and *I remembered buying her flowers* (= I could remember an occasion when I bought her flowers). This will be covered in more detail in the next section.

3

- Put the students into pairs and ask them to take turns completing the blanks. Mark any of the blanks that they disagree on.
- When they've completed their accounts, ask them to compare them and discuss their answers. Don't give the correct answers at this stage.

ANSWERS:
1 laughing
2 to bring
3 putting
4 to get
5 to sit
6 to sleep
7 to take
8 to ask
9 to convince
10 to close
11 being
12 to get
13 paddling
14 going out
15 to order
16 eating
17 to have

4 1.48

Play the recording for the students to check their answers. Then have a class discussion about the problems mentioned in the story.

> 1.48
>
> My "perfect" Caribbean honeymoon started at the airport. I can't help laughing at our bad luck, it was so horrible, but so funny in a very unfunny way. First, my husband forgot to bring his passport. I always tell him he has to check three things: passport, wallet, and tickets. He said that he remembered putting it in his backpack, but he didn't . He had to go all the way back to the house to get it. "I remembered to bring my passport. Here it is." I thought. By the time he got back, we had missed our flight. I'll never forget looking at his frustrated face and thinking "It's my honeymoon. Everything is going to be okay". We did manage to get another flight but it would mean arriving at 11:00 pm instead of 11:00 am. I wanted to sit in a window seat, but the only seats they had were in the middle seats. I had intended to sleep on the way, but we sat next to a very noisy family. I can't stand flying with crying kids!
>
> We had expected to take a limo from the airport, but there were none available at that hour, so we rented a car instead. It was hard to find the hotel and we had to stop to ask for directions a couple of times. By the time we got to the hotel it was 2:30 in the morning. The receptionist said that they couldn't hold our reservation and there were no more rooms with an ocean view. The one room they had small, dark and had a great view of the parking lot. We tried to convince him to help us, that it was our honeymoon, but he said there was nothing he could do about it. To top it all off, Mike forgot to close the shampoo bottle completely and there was shampoo everywhere when I opened the suitcase.
>
> Mike enjoys being active, while I prefer to take it easy, so I watched him taking surfing lessons from a lounge chair on the beach. "The important thing when you're trying to get up on the board is to keep paddling. Otherwise, you'll never catch a wave," said the tanned instructor. Well, he stopped paddling too soon, got clobbered by a huge wave and threw his back out. We didn't feel like going out for dinner after all that, and decided to order room service. Something I ate did not agree with me, of course, and I was sick all night.
>
> I had wanted an unforgettable honeymoon. I guess I should be careful of what I ask for. It was forgettable and regrettable! But though I may regret eating that shrimp cocktail, I'm happy to be married.
>
> Now, we deserve to have another vacation! We should try spending a romantic weekend... Maybe we'll make it a staycation!

Vocabulary & Grammar (SB page 57)

Verb patterns (2)

1

Ask the students to look back at the text on page 56 and find the four verbs that can be followed by either a *to*-infinitive or a gerund. They may find it helpful to underline the sentences in which these occur.

> **ANSWERS:**
> remember, forget, try, stop

2 1.48

- Focus attention on the table and go through the examples with the class. Make sure they understand the difference in meaning between *remember* + *to*-infinitive and *remember* + gerund.
- Play the recording one more time. Ask them to complete the table with the four verbs they identified in Exercise 1 and the example sentences from the listening text on page 56.

> **ANSWERS:**
> **a** remember doing sth: 1 – He remembered putting the passport in his backpack.
> **b** remember to do sth: 2 – I remembered to bring my passport. Here it is.
> **c** (never) forget doing: 3 – I'll never forget looking at his frustrated face and thinking "It's my honeymoon. Everything is going to be okay".
> **d** forget to do sth: 4 – First, my husband forgot to bring his passport.
> **e** stop doing sth: 5 – Well, he stopped paddling too soon, got clobbered by a huge wave and threw his back out.
> **f** stop to do sth: 6 – It was hard to find the hotel and we had to stop to ask for directions a couple of times.
> **g** try doing sth: 7 – We should try spending a romantic weekend ...
> **h** try to do sth: 8 – "The important thing when you're trying to get up on the board is to keep paddling. Otherwise, you'll never catch a wave,"

Language note

Grammar: verb patterns – *to*-infinitive or gerund
(See Student's Book page 144.)

3

- Ask the students to choose the correct verb structures in the sentences. Allow them to compare in pairs before checking answers with the class. Point out that the difference between *try doing* and *try to do* is very subtle, and in many cases they can be used interchangeably.
- Ask the students to check any of the sentences that are true for them. They should then rewrite the others to make them true and compare with a partner.

ANSWERS:
a buying
b to bring
c traveling
d to pack
e to have
f eating
g coming
h to take

4 Grammar Extra 5, Part 2

Ask the students to turn to Grammar Extra 5, Part 2 on page 144 of the Student's Book. Here they'll find an explanation of the grammar they've been studying and a further exercise to practice it.

ANSWERS:
2
1 to get along with
2 flirting
3 seeing
4 arguing
5 having
6 to bring
7 to get
8 to buy

Listening (SB page 57)

1 1.49

- Write the word *romantic* on the board and brainstorm a few things that the students associate with being romantic. They'll discuss this later, so don't spend too much time on it at this stage.
- Focus attention on the pictures and tell the students that they're going to listen to these people's answers to the question *Do you think you're romantic?* Ask them to listen and number the people in order from most romantic to least romantic.

ANSWERS:
1 **b**
2 **a**
3 **c**
4 **d**

1.49
a
Well, I try to remember my wife's birthday every year, and on the way home yesterday I stopped to buy her some flowers – I think that's romantic, but she just thought I'd done something wrong.
b
I'm very romantic, but I think most women are. I remember meeting my boyfriend for the first time. It was in a club and I remember seeing him across the room and thinking, "He looks nice." He was wearing a black T-shirt and really nice jeans. I even remember what he said to me – he said, "Do you want to dance?" When I asked him recently if he remembered meeting me for the first time, he had no idea.
c
I don't know. I don't think my boyfriend would say I'm romantic because I always forget to buy him gifts or say nice things to him. But deep down I think I am romantic. Since I met my boyfriend, I've stopped looking at other men. Well, I haven't stopped looking, but I have stopped hitting on them.
d
No, I don't think I'm romantic really. I don't like all that romantic nonsense. Women expect you to buy them gifts and remember their birthdays. And they try to make you give up sports and all those things I enjoy. I can't be bothered with all that. Maybe that's why I haven't managed to find a girlfriend!

Cultural note

You may need to explain that in the USA men sometimes buy flowers to apologize or make up with their wives or girlfriends for something that they did wrong. So, if it's unusual for the man to buy flowers, his wife or girlfriend may be suspicious about his motive for buying her flowers.

2

- Pairwork. Ask the students to work together to complete the sentences. Then ask them to decide whether they are *dos* or *don'ts* for being romantic and to put them into the correct column on the table.
- Check answers before asking the students to suggest other *dos* and *don'ts* that can be added to the table.

> **ANSWERS:**
> **a** Try to remember: Do
> **b** Stop to buy: Do
> **c** Remember meeting: Do
> **d** Forget to say: Don't
> **e** Stop looking: Do
> **f** Try to make: Don't

Cultural note

H.V. Prochnow /ˈeɪtʃ vi ˈprɑknaʊ/ (1897–1998) American banker, author, and public speaker, Prochnow is best remembered for his witty quotes.

Language for Life & Pronunciation (SB page 58)

1 1.50

- Focus the students' attention on the illustration and give them time to take in what they can see. Tell them that they're going to read and listen to six people talking about things that really annoy them. Play the recording and ask the students to read the texts. Then ask them to match one of the people to the illustration.
- Check the answer and then ask the students to discuss which of the habits mentioned they'd find most annoying.

> **ANSWER:**
> 6 Martin

> 1.50
> **1 Naomi**
> I hate it when men wear too much aftershave. My brother-in-law, for example. He will insist on covering himself in this really strong aftershave – it makes me sneeze.
> **2 Kevin**
> There are so many things that annoy me! But I think the thing that annoys me most is when I watch a movie with my girlfriend. She's always asking me questions about what's happening: "Who's this? What happened there? Why did he do that?" Argh. That really gets on my nerves.
> **3 Roz**
> It really annoys me when people talk about how fat they are when they are stick thin! I've got this friend who's really slim – much slimmer than me. But she will go on about being fat. It's so annoying.
> **4 Dan**
> It really annoys me when my brother and his girlfriend are together. They're forever hugging and kissing in front of me. Ugh – it makes me sick!
> **5 Sally**
> I can't stand it when people say they haven't done any work for an exam, and then they get the highest score. One of my friends is like that. She's always telling us how worried she is because she hasn't done any work, but then she gets a 90%.
> **6 Martin**
> I find it irritating when people keep losing things. For example, my mom's always losing her glasses. Why doesn't she put them on a chain? Or get a spare pair? She drives me crazy.

2

Ask the students to listen again and to complete the descriptions with the correct verb structures. Play the recording and then check answers with the class.

> **ANSWERS:**
> 1 will insist on
> 2 's always asking
> 3 will go on about
> 4 're forever hugging and kissing
> 5 's always telling
> 6 's always losing

3 1.51

- Play the recording for the students to listen and repeat the phrases. After they've done this chorally, ask several students to repeat the phrases individually, and check to see that everyone is pronouncing the words correctly.
- Ask them to mark the stressed words, and play the recording again for them to check and to note the speakers' intonation. They should then practice the phrases again. Tell them to try to imitate as closely as possible the stressed-timed phrases to achieve their maximum effect.

> 1.51
> 1 He will insist on covering himself in this really strong aftershave.
> 2 She's always asking me questions about what's happening.
> 3 She will go on about being fat.
> 4 They're forever hugging and kissing in front of me.
> 5 She's always telling us how worried she is.
> 6 My mom's always losing her glasses.

Life Skills (SB page 58)

The Practice of Gratitude

1

In pairs, ask the students to think about things that they can be thankful for (happy moments) and that are usually neglected during the routine and busy days.

2 1.52

Play the recording and ask the students to number the sentences in the order you hear them.

> **ANSWERS:**
> **a** 2, **b** 5, **c** 1, **d** 4, **e** 3

3

The students can start practicing on a separate slip of paper.

Writing Extra (SB page 59)

Article: expressing an opinion

1

Focus the students' attention on the picture and get them to identify that it shows a wedding on a beach. Ask them to read the article and choose the best title.

> **ANSWER:**
> **b** Weddings are for the family

Cultural notes

The Little White Wedding Chapel
The Little White Wedding Chapel was established in 1951 in Las Vegas. It's famous for its "quickie" weddings, where people can show up and get married shortly afterwards. Famous brides and grooms who have married in the chapel include Frank Sinatra, Bruce Willis, and Britney Spears.

Renée Zellweger /rəˈneɪ ˈzelwegər/ (born 1969)
Renée Zellweger is an American actress who starred in the movies *Bridget Jones's Diary* (2001) and *Cold Mountain* (2004). She also played Roxie Hart in the musical *Chicago* (2002), which won the Academy Award for Best Picture.

Mauritius /məˈrɪʃəs/
Mauritius is an island nation in the south-west Indian Ocean with a population of 1.3 million. It was the only known habitat of the now extinct dodo. The official language of Mauritius is English.

2

- Remind the students that dividing your writing into paragraphs makes it easier for people to read. New paragraphs often begin where there is a change of function or a change of idea. Go through the paragraph plan with the class. Then ask them to read the article again and use this plan to divide up the paragraphs.
- When they've finished, ask them to compare their answers with a partner. Then check with the class.

> **ANSWERS:**
> Paragraph 2 begins at line 4: *First and foremost, ...*
> Paragraph 3 begins at line 11: *Celebrities are renowned ...*
> Paragraph 4 begins at line 18: *It is worth considering ...*
> Paragraph 5 begins at line 24: *In my opinion ...*

3

Focus attention on the highlighted sections of the article and ask the students to work individually to find the things in the list. Allow them to compare their answers in pairs before checking with the class.

> **ANSWERS:**
> **a** in my view; in my opinion
> **b** for instance
> **c** But are they making a terrible mistake?
> **d** Understandably; not surprisingly; personally
> **e** First and foremost; it is worth considering; what strikes me is that

4

This writing exercise could be done for homework. Remind the students that they should use linking words to make their articles flow well and should use paragraphs to divide the different sections. With weaker classes, make a paragraph plan on the board similar to the one in Exercise 2 for one of the subjects first. It's a good idea to recommend that the students always start with a paragraph plan.

Writing

Workbook page 23
Writing an email of complaint
Formal expressions

Further practice material

Need more classroom practice activities?

Photocopiable resource materials in the Teacher's Presentation Kit / Extra Resources

Need more tests?

Test Generator
Teacher's Presentation Kit / Extra Resources / Tests

Need more on important teaching concepts?

Key concepts in *American Inside Out Evolution* pages xxi-xxxvi

Need student self-study practice?

Workbook pages 20-23

Need more information and ideas?

American Inside Out Evolution website
www.macmillan.com.br/americaninsideoutevolution

Need to check what your students can do by the end of this unit?

Self-evaluation checklists on pages xxxix-xlvi

6 Eat *Overview*

Section	Aims	What the students are doing
Reading & Speaking SB page 60	Reading for specific information Fluency work	Reading about a bad experience in a restaurant. Talking about restaurant experiences.
Reading & Vocabulary SB page 61	Reading for specific information	Reading a text about food customs around the world. Reading for specific information: identifying the main idea of paragraphs. Comparing and talking about intercultural experiences.
Listening & Vocabulary SB page 62	Listening for specific information Food collocations	Listening to an interview and identifying true and false statements. Making collocations with food words. Talking about the best and worst restaurants in their area.
Speaking: anecdote SB page 62	Fluency practice	Talking about their favorite restaurant.
Grammar SB page 63	Present perfect: simple and progressive	Studying the form and use of the present perfect, simple and progressive. Describing pictures using the present perfect progressive. Discussing when progressive forms are incorrect or sound strange.
Reading & Vocabulary SB page 64	Reading for gist Guessing meaning from context	Listing how food customs will change in the future. Completing a glossary by guessing meaning from context. Discussing about food trends.
Vocabulary & Writing SB page 65	Linkers	Completing a summary of an article using linking words. Categorizing linkers by their function. Choosing the correct linkers in a text.
Reading SB page 67	Reading for specific information	Guessing the correct statistics to complete sentences about food waste, then reading an article to check their ideas. Discussing food waste.
Grammar SB page 67	Passives review	Completing sentences with information from an article, then rewriting them in the passive. Rewriting the review with passives so it reads more naturally.
Pronunciation & Vocabulary SB page 67	Numbers review	Studying different types of numbers. Practicing reading different types of numbers. Looking at different ways of pronouncing *O* (zero).
Language for Life SB page 68	Food idioms and expressions	Matching words to things people complain about in restaurants. Listening to people complaining and completing useful phrases. Replacing phrases with idioms.
Life Skills SB page 68	Tuning into others	Suggesting a more understanding, alternative explanation for some situations.
Writing Extra SB page 69	Exploring synonyms	Ordering expressions from least hungry to most hungry. Choosing the correct collocations and talking about food and eating. Completing a table with synonyms, then describing people with them.

6 Eat *Teacher's notes*

Warm up

Ask the students how often they eat out in restaurants. Do they have "takeout" in their country (cooked food that you buy from a restaurant but take home to eat)? What kinds of restaurants do they prefer?

Reading & Speaking (SB page 60)

1 1.53

- Tell the students that they're going to read and listen to a text about a bad experience in a restaurant. Ask them what kind of things this might constitute.
- Play the recording and ask them to listen and read the text at the same time. Then ask them why Jeff is a bad waiter.

ANSWER:
Because he told them about the day's special, even though it was already sold out. Afterwards, he abandoned them in the middle of taking their order.

1.53

I am not quite sure if he was the worst waiter I have ever encountered, but he was comically bad. To this day, every time we meet someone named Jeff, we start laughing. It's a running joke in our family. A couple of years ago my wife Jesse and I went to this fancy little restaurant that had just opened in our neighborhood. We were greeted by Jeff.

Waiter: Good evening, my name is Jeff. I'll be your server this evening. Can I take your drink order?
Me: Give us a couple of minutes to sit down and take a look at the menu, please.

He gave us a big smile and bounced back toward the kitchen. A couple of minutes later, Jeff was back.

Me: Jeff, are there any specials today?
Waiter: Today we have a lovely grilled branzino with a caper and butter sauce. It comes with panroasted baby vegetables and is served on a bed of wild rice.
Jesse: Sounds wonderful, I'll have the special.
Me: Make that two.

After a few minutes, he returned.

Waiter: Oh, I'm sorry, we're all out of the special. You missed out!

Bizarrely enough, Jesse kept smiling like it was completely normal and seemed not to notice anything strange in his behavior. When I finally recovered, I ordered a carbonara and Jesse, not at all upset, the smoked salmon.

Waiter: Would you like that hot?
Jesse: You mean spicy hot?
Waiter: No, hot hot.
Jesse: I'm sorry, I don't understand.
Waiter: Some people like to eat their salmon cold.
Jesse: Um, I ...
Waiter: Hey, my shift is over. Could you repeat your order to Melissa? She'll be your server. Have a great night, folks!

Without saying anything else, and just very naturally, he bounced off before we could say a word, leaving us absolutely speechless and terribly hungry.

2

- Focus attention on the questions. Ask the students to think about their answers. Give them time to do this and allow them to make brief notes if they wish.
- Put the students into pairs and ask them to compare their answers. Encourage them to ask each other follow-up questions to find out more details and to report back to the class on what they've found out.

Reading & Vocabulary (SB page 61)

1

Go through the text with the students and ask them to think about the main topic of the text.

ANSWER:
b Customs at the table around the world

2

- Ask the students to read the text again paying attention on the available options for them to fill in the blanks. Put students into pairs and give them time to read and discuss their answers.
- Have students explain why they chose those answers and which clues in the titles match with clues in the text.

> **ANSWERS:**
> **1 b, 2 d, 3 a, 4 e, 5 c**

3

- Divide the class into two groups, (A) students who have traveled abroad and (B) those who have not. Have the group B ask students in group A questions about their experiences. Ask group B to take notes, then choose students from group B to report about what they learned from group A. If the students are well-traveled you can make groups of students who have been to a particular country.

Language note

Vocabulary: collocation

Note that although *clench* means *close tightly*, it's only used with certain nouns. You might *clench your teeth* or *clench your fists* if you were angry, but you wouldn't *clench your eyes*.

Listening & Vocabulary (SB page 62)

1 1.54

- Make sure the students understand that a restaurant critic is a journalist who writes restaurant reviews. Ask them to think about what Jean Crowshaw's job involves and write their suggestions on the board.
- Pairwork. Go through the statements with the class and ask them to discuss in pairs whether they think they are true or false. Then play the recording for the students to check their answers.

> **ANSWERS:**
> (Answers for Exercise 2 are in parentheses.)
> **a** False. (She eats out two or three times a week.)
> **b** True
> **c** False. (She doesn't write anything down. She takes mental notes.)
> **d** False. (She doesn't wear any disguise.)
> **e** True
> **f** False. (The newspaper pays.)
> **g** True
> **h** False. (She can't stand them.)
> **i** False. (It was in a very rural place in Umbria, Italy.)

1.54 **(I = Interviewer; JC = Jean Crowshaw)**

I: How did you become a restaurant critic?

JC: Well, I've been working for newspapers for more than twenty years. I started out as a journalist when I was twenty-three, and I've worked for several newspapers since then, including this one. Then, when the last restaurant critic retired, I was asked to take his place. And I've been doing it for the last thirteen years.

I: How can you do this job and stay so slim?

JC: Yeah, that's a good question. I mean, I eat out two or three times a week. But as a matter of fact, to write about a restaurant and its cuisine, I need to taste the food, but I don't need to clean my plate. When I'm covering a restaurant, I always take three friends with me. Everyone has to order a different dish. So then I taste about two bites of everything on their plates, and then I eat the same amount of food on my plate. Then I stop eating. And that's not just so that I stay thin, it's so that I can remember all the different flavors.

I: Do you take notes?

JC: No, I don't write anything down because I don't want to draw attention to myself. So while I'm eating, I'm making mental notes about the restaurant. How does the room look? Is the lighting too dim, too bright? Is the service efficient or is it slow? How is the food presented? Are the waiters doing their job well? Do the customers look happy? Then, as soon as I get home, no matter how late it is or how tired I am, I write down my impressions - I write pages and pages of notes.

I: You must be pretty well-known on the restaurant circuit. Do you wear a disguise?

JC: What, like a wig? Ha ha, no, I couldn't do that. Like I said, I've been working around the Washington area for some thirteen years now, so inevitably, I do sometimes get recognized, but by that time it's too late for the management to call in another chef or change the serving staff.

I: Do people get upset if you give them a bad review?

JC: Oh yes, but the bad reviews are the most fun to write! Once, a restaurant owner called my editor and threatened to come in with a gun – I don't think he did in the end.

I: Who pays for your food?

JC: The newspaper pays for the food. Nothing is accepted for free.

I: Have you had any particularly good or bad experiences that stand out in your memory?

JC: There was the waitress who tripped and poured my son's dessert and a glass of wine in my lap. I wasn't too happy at the time, but I managed to see the funny side of it later. But there's one thing I really hate and that's when the waiter keeps asking "Is everything all right?" Good, experienced waiters never ask that – they don't need to because they can tell if everything's all right just by looking at the customers' faces.

I: Have you met any rude waiters or waitresses?

JC: I've experienced every kind of waiter and waitress – rude and moody, chatty and enthusiastic, and over-familiar. The best waiters are those who are attentive but not intrusive. I can't stand those waiters who squat down beside you to take your order, and then proceed to tell you their favorite items on the menu, because they ate it on their vacation in Italy ... this kind of invasion of your privacy is totally unacceptable.

I: What's the best meal you've ever eaten?

JC: It was in Italy, in Umbria. I was traveling with my husband, and we stopped in a very rural place where we had the dinner I'll remember for the rest of my days. Olive oil pressed from the restaurant's own trees, lamb with so much flavor that it defines what the meat should taste like – wonderful bread, handmade pasta, local wines. It wasn't a formal restaurant, but I've never forgotten it and I've never enjoyed a meal more.

2

Ask the students to correct the false statements. Play the recording again for them to check their answers.

(See answers in parentheses in Exercise 1.)

3

- Make sure the students understand the words in the box. Ask them to think about which one collocates with all the items in each list. Point out that while individual items from each list may collocate with more than one word from the box, only one word from the box collocates with all the items in each list.
- Check answers with the class before asking the students to circle the collocations that they don't know. They can then look these up in a dictionary and write example sentences for them.

ANSWERS:
a food
b meal
c dish
d plate
e flavor
f menu

4

Pairwork. Put the students into pairs and ask them to decide which is the best and worst restaurant in your area. This could be in the area where you are now or in their hometown. Ask the pairs to report back to the class, giving reasons for their choices.

Speaking: anecdote (SB page 62)

For more information about how to set up, monitor, and repeat anecdotes, see pages xix to xx in the Introduction.

- Go through the instructions and the questions with the class. Give the students a minute or two to decide which restaurant they're going to talk about. Then ask them to look at the questions and think about their answers to them. Allow them to make notes of what they're going to say and how they're going to say it, but discourage them from writing a paragraph that they can simply read aloud. Go around, monitoring and giving help where necessary.

- Pairwork. Put the students in pairs and ask them to take turns telling their partner about their favorite restaurant. Encourage them to ask each other follow-up questions to get further information. Then ask some pairs to report back to the class about what they found out.

Cultural note

Restaurant chain

A restaurant chain is a group of restaurants that have the same name but are found in different locations, sometimes within one country, and other times internationally (e.g. McDonald's; Pizza Hut).

Grammar (SB page 63)

Present perfect: simple and progressive

1

- Focus the students' attention on the information in the margin. Make sure they understand the difference between actions and states.
- Ask the students to look at the extract from the interview. Point out the words in bold and ask them to name the tenses and match each to one of the descriptions.

ANSWERS:
I've been working: present perfect progressive – c
I started out: simple past – a
I've worked: simple present perfect – b

Language note

Grammar: present perfect: simple and progressive
(See Student's Book page 144.)

2

- Go through the example with the class, and then ask the students to work individually to write their three sentences. Remind them that they must use the three tenses in the given sequence and that one of their sentences should be false. As they work, go around giving extra help where needed and making sure that the students are all forming their sentences correctly.
- Put the students into pairs and ask them to take turns reading their sentences aloud. Their partner should try to guess which sentence is false. Encourage them to report back to the class on what they found out.

3

- Do the first one as an example with the class, and then ask the students to choose the most appropriate forms.
- Put the students into pairs to discuss their answers before checking with the class.

ANSWERS:
1 a learned
b been learning
2 a read
b been reading
3 a been eating
b eaten
4 a worked
b been working

4

Go through the explanation and instructions with the class. Then focus attention on the first picture and ask the students to say what the man has been doing (he's been chopping onions). Ask them to make similar sentences about the remaining pictures.

ANSWERS:
a He's been chopping onions.
b He's been eating dinner.
c She's been cleaning/mopping the floor.
d He's been putting up shelves.

5

- Read the sentences with the class, and then ask them to think about why they sound strange or wrong. Remind them to think about the difference between states and actions. Then check answers.
- As the students rewrite the sentences, go around giving extra help where needed. After checking their answers, ask if any of the statements are true for them. If you have time, ask them to change the statements so that they are true.

ANSWERS:
a *hate* describes a state: it isn't an action, so the progressive form is wrong.
b *stop* describes a single action: you do it once. It isn't normally possible to repeat it.

c *decide* describes a single action: you do it once. It isn't normally possible to repeat it.
d *cut* describes a single action: you do it once. Repeating it would be considered "self-harm."
e *have* describes a state: it isn't an action, so the progressive form is wrong.
f *understand* describes a state: it isn't an action so the progressive form is wrong.

a I've always hated ...
b I've stopped ...
c I've decided ...
d I've cut myself ...
e I've had ...
f I've never understood ...

6 Grammar Extra 6, Part 1

Ask the students to turn to Grammar Extra 6, Part 1 on page 144 of the Student's Book. Here they'll find an explanation of the grammar they've been studying and further exercises to practice it.

ANSWERS:
1
a I've been learning English for six years.
b I've known my best friend since I was a child.
c I'm exhausted. I've been working hard all day.
d I haven't seen my parents for ages.
e I'm tired. I haven't been feeling well lately.
f I haven't done any housework for weeks.
g I've been sitting here for more than an hour.
h I've been thinking about changing my job lately.
2
a since
b for
c since
d for
e since
f for
g since

Reading & Vocabulary (SB page 64)

1

- Ask the students to work in pairs to make lists of how technology has changed the way we deal with food. Ask them to think back historically and chose the most important technological advance.
- Ask the pairs to report to the class and compare and contrast answers. Ask them to come to a consensus about the most important technological advance.

2

- Focus attention on the words in the article that are highlighted in yellow (tell them to ignore the ones highlighted in blue; these will be dealt with in the next section).
- Ask the students to figure out the meanings of the highlighted words from their context and to complete the glossary. When checking answers, ask them to say which strategy they used for each word.

ANSWERS:
a trend
b crunchy
c the jury is still out
d tactile
e produce
f raw
g viable
h stale
i snap
j picky
k discard
l novelty

3

- Promote a debate on the virtues of local versus global. Give the groups time to list the advantages and disadvantages. Give each team one minute to speak, plus 30 seconds for rebuttal. At the end of the debate, explain the portmanteau "glocalization."
  Glocalization is the adaptation of international products around the particularities of a local culture in which they are sold. The process allows integration of local markets into world markets. Ask the students for examples of *glocalization* in their country.

Vocabulary & Writing (SB page 65)

1

- Focus the students' attention on the table of linkers. Draw their attention to the headings and point out that different linkers perform different functions in a text. (See Language note below.)

- Ask the students to use the linkers in the table to complete the summary of the article from page 64.

> **ANSWERS:**
> **a** Furthermore
> **b** Consequently (or So)
> **c** Although (or Even though)
> **d** so
> **e** even though
> **f** however (or even though)
> **g** To sum up

Language note

Vocabulary: linkers
These discourse markers provide us with a logical sequence (organizing ideas / adding more information / concluding) to the text and show us how the different parts of the text relate to each other (showing contrast / demonstrating cause and effect).

2

- Ask the students to look back at the article on page 64 and find the nine highlighted linkers within it. Ask them to put them in the correct column on the table.
- Allow the students to compare their tables with a partner before checking answers with the class.

> **ANSWERS:**
> **Organizing ideas**
> First and foremost, Secondly, Finally
> **Adding more information**
> that is, In other words, What's more
> **Connecting contrasting ideas**
> however
> **Showing cause and effect**
> As a result
> **Concluding**
> In summary

3

- Ask the students to read the text about becoming a vegetarian. Tell them to ignore the choices in bold for the time being. This will give them an idea of the overall structure and content of the text. Then ask them to go back through the text and choose the correct linkers. Remind the students that they need to think about the function of the linker in each place and choose the appropriate one for that function.
- Check answers with the class before having a class discussion on vegetarianism.

> **ANSWERS:**
> **a** However
> **b** The first reason
> **c** As a result,
> **d** What's more
> **e** In other words
> **f** Secondly
> **g** In fact
> **h** Finally
> **i** Furthermore
> **j** But
> **k** To sum up

Reading (SB page 67)

1

- Pairwork. Ask the students to read the five statistics about food waste around the world and to discuss in pairs which number they think is correct for each one. Ask the pairs to report back to the class on their choices and see how much agreement there is.
- Ask the students to read the article and check their ideas. Ask them if they find the information surprising or not.

> **ANSWERS:**
> **1 b** 1/3
> **2 b** \$990 billion
> **3 b** around 35%
> **4 a** 10 billion
> **5 c** 300,000,000

2

Groupwork. Go through the questions with the class and make sure that everyone understands them. Put the students into groups and ask them to discuss the questions. Go around, monitoring and offering help with vocabulary where needed. Then ask the groups to report back to the class on their discussions.

Grammar (SB page 67)

Passives review

1

- Focus the students' attention on the words in the box. Ask them to use these words to complete the sentences underneath, according to the information they read in the text on page 66. Tell them to ignore the underlined words for the moment. Check answers before moving on to the next stage of the activity.
- Focus attention on the information and the examples in the margin. Ask the students to rewrite the sentences in the exercise, using passive forms for the underlined verbs. Encourage them to do this without looking back at the article. When they've finished, allow them to look back and check their answers. Then ask them to say why passive structures have been used in the article rather than active ones.

ANSWERS:

a tubers
b day
c sea
d date
e lose

a 45% of fruits, vegetables, roots and tubers is lost or wasted.
b On average 10 billion apples are thrown away every day.
c 8% of all fish is thrown directly back into the sea.
d 39% of food in Canada, New Zealand, Australia, and the US is wasted in part because it is past it's "use by" date.
e Roughly 990 billion dollars of food a year is wasted or lost.

The passive is preferred because as the article is about food waste you want "food" or "food waste" (the object of the active verb) to be the topic of each sentence. The subject of the active verb ("people") is obvious in the context.

Language note

Grammar: passive review
(See Student's Book page 144.)

2 Grammar Extra 6, Part 2

Ask the students to turn to Grammar Extra 6, Part 2 on page 144 of the Student's Book. Here they'll find an explanation of the grammar they've been studying and a further exercise to practice it.

ANSWERS:
3
a That chair was made by my brother.
b We were introduced yesterday.
c More than 80% of our waste could be recycled.
d Your application is being processed now.
e The telephone was invented by Alexander Graham Bell.
f English is spoken as a first language by 400 million people.
g A man has been arrested in connection with the robbery.
h An announcement will be made later on in the week.

Pronunciation & Vocabulary (SB page 67)

Numbers review

1 1.55

- Focus the students' attention on the information in the margin. Point out that numbers can take many forms and that they can be pronounced in different ways. Ask the students to say the numbers in the box and to put them in the correct columns in the table.
- Play the recording for them to check their answers. Then play it again for them to repeat the numbers. When they've done this chorally, ask for individual repetition of the numbers.

ANSWERS:
1 and 2
(Answers for Exercise 2 in the second line)

Cardinal numbers	Ordinal numbers	Fractions
246,813,579 1,234,567	53rd 75th	4/5 5/6

Decimals	Dates	Telephone numbers
99.9 0.25	01/01/1901 07/27/2012	207-419-3211 301-962-7877

1.55
Cardinal number: two hundred and forty-six million, eight hundred and thirteen thousand, five hundred and seventy-nine
Ordinal number: fifty-third
Fraction: four fifths
Decimal: ninety-nine point nine
Date: January first nineteen oh one
Telephone number: two oh seven, four one nine, three two one one

Language notes

Vocabulary

Numbers

- The number *0* is often pronounced like the letter "O" when saying numbers one figure at a time, e.g. for a telephone number. It can also be pronounced *zero* or *nil* in a sports score (except tennis, where it's *love*).
- British English: always put *and* before the tens in a number, e.g. *six hundred and twenty*. In American English, it's sometimes *six hundred twenty*.
- You write a comma after the thousands, but if the number has just four figures, you can write the number without a comma, e.g. *1,500* or *1500*.
- You don't use the comma to indicate decimals. You use the period as the decimal point.

Fractions

It's common to use *a/an* (/ə/ /ən/) rather than *one* when saying any fraction that has number "1" in the top half (⅛, ¼, ⅓, ½, etc.), e.g. *a third* is more common than *one third*, while *one half* is never said.

Dates

In American English, you write *May 10*, and you say *May tenth*. When you write the date in figures, you write *5/10/2007*. In standard British English, you write *10th May*, and you say *the tenth of May*. Because you say the day first, you write *10/5/2007*.

2 1.56

Ask the students to listen to five more numbers on the recording and put them in the correct column of the table in Exercise 1. They then practice saying them.

(See answers in Exercise 1.)

1.56
zero point two five
one million, two hundred and thirty-four thousand, five hundred and sixty-seven
seventy-fifth
three zero one, nine six two, seven eight seven seven
five sixths
July twenty-seventh, twenty twelve

3 1.57

- Ask the students to write the letters ***a*** to ***c*** on a piece of paper. Tell them they're going to hear three different ways of saying the number *0*. Ask them to write these down as they hear them.
- Check answers with the class before asking them to match each way of saying *0* to one of the situations.

ANSWERS:
1 c -10°
2 b 1908
3 a 2 - 0

1.57
a Rafael Nadal is winning two sets to love.
b My grandfather was born in nineteen oh eight.
c It's really cold – ten degrees below zero.

Language for Life (SB page 68)

1 1.58

- Get students to discuss the first question and write their suggestions on the board. Then ask them to match the items in the box with the list of things that people might complain about.
- Play the recording for them to see how many of their suggestions are mentioned.

ANSWERS:
a The service – (un)helpful, rude, slow
b The lighting – bright, dark
c The food – bland, bad, overcooked, overdone
d The other customers – noisy, rude
(See complaints underlined in the audioscript below.)

1.58
(W1 = Waiter; W2 = Waitress; M = Man; Wom = Woman)

W1: Busy tonight, isn't it?
W2: Yeah. Who's the man at table four? He looks familiar.
W1: Oh, that's Burt Sinclair. He's a big cheese in the hotel industry, so if you butter him up, he'll give you a nice big tip.
W2: Oh – I could use some extra cash.
M: Excuse me! Excuse me!
W2: Yes, sir. Can I help you?
M: Yes, you can. The service in here is very slow this evening. We've been sitting here for ten minutes and we haven't even seen the menu yet.
W2: Oh, I'm terribly sorry, sir. We're very busy tonight. I'll get you the menus immediately.
W1: How are you doing with the big cheese at table four?
W2: Well, he obviously thinks he's the greatest thing since sliced bread, and so does the woman with him.
W1: That's his wife.
W2: His wife! Oh!
M: Excuse me!
W2: Yes, sir. Are you ready to order?
M: I'm afraid not. It's so dark in here that we can't read the menu.
W2: Oh, one moment, sir. I'll bring you a bigger candle. There, is that OK?
M: Yes, yes, that's fine.
W2: Would you like a few more minutes, sir?
M: No, no. I'll have the steak.
W2: OK, and how would you like it, sir?
M: Medium rare.
Wom: And I'll have seafood pasta and a salad.
W2: That's one steak, medium rare, and one seafood pasta.
W1: Everything OK with table four?
W2: They're tricky customers. I feel like I'm walking on eggshells.
W1: Just remember the tip.
M: Excuse me!
W2: Yes, sir?
M: I'm afraid this steak is overcooked. I asked for medium rare.
W2: I'm sorry, sir.
M: And there's another problem.
Wom: It's my seafood pasta – I think the scallops are bad.
W2: Oh, no. I'm very sorry. I'll talk to the chef.
W1: It's not looking very good for the tip, is it?
W2: That's not funny.
M: Excuse me!
W2: Grrr.
W1: Calm down. You have to take it all with a grain of salt. If you start taking it personally, you've had it.

Language note

Vocabulary

- *Bad* can refer to the quality of the food having deteriorated to the point where it's unpleasant or dangerous to eat, and it's generally used for things like fish and seafood, which can deteriorate quickly. *The fish is bad* means that the fish is inedible.

2 1.59

- Ask the students to complete the useful phrases. Ask them to compare in pairs, then check with the class.
- Play the recording for the students to listen and repeat. When they've done this chorally, ask for individual repetition of the useful phrases.
- Put the students into pairs and ask them to discuss their own experiences of complaining in restaurants.

ANSWERS:
a slow
b dark
c overcooked
d bad

1.59
a The service is very slow this evening.
b It's so dark in here that we can't read the menu.
c I'm afraid this steak is overcooked.
d I think the scallops are bad.

3

Draw the students' attention to the list of idioms 1-5. Remind them that they heard them all in the conversation in Exercise 1. Ask them to use the idioms to replace the underlined phrases in the sentences. Tell them to do this without looking at the audioscript on page 160, but allow them to look at it to check their answers.

ANSWERS:
a 5
b 1
c 4
d 3
e 2

4

Put the students into pairs to discuss people and situations where these idioms are appropriate. Then ask them to report back to the class on what they found out.

Life Skills (SB page 68)

Turning off and Tuning in

- The aim of this activity is to raise awareness of how we often look at a situation or person and judge them in a negative way, and how perhaps these people may actually be dealing with a difficult situation.
- Discuss the text with students and ask them to work in pairs to come up with situations people might be going through that may explain their behavior but do not come to our minds in daily situations.

Writing Extra (SB page 69)

Exploring synonyms

1

Pairwork. Ask the students to look at the sentences and put them in order as indicated. Then ask them to read the dictionary extract to check their answers.

ANSWERS:
1 "I'm hungry."
2 "I'm starving."
3 "I'm famished."
4 "I'm absolutely ravenous."

2

- Go through the instructions with the class, and then ask the students to work individually to form the collocations. When they've finished, ask them to check in the dictionary extract.
- Check answers with the class, and then ask the students to find out how the other verbs are used. Ask them to identify which verb suggests you have only a short time to eat.

ANSWERS:
c *grab* and **d** *have*
Grab suggests you only have a short time to eat.

3

Ask the students to go through the list and note down their answers. Then ask them to compare their ideas with a partner.

4

Focus attention on the table and point out that there are different ways of saying *fat* and *thin*. (Some are more polite than others.) Ask them to read the two dictionary extracts on *fat* and *thin* and to complete the table.

ANSWERS:

Fat

Positive	**Negative**
plump chubby	big, large dumpy overweight obese

Thin

Positive	**Negative**
slim slender lean trim	skinny anorexic emaciated gaunt bony

5

Pairwork. Ask the students to discuss in pairs which words they would use to describe the people listed.

ANSWERS:
a chubby
b anorexic
c trim
d emaciated

6

Ask the students to look in their own dictionaries to find out what synonyms are given for *hungry*, *eat*, *fat*, and *thin*. Then ask the students to find all the different ways of saying *cook* (e.g. *roast*, *boil*, *grill*). Encourage them to record them in their vocabulary notebooks in example sentences to show the difference in meaning.

Further practice material

Need more classroom practice activities?

Photocopiable resource materials in the Teacher's Presentation Kit / Extra Resources

Need more tests?

Test Generator Teacher's Presentation Kit / Extra Resources / Tests

Need more on important teaching concepts?

Key concepts in *American Inside Out Evolution* pages xxi-xxxvi

Need student self-study practice?

Workbook pages 24-27

Need more information and ideas?

American Inside Out Evolution website www.macmillan.com.br/americaninsideoutevolution

Need to check what your students can do by the end of this unit?

Self-evaluation checklists on pages xxxiv-xlvi

Review B *Teacher's notes*

These exercises act as a check of the grammar and vocabulary that the students have learned in Units 4–6. Use them to find any problems that students are having, or anything that they haven't understood and that will need further work.

Grammar (SB page 70)

Remind the students of the grammar explanations they read and the exercises they did in the Grammar Extra on pages 142 to 145.

1

This exercise reviews narrative tenses from Unit 4.

ANSWERS:

1	decided	7	heard
2	had traveled	8	was coming
3	were counting	9	looked
4	had been living	10	had been putting
5	picked	11	heard
6	was cutting	12	saw

2

This exercise reviews the future progressive from Unit 4.

3

This exercise reviews *will*, *would*, and *used to* for habits from Unit 5. Check answers before asking the students to discuss in pairs which sentences are true for them.

ANSWERS:

a ✔

b ✗ Change *'d* to *used to*. (*would* can only be used for past actions, not states.)

c ✗ Change *used to* to *will*. Or change *used to work* to *work*. (*used to* can only be used for past actions or states, not present ones.)

d ✔

e ✗ Change *'ll like* to *like*. (*will* can only be used for present habits, not states.)

f ✔

4

This exercise reviews verbs with the *to*-infinitive or gerund from Unit 5. Check answers before asking the students to check the sentences that are true for them.

ANSWERS:

a seeing **b** to buy **c** to call **d** eating

5

This exercise reviews the present perfect: simple and progressive from Unit 6.

ANSWERS:

1	Correct.	7	I've had
2	I've worked	8	I've always loved
3	Correct.	9	Correct.
4	has happened	10	Correct.
5	I've cut	11	I've enjoyed
6	Correct.		

Vocabulary (SB page 71)

1

This exercise reviews the prefix *self-* and the suffix *ible/able* from Unit 4.

ANSWERS:

a	self-conscious	**e**	doable
b	reasonable	**f**	unbearable
c	self-employed	**g**	self-discipline
d	visible	**h**	edible

2

This exercise reviews phrasal verbs from Unit 4.

ANSWERS:

a get **b** let **c** take **d** call **e** picked
f keep **g** given **h** feel

3

This exercise reviews wedding vocabulary from Unit 5.

ANSWERS:

a bride	**g** bridesmaid
b groom	**h** vows
c best man	**i** propose a toast
d confetti	**j** wedding cake
e veil	**k** bouquet of flowers
f honeymoon	

4

This exercise reviews collocations involving body parts from Unit 6.

ANSWERS:
a Stick **b** Hold **c** Bend **d** Shake

5

This exercise reviews collocations involving food from Unit 6.

ANSWERS:

a three-course	**c** unmistakable
b hard	**d** fast

6

This exercise reviews different types of numbers from Unit 6. When they've completed their lists, put the students into pairs to read them aloud to each other.

ANSWERS:
(Answers will vary according to the students' personal circumstances.)

Pronunciation (SB page 71)

1

Remind the students that the boxes show the syllables of a word and the large boxes indicate the stressed syllables. Here they're being asked to classify words according to how many syllables they have and where the main stress falls. Encourage them to say each word aloud to get a feeling for what sounds right.

ANSWERS:
1 and 2

A: □□□	**B:** □□□	**C:** □□□□
candlelight	however	competition
hazardous	organic	expedition
neighborhood	reception	invitation
organized	tomato	superstitious

2 1.60

Ask the students to underline the stressed syllables in the words in the table. Then play the recording for them to check their answers. Play it a second time for them to listen and repeat.

ANSWERS:
(See answers underlined in Exercise 1.)

Further practice material

Need more classroom practice activities?

Photocopiable resource materials in the Teacher's Presentation Kit / Extra Resources

Need more tests?

Test Generator
Teacher's Presentation Kit / Extra Resources / Tests

Need more on important teaching concepts?

Key concepts in *American Inside Out Evolution* pages xxi-xxxvi

Need more information and ideas?

American Inside Out Evolution website www.macmillan.com.br/americaninsideoutevolution

7 Escape Overview

Section	Aims	What the students are doing
Reading & Vocabulary SB page 72	Beach activities; scanning Reading for gist	Talking about beach vacations and comparing their ideas with a text. Marking statements true or false. Scanning the text for vocabulary items to complete definitions.
Vocabulary & Grammar SB page 74	Reporting verbs	Putting a summary in order. Studying the use of reporting verbs.
Speaking: anecdote SB page 74	Fluency practice	Talking about a family vacation they took as a child.
Listening & Grammar SB page 75	Listening for gist Past modals of obligation	Discussing potential vacation problems. Then listening to accounts of the vacations to find out what went wrong. Studying the use of modal verbs to talk about past obligation. Talking about recent travel experiences.
Reading SB page 76	Reading for gist	Talking about posting vacation photos on social media. Matching character types to postcards according to a text. Talking about people they know who fit the character types.
Vocabulary SB page 77	Word formation: *ful*, *ish*, and *less*	Underlining the suffixes *ful*, *less*, and *ish* in the reading text. Forming adjectives with suffixes. Then writing example sentences. Completing a table with adjectives. Completing a text by modifying words.
Listening & Speaking SB page 78	Listening for specific information Fluency practice	Talking about friendships formed on vacation. Then listening to someone talking about friendships formed on vacation and answering questions. Completing extracts from the recording. Matching discourse markers with interpretations. Underlining appropriate discourse markers in a dialogue. Writing and practicing conversations about a summer friendship.
Reading & Grammar SB page 79	Reading for gist Articles	Completing a story with articles and identifying the moral. Finding examples in the text for rules on using articles.
Pronunciation SB page 79	Pronunciation of articles in place names	Listening and repeating place names. Then identifying the different ways in which *the* is pronounced. Adding more examples of place names with *the*.
Language for Life SB page 80	Advice and recommendations	Talking about things to see in Paris. Then listening to a conversation and finding how many museums are mentioned. Matching sentence halves. Completing travel tips and matching them to the correct cities. Writing travel tips for their own city.
Life Skills SB page 80	Stress Management	Listening to a radio show with advice on escaping stress and anxiety with relaxation techniques. Discussing how to incorporate these techniques into one's routine.
Writing Extra SB page 81	Travel guide	Matching paragraphs with the correct city and writing headings. Matching words with their synonyms. Replacing the word *very* with adverb + adjective combinations. Writing a travel guide for their own city.
Writing WB page 31		Writing a description of a place.

7 Escape *Teacher's notes*

Warm up

Ask the students where they'd love to be right now. Ask them to give details about the place, the people they'd be with, and what they'd be doing, providing reasons for their choices.

Reading & Vocabulary (SB page 72)

1

- Focus the students' attention on the picture at the bottom of the page. Ask them if this is the kind of beach they like to go to when they go on vacation.
- Go through the questions with the class. Then put the students into small groups to discuss them. Appoint a representative of each group to report back to the class. Make sure they keep a written list of their ideas for things that might spoil living on the beach.
- Ask the students to read the text on page 73 and see how many of the things they put on their list are mentioned. Find out if any of these things have ever happened to anyone in the class. If so, ask them to explain what happened.

ANSWER:

c The author mentions:
- bugs and insects
- things like houses, cars, and furniture corrode more easily
- there is a lot of work to keep everything free of salt
- cost of living can be higher
- need to replace some items more frequently
- risk of hurricanes

Cultural note

Barbados /bɑɹˈbeɪ.doʊs/
Barbados is an island in the tropical Caribbean. Its capital is Bridgetown and the language spoken is English. Although it lies outside the hurricane belt, it has endured a few hurricanes in the past, such as Hurricane Ivan in 2004.

2

Ask the students to decide if the statements are true or false. Then allow them to compare notes with a partner. When checking answers, ask them to correct the false statements, using evidence from the text to support their answers.

ANSWERS:

a False. "I knew that life near the beach was not as idyllic as it may seem on TV, in a magazine, or even on a two-week vacation."
True
False. "Having lived in Barbados until twenty years of age, [...]"

b True
True
False. "[...] my daughters and my wife had never experienced anything like this"

c True
True
False. "At that point I put my foot down – there would be no move to Barbados."

3

- Focus the students' attention on the definitions. Ask them if they can complete any of them without looking back through the text. When they've done this, they can check with the text and find the remaining ones.
- Check answers before asking the students to write their own example sentences.

ANSWERS:

a dip
b foot down
c compromise
d raft
e nibble
f nap

4

Pairwork. Put the students into pairs and ask them to discuss the question. Encourage them to report back to the class and take a class vote to find out who sides with the author and who with the author's wife.

Vocabulary & Grammar (SB page 74)

1

Read the first two lines of the summary to the class and then go around the class, student by student, establishing the correct order for the remaining lines in the summary.

> **ANSWERS:**
> 1 A little over a year ago, my twelve-year-old daughter **announced**
> 2 that she would be moving to Barbados. She **insisted** that
> 3 Scotland was too cold and rainy.
> 4 "Growing up on the beach is more fun," she tried to **persuade**
> 5 me. I understood her point of view, I **reassured**
> 6 her, but also felt it necessary to **mention**
> 7 the cons of living near the beach. I **explained** my
> 8 own experience of growing up on the beach, but in the end, came up with a compromise by **suggesting**
> 9 that she spend the summer holidays in Barbados. After her return, my daughter **confessed**
> 10 that she could understand my point of view as well.

2

Elicit examples from the students that demonstrate the difference between *tell* and *say* before they categorize the verbs in bold from Exercise 1.

> **ANSWERS:**
> A: persuade me, reassured her
> B: mention, announced that, insisted that, explained, suggesting that, confessed that

Language notes

Vocabulary & Grammar: reporting verbs

- *Say*, *tell*, and *ask* are the most common reporting verbs.
- *Tell*, *reassure*, *inform*, *advise*, *assure*, *convince*, *encourage*, *persuade*, and *warn* are usually followed by an object pronoun (*me*, *him/her*, etc.), e.g. *He told me he wanted to go home.*
- *Say*, *mention*, *confirm*, *claim*, *admit*, *announce*, *insist*, *explain*, and *suggest* aren't necessarily followed by an object pronoun, but can be followed by an optional *that*, e.g. *She mentioned to me (that) she was on a diet.* Or *She mentioned (that) she was on a diet.*

3 2.02

- Ask the students to think about which column the verbs should go in before they turn to their dictionaries to check the patterns.
- Play the recording for the students to listen to five people talking about their favorite beaches and to confirm their answers.

> **ANSWERS:**
> A: advise sb to; assure sb that; convince sb that; encourage sb to
> B: admit that; claim that; confirm that

> 2.02
>
> **1**
> My favorite beach is in Cape Town. It's called Camps Beach, and I love it, because the location is spectacular. But if you want to swim there, I'd advise you to wear a wetsuit because the water is freezing.
>
> **2**
> My favorite beach is in Florida, but nobody knows about it. It took a while to convince my friend that it was worth climbing down a very dangerous cliff to get there, but she had to admit that it was worth it.
>
> **3**
> My favorite beach is in Maui. I've traveled to hundreds of beaches in different countries, and I can now confirm that the best beach in the world is Kapalua Beach.
>
> **4**
> Travel brochures claim that the best beaches are in faraway places like the Caribbean or the Indian Ocean, but I can assure you that there are wonderful beaches closer to home. For example, my favorite beach is in Valparaiso, and I can drive there in a day.
>
> **5**
> My favorite beach is the man-made beach along the river Seine in Paris. In the summer, they import a load of sand and encourage people to go there to hang out and relax. I think it's great for families who can't afford to go away on vacation.

Speaking: anecdote (SB page 74)

For more information about how to set up, monitor, and repeat anecdotes, see pages xix to xx in the Introduction.

- Go through the instructions and the questions with the class. Give the students a minute or two to decide what they're going to talk about. Then ask them to look at the questions and think about their answers to them. Allow them to make notes of what they're going to say and how they're going to say it, but discourage them from writing a paragraph that they can simply read aloud. Go around, monitoring and giving help where necessary.

- Pairwork. Put the students in pairs and ask them to take turns telling their partner about a family vacation they had as a child. Encourage them to ask each other follow-up questions to get further information. Then ask some pairs to report back to the class about what they found out.

Listening & Grammar (SB page 75)

Past modals

1 2.03-2.05

- Pairwork. Put the students into pairs and ask them to look at the pictures and discuss what kinds of things might go wrong on vacations like these. Encourage them to make a list for each one and to report back to the class on their ideas.
- Go through the instructions and the three questions with the class, and then play the recording for them to listen, compare their ideas with what happened on each vacation, and find the answers to the questions.

ANSWERS:
a Rachel.
b Sarah and Paul.
c Amy and Josh.

2.03
Paul
We decided to do something really special for Christmas. We both love skiing, so we managed to book ten days in a small ski resort in Alberta, Canada. When we arrived there, though, we found out that the temperatures had been unseasonably warm. Basically, there was no snow. Well, there were a few centimeters of snow very high up on the black runs, but we weren't allowed to go there, because it was too high and too dangerous. So we had to find other ways to entertain ourselves, and in the end, this was really good because we were forced to relax. We didn't have to get up early to go skiing, so we could go out until late at night and sleep in the morning. We read books, had long lunches, went for walks, and drank lots of hot chocolate. At the end of the vacation, we felt completely relaxed.

2.04
Amy
When I was 18, I was desperate to go to Guatemala to see the volcanoes, but I wasn't allowed to go there alone – my parents thought I was too young. So my brother agreed to come with me, and we carefully planned a three-week tour. We set off from Chicago, and our destination was the Guatemalan city of Antigua, but we had a lay-over in Miami for a few hours. Anyway, we finally took off from Miami, and, during the flight, my brother asked a fellow passenger if he'd been to Antigua before. He replied that he had, and it was one of the most beautiful islands he'd ever come across. At that point, we realized we were on the wrong plane, going to the wrong place. Obviously we couldn't get off the plane there and then, so we had to go on and then figure it all out when we landed. There were no direct flights from the Caribbean island of Antigua to the Guatemalan city of Antigua, so we had to go back to Miami and start again. We lost a week of our vacation, but in the end it just made us appreciate Guatemala all the more.

2.05
Rachel
When I told my friends I was going on a cycling vacation in Spain, they thought I was kidding. But I thought it would be fine. OK, I don't actually own a bicycle, but I do go to the gym twice a week. In preparation, I went to a specialist bike store to buy some gear. The helmet was compulsory, so I got one of those, but I didn't think I needed the padded cycling shorts. The guy in the store recommended them, but I thought they looked stupid, so I didn't get them. I should have listened to that guy. As soon as I met the other people, I knew I was in trouble. One man had recently ridden from Paris to Madrid – for fun! Our Spanish tour leader looked like she was about to set off on the Tour de France. I made a big effort to keep up on the first day, but by evening my rear end was in agony, and I couldn't the sit down. Fortunately, we didn't have to carry anything – there was a car that took all our baggage from one place to the next. But I have to admit that I got a ride in the baggage car a couple of times. I never realized that that part of Spain was so mountainous.

2

- Pairwork. Go through the instructions with the class and make sure they understand that two phrases are appropriate in each list. Ask the students to discuss in pairs which answer isn't appropriate in each case.
- Play the recording again for them to check. Ask them to check the modal verb or phrase that each speaker actually uses.

ANSWERS:
1 **a** and **b**
2 **b** and **c**
3 **a** and **b**
4 **a** and **c**
5 **b** and **c**
6 **a** and **b**

The modal verbs actually used in the recordings:
1 **b**
2 **b**
3 **a**
4 **c**
5 **c**
6 **a**

Language note

Grammar: past modals
(See Student's Book page 146.)

3

Go through the example sentences in the margin and ask the students to match each one with the functions listed in the exercise. Then do the exercise with the class.

ANSWERS:
a I had to / needed to
b I didn't have to / didn't need to
c I could / was allowed to
d I couldn't / wasn't allowed to
e I shouldn't have done
f I should have done / ought to have

4

- Go through the instructions with the class and make sure they understand that they should make as many true sentences as they can using the prompts.
- Put the students into pairs and ask them to tell each other their sentences.

5 Grammar Extra 7, Part 1

Ask the students to turn to Grammar Extra 7, Part 1 on page 146 of the Student's Book. Here they'll find an explanation of the grammar they've been studying and a further exercise to practice it.

ANSWERS:
1
a didn't have to
b didn't need to
c ought to have
d wasn't allowed to
e shouldn't have
f had to
g couldn't
h should have

Reading (SB page 76)

1

- Pairwork. Focus attention on the photos and ask the students when they last saw a post on Instagram, who made the post, and what it was about. Ask them to say what kinds of things they post on social media.
- Go through the questions with the class and ask the students to discuss them in pairs. Encourage the pairs to report back to the class on their discussion.

2

Give the students time to read the article carefully and to match the character types to the postcards. They can check their answers at the end of the article.

ANSWERS:
A 3
B 4
C 5
D 2
E 1

3

Pairwork. Ask the students to discuss the five character types described in the article and to say if they know anyone who fits the descriptions.

Vocabulary (SB page 77)

Word formation

1

Go through the instructions with the class, and then ask them to turn back to the article on page 76 and underline all the adjectives they can find with the three suffixes. Check answers before getting the students to say which suffix has which meaning.

> **ANSWERS:**
> tasteful, bookish, humorless, cheerful, thoughtful, stylish, tasteless
>
> **a** ful or ish
> **b** less

Language note

Vocabulary: word formation
Many words combine with *ful* if you want to describe something that possesses those qualities (*useful, tasteful*), or *less* if you want to describe something that lacks those qualities (*useless, tasteless*). Although many words can combine with both *ful* and *less* (see above), there are some words that only fit with one or the other (*delightful, stressful, wonderful*, and *endless, homeless, relentless*).

2

- Make sure the students understand that for each list they have to decide which suffix combines with all the words (individual words within a list may also combine with the other suffixes).
- Ask the students to check their answers by looking in the Word formation panel in the margin. This gives more examples of words that have the three suffixes. Ask them to check the ones they know and to choose three more to learn.

> **ANSWERS:**
> **a** less
> **b** ish
> **c** ful

3

- Focus attention on the prefixes in the table and point out that these prefixes usually give a negative meaning to the words they combine with. Ask the students to look back through the article on page 76 and find ten adjectives with these prefixes. They should write these in the correct columns of the table. Check answers before moving on to the next stage.
- Ask the students to form negative adjectives from those in the box and add them to the table.

dis	il	im
dissatisfied	illegible	impatient
dishonest	illegal	immature
disloyal	illiterate	immoral
disobedient	illogical	impolite

in	ir	un
indecisive	irresistible	unadventurous
incapable	irrational	uninteresting
inadequate	irrelevant	unusual
inappropriate	irresponsible	unself-conscious
		undivided
		unwilling

4 2.06

- Point out that the students will need to modify the words at the ends of the lines to make them fit the blanks. This could mean adding a prefix or a suffix or both, making the word negative, etc. The words needed are all ones that have been looked at in this section. The students may need help with the 8th blank, where *response* also needs the suffix *ible* and with the final blank, where the writer is being sarcastic. If they fail to grasp this, they may try to complete it with *unhelpful.*
- Play the recording for the students to check their answers.

> **ANSWERS:**
> **1** unwilling
> **2** irresistible
> **3** relentless
> **4** disobedient
> **5** devilish
> **6** undivided
> **7** stressful
> **8** irresponsible
> **9** careful
> **10** hellish
> **11** tearful
> **12** helpful

5

Pairwork. Ask the students to discuss the question in pairs and to report back to the class any surprising or amusing things they find out.

Listening & Speaking (SB page 78)

1

Get students to discuss this question as a class. The listening text in the next exercise is about friendships formed during vacations. Students may feel free to talk about other kinds of friends as well, such as friends from school.

2 ▶ 2.07

Tell students that they are going to listen to a woman talking about a friendship she formed when she was on vacation. Go through the questions with the class so that they know what information to listen out for and then play the recording.

ANSWERS:
a She was on vacation in Brazil.
b Her visa ran out.
c São Paulo.

▶ 2.07 **(F = Frank; A = Anna)**

F: Do you usually make friends while on vacation, Anna?

A: Not really but I made a good friend many years ago! When I was twenty I went to Brazil – I went to Rio de Janeiro – and while I was there I met Paulo.

F: What was he like?

A: Come to think of it, he was very funny, and we had a lot in common. We hit it off right away when we were introduced by a mutual friend at a party. From the very beginning he would always make me laugh. Just thinking about that time in my life puts a smile on my face. Anyway, it was the beginning of a great friendship.

F: Nice!

A: We got along so well together ... we would have conversations for hours about books we had read and movies we had seen. And he was always so insightful. I could really talk to him about fun things and more serious things as well, do you know what I mean? In fact, I thought we would be friends forever.

F: Yeah I know what you mean. So what happened next?

A: Well, eventually, my visa ran out and I returned to Texas. We then spent six months calling each other, writing letters, and sending packages. But long distance friendships were more difficult before we had so much technology to keep in touch.

F: What happened?

A: Basically, we just got busy with other things – university, work ... and we eventually lost touch.

F: Oh, that's sad.

A: Well, in the end I reconnected with him on social media, and we have been catching up. He is the same Paulo – funny and wise, just older, like me! He moved to São Paulo, where his wife is from. Now that it is easier than ever to stay in touch, we have rekindled our friendship. To tell you the truth, social media certainly has its upside!

3

Give the students time to look through the extracts so that they know what to listen out for. Play the recording again and ask the students to write in the missing words.

ANSWERS:
a ago
b funny
c friendship
d forever
e touch
f media
g upside

4

Focus attention on the words in bold in Exercise 3. Explain that these are known as *discourse markers*. Go through the list of eight interpretations and ask them to match them to the discourse markers.

ANSWERS:
1 f
2 d (Do you know what I mean?)
3 a
4 b
5 d (In fact)
6 c
7 g
8 e

Language note

Vocabulary: spoken discourse markers
These discourse markers are either spoken or found in informal writing such as an email or a message to a friend. During a conversation, many of them are signals to provide the listener with the information they need to react. *Actually* can be used as a way of contradicting someone, e.g. *You're not the type to have a romance while on vacation, are you? – Actually, I am.* If you've strayed from the topic you were discussing, *Anyway* is the perfect way of saying so, e.g. *Anyway, let's get back to what we were talking about.*

5 2.08

- Tell the students they're going to read about another friendship. Tell them to read it carefully and decide which discourse marker is the most appropriate for each choice.
- Play the recording for the students to check their answers. Then ask them to practice the conversation with a partner, taking turns being Gill and Tony. Play it again if they need help with intonation. Ask a confident pair to perform the conversation for the class.

ANSWERS:
1 Actually
2 come to think of it
3 Anyway
4 Do you know what I mean?
5 Basically
6 to tell the truth
7 In fact
8 in the end

6

- Pairwork. Put the students into pairs and ask them to write a similar conversation about meeting someone on vacation, using as many discourse markers as they can.
- When they've finished, ask them to practice their conversations. Take note of any particularly good ones, which could be performed for the class.

Reading & Grammar (SB page 79)

Articles

1 2.09

- Ask the students to look quickly through the story and ask a confident student to give a quick summary of what it's about. Then ask them to read it more carefully and to decide which articles need to be added to the story.
- Play the recording for them to check their answers. Ask them what they think the moral of the story is.

ANSWERS:
1 A
2 a
3 a
4 -
5 an
6 The
7 a
8 the
9 a
10 a
11 the
12 -
13 the
14 a
15 the
16 a
17 the
18 the
19 the
20 the
21 a
22 a
23 -
24 the
25 a
26 the
27 the
28 the
29 the
30 a

Moral of the story: Be careful what you wish for.

2.09

A poor treasure hunter was using a metal detector to search for valuables on a beach in Monaco. He had searched for hours but only found an old rusty key. Tired and disappointed, he sat down to rest when he heard sounds of distress. The cries were coming from a cove close by. He waded into the water and saw to his surprise that it was a mermaid. Her tail was caught in a discarded fishing net and she could not free herself. When he rescued her, the mermaid was so grateful she said, "Because you have saved me I will grant you one wish." He could not believe his luck. As he looked out into the harbor, sounds of a party were coming from the largest yacht that he had ever seen. It belonged to a successful millionaire businessman, the richest man in Monaco. "I want everything the owner of that yacht has!" he said.
"Go home, your wish has been granted," she said, and she dived into the surf and disappeared.
He hurried home and to his amazement the tiny shack he lived in had been transformed into a mansion with a garage full of expensive cars. As he approached, the door opened and his wife came out, with a huge smile on her face.
"Isn't it wonderful, my love?" the man asked. "We are now very rich and can afford all the things we ever wanted."
"Yes," she exclaimed. "Including the zoo out back. We now have all the animals we have ever wanted, including a giraffe."

2

- Go through the rules with the class and then ask them to find an example of each in the text in Exercise 1.
- When you've checked answers, ask them to look at the information about articles in the box in the margin.

ANSWERS:
Rule **a**: 1, 2, 3, 5, 7, 9, 10, 14, 16, 21, 22, 25, 30
Rule **b**: 23
Rule **c**: 6, 11, 18, 26
Rule **d**: 20, 24, 27, 28, 29
Rule **e**: 15, 17
Rule **f**: 4

Language note

Grammar: articles
(See Student's Book page 146.)

3 Grammar Extra 7, Part 2

Ask the students to turn to Grammar Extra 7, Part 2 on page 146 of the Student's Book. Here they'll find an explanation of the grammar they've been studying and further exercises to practice it.

ANSWERS:

2

a the
b -, -
c -, -
d -, -
e -, -
f -, -
g -, -
h -, -
i the, the
j the, the
k the, the

3

1 An
2 the
3 -
4 a
5 a
6 the
7 the
8 -
9 The
10 the
11 the
12 a
13 the
14 the
15 the
16 the
17 The
18 -
19 -

Pronunciation (SB page 79)

1 2.10

Play the recording and ask the students to listen and repeat the place names, paying particular attention to the pronunciation of *the*. Ask them what the difference is between A and B.

ANSWERS:
In list A, *the* is pronounced /ðə/.
In list B, *the* is pronounced /ði/.
The difference is because the items in list B all begin with a vowel sound.

Cultural notes

The Danube /ðə ˈdænjub/
The Danube is the second-longest river in Europe after the Volga. It flows for 2,850 km through ten countries (Austria, Bulgaria, Croatia, Germany, Hungary, Moldova, Romania, Serbia, Slovakia, and Ukraine).

The Panama Canal /ðə ˈpænəmɑ kəˈnæl/
The Panama Canal is a canal that joins the Caribbean Sea to the Pacific Ocean. It opened in 1914.

The Himalayas /ðə hɪməˈleɪjəz/
The Himalaya Range sits between Bhutan, India, Nepal, and the Tibetan region of China. Its highest point is Mount Everest (8,874 m), the highest point on Earth.

The Mississippi /ðə mɪsɪˈsɪpi/
The Mississippi River is 6,300 km long. It's the second-longest river in the USA – the longest is the Missouri River. It flows through ten states before running into the ocean in the Gulf of Mexico.

The Yucután Peninsula /ðə jukəˈtæn pəˈnɪnsjʊlə/
The Yucután Peninsula, in south-east Mexico, separates the Caribbean Sea from the Gulf of Mexico.

The Andes /ði ˈændiz/
The Andes is the longest mountain range in the world, running along the length of the western side of South America for 7,000 km through Argentina, Bolivia, Chile, Colombia, Ecuador, Peru, and Venezuela. The average height of the range is 4,000 m.

The Eiffel Tower /ði ˈaɪfəl ˈtaʊər/
The Eiffel Tower was constructed in central Paris under the supervision of Gustave Eiffel for the Grand Exposition of 1889. At 243 m high, it was the tallest building in the world and remained so until 1930.

The Empire State Building /ði ˈempaɪər ˈsteɪt ˈbɪldɪŋ/
The Empire State Building is 102 stories high and was the world's tallest building from 1931 to 1972.

The Indian Ocean /ði ˈɪndiən ˈoʊʃn/
The Indian Ocean sits between Africa (to the west) and Indonesia/Australia (to the east), India (to the north), and Antarctica (to the south). It covers about one fifth of the Earth's water surface and is the third-largest ocean.

The Orinoco /ði ɔrɪnˈnoʊkoʊ/
The Orinoco is a South American river running for more than 2,000 km through Colombia and Venezuela.

Language note

Pronunciation: *the*
When pronouncing place names starting with a consonant or the vowel *u* pronounced /ju/, *the* is pronounced /ðə/, e.g. *The Danube* /ðə ˈdænjub/, *The USA* /ðə ˈjuesˈeɪ/. For names starting with any other vowel sound, *the* is pronounced /ði/, e.g. *The Andes* /ði ˈændiz/, *The Eiffel Tower* /ði ˈaɪfəl ˈtaʊər/.

2

Ask the students to think about the question and add any more examples that they can think of to the table, when they've checked the pronunciation in a dictionary.

Language for Life (SB page 80)

1 2.11

- Pairwork. Focus the students' attention on the picture and ask them to identify the place the woman is dreaming about (Paris). Ask them to discuss with their partner the sights they'd want to see on a first visit to Paris.
- Play the recording and ask the students to listen and find out how many museums are mentioned.

ANSWERS:
Three museums are mentioned: the Louvre, the Musée d'Orsay, and the Picasso Museum.

2.11 **(T = Tim; S = Shannon)**

T: Where are you going on vacation this year?
S: I'm off to Paris.
T: Oh, great – I love Paris.
S: Oh, yes, you know it pretty well, don't you? Can you believe this is my first time there? Do you have any tips?
T: Well, there's so much to see. I'd definitely recommend the Eiffel Tower. Take the glass-sided elevator – when it comes out into the daylight, the views are spectacular.
S: That sounds like a must. What about museums?
T: Well, of course the most famous museum is the Louvre, but it's probably best to avoid it because of the long lines, but make sure you go to the Musée d'Orsay. It's one of the best museums in the world. You'll have to wait in line there too, but it's worth it. Where are you staying?
S: In a little hotel in the third arrondissement.
T: Oh, that's a really nice area. While you're there, make sure you walk around the backstreets, because there are some nice little stores – oh, and while you're there you should go to the Picasso Museum. You won't be disappointed.
S: Oh, I love Picasso. And how should we get around? What are the taxis like?
T: Um, I think it's probably best to avoid taxis, because the traffic can be very slow. If I were you, I'd use the buses or the metro. They're very good.
S: Wow, that sounds great.
T: And whatever you do, don't leave Paris without tasting the oysters at Bofinger.
S: Bofinger?
T: Yes, it's a restaurant on Rue de la Bastille. It's the best place for seafood, and the décor is fantastic.
S: I think I need to write this down. How do you spell Bofinger?

2 2.12

- Point out that matching the sentence halves produces useful phrases for giving advice about places to visit.
- Play the recording for the students to check their answers. Then play it again for them to repeat.

ANSWERS:

a 6	**e** 3	**i** 7
b 9	**f** 5	**j** 11
c 10	**g** 8	**k** 4
d 1	**h** 2	

2.12

a I'd definitely recommend the Eiffel Tower.
b The views are spectacular.
c That sounds like a must.
d It's probably best to avoid it.
e Make sure you go to the Musée d'Orsay.
f It's worth it.

g You should go to the Picasso Museum.
h You won't be disappointed.
i If I were you, I'd use the buses or the metro.
j Whatever you do, don't leave Paris without tasting the oysters.
k It's the best place for seafood.

Cultural notes

The Louvre /ðə ˈluvrə/
The Louvre is one of the largest museums in the world. Among the thousands of famous paintings housed there is Leonardo da Vinci's *Mona Lisa*.

The Musée d'Orsay /ðə ˈmjuseɪ ˈdɔrseɪ/
Once a railway station, the Musée d'Orsay was converted into a museum in 1986. It now houses nineteenth-century French art and design, including a large collection of French Impressionist paintings.

The Eiffel Tower
(See notes about the Eiffel Tower on page 91.)

The Picasso Museum /ðə prˈkæsoʊ mjuˈziəm/
The Picasso Museum in Paris has 3,000 works by Pablo Picasso, as well as work by other artists including Degas, Matisse, and Seurat, from Picasso's private collection.

3

- Ask the students to complete the tips using the useful phrases.
- Check answers before asking the students to match each tip to one of the cities in the box.

ANSWERS:
a views ... spectacular
b you; don't ... without
c best ... for; should
d make ... you; won't ... disappointed
e best ... avoid
f a; worth

a Cape Town b Barcelona c Bangkok
d Sydney e New York f Mexico City

Cultural notes

Table Mountain
A flat sandstone mountain (1,086 m) overlooking the city of Cape Town, South Africa.

Antoni Gaudi /ænˈtoʊni ˈgaʊdi/ (1852-1926)
Antoni Gaudi was a Catalan architect who worked in the Spanish city of Barcelona. He was influenced by gothic and Catalan architecture, but he developed his own unique and eccentric style.

Bondi Beach /ˈbɑndaɪ ˈbitʃ/
The name of a famous beach and suburban area close to the center of Sydney, Australia.

Coogee /ˈkʊdʒi/
A suburb on the south-east coast of Sydney, Australia.

Central Park /ˈsentrəl ˈpɑrk/
Central Park is an 843-acre public park in the middle of New York City. It was created in 1853. It includes several artificial lakes, two ice-skating rinks, and a sports area.

Teotihuacan /teɪoʊˈtiwæˈkæn/
Teotihuacan is an ancient city in central Mexico. Between A.D. 300 and 650, Teotihuacan controlled a wide area. It was destroyed in about 750.

4

- Pairwork. Put the students into pairs and ask them to write some tips for their own city. If they don't come from the same place, get them to write tips for the city they are in at present or a place that they both know.
- Go around, giving help and making sure they're using the useful phrases wherever possible. Ask several pairs to read aloud their tips to the class.

Life Skills (SB page 80)

Ways to Relieve Stress

1 2.13

Tell students to discuss in pairs or small groups the different factor that cause stress and anxiety in their daily lives. Students will listen to a radio talk show on how to reduce stress. After the listening, have students answer the questions.

ANSWERS:
Answers may vary.

2

Ask the students to think about alternatives to make the routine less stressful or to stay balanced, even during difficult days.

POSSIBLE ANSWER:
Students may suggest any of the following or others not listed here: breathing techniques, yoga, exercise, listening to music, massage.

3

Play the recording once more and ask the students to pay attention in the stress reduction techniques in order to complete the table with their benefits.

Stress Reduction Technique	Benefits
Meditation	1 lowers heart rate 2 boosts immunity
Strengthen social circles	1 reduces stress levels 2 improves immune functions
Laughing	1 reduces stress hormones 2 reduces blood pressure 3 increases T-cells 4 increases endorphins (any 2 of the above)

Writing Extra (SB page 81)

Travel guide

1

- Pairwork. Focus the students' attention on the pictures and tell them to discuss the questions in pairs.
- Find out how much the students can say about the different cities and make notes of their ideas on the board.

2

Ask the students to match the paragraphs in the guide to the cities shown in the pictures. When they've finished, ask them to compare their answers with a partner. Then check with the class. Ask them what details helped them decide on the answers (e.g. *famous canals* number 1).

ANSWERS:
1 Amsterdam
2 Madrid
3 San Francisco
4 Buenos Aires
5 Sydney

3

Point out that guidebooks often have questions as headings for different sections. These are the kinds of questions that tourists visiting the places described might want to ask. Ask the students to think of suitable questions to use as headings for the paragraphs of the guide. When they've finished, put them into pairs and ask them to compare the headings they've thought of.

POSSIBLE QUESTIONS:
2 What is the weather like?
3 What is there to do outside the city?
4 What foods should I try?

4

Focus attention on the highlighted words in the guide and ask the students to match them with the synonyms in the table. Allow them to compare their answers in pairs before checking with the class.

ANSWERS:
Saying how things usually are
is sometimes = can be
normally = in general
most = the majority of
are usually = tend to be
Linking words
owing to = because of
Despite this = However
Even though = In spite of the fact that
Or else = Alternatively

5

Point out that there are many different ways of saying *very*. Draw the students' attention to the example: *incredibly expensive*. Ask them first to underline all the instances of *very* in the guide, then to replace each one with an appropriate alternative from the box. Remind them to use each one only once.

ANSWERS:
Paragraph 1: extortionately expensive
Paragraph 2: extremely hot; bitterly cold
Paragraph 3: particularly pleasant
Paragraph 4: surprisingly popular; totally addictive
Paragraph 5: dazzlingly white

6

- This writing exercise could be done for homework. Remind the students to use linking words to make their texts flow well and to include adverb + adjective combinations to make them more interesting.
- You could ask the students to exchange their accounts in pairs or small groups and read each other's. Alternatively, they could be displayed in the classroom for everyone to read and enjoy.

Writing

Workbook page 31
Writing a description of a place
Sentence frames

Further practice material

Need more classroom practice activities?

Photocopiable resource materials in the Teacher's Presentation Kit / Extra Resources

Need more tests?

Test Generator
Teacher's Presentation Kit / Extra Resources / Tests

Need more on important teaching concepts?

Key concepts in *American Inside Out Evolution* pages xxi-xxxvi

Need student self-study practice?

Workbook pages 28-31

Need more information and ideas?

American Inside Out Evolution website www.macmillan.com.br/americaninsideoutevolution

Need to check what your students can do by the end of this unit?

Self-evaluation checklists on pages xxxix-xlvi

8 Attraction *Overview*

Section	Aims	What the students are doing
Listening & Vocabulary SB page 82	Listening for gist Facial features	Completing collocations about facial features. Listening to people talking about features they find attractive. Describing people with interesting faces.
Reading SB page 82	Scanning for information Guessing meaning from context	Agreeing or disagreeing with statements about the nature of beauty. Scanning a text to find if statements are true. Guessing the meaning of unknown words and compiling a glossary.
Grammar SB page 84	Passive report structures	Studying the use of passive reporting in written texts. Completing passive reporting sentences. Rewriting statements in a more informal style.
Listening SB page 84	Listening for gist	Matching people with opinions on cosmetic surgery. Completing extracts from a radio debate.
Reading & Grammar SB page 85	*have/get something done*	Completing a text about a woman who had a total makeover. Identifying when to use *have/get* + object + past participle. Putting sentences in order. Talking about the best places to *get/have* things done.
Reading & Speaking SB page 86	Reading for detail Fluency practice	Discussing being attracted to someone. Reading an article and completing a table.
Vocabulary SB page 86	Character adjectives	Deciding whether adjectives are positive or negative. Replacing words in sentences with others of similar meaning.
Pronunciation SB page 86	Stress in character adjectives	Marking the stress on adjectives describing character. Identifying changes of stress when adjectives are turned into nouns.
Listening & Speaking SB page 88	Listening for specific information	Discussing sayings. Listening to a radio show and answering the questions. Discussing the ideas presented in the show.
Grammar SB page 89	Unreal conditional structures	Completing hypothetical questions with *would* and *were*. Then underlining the alternatives to *if* in the questions. Completing questions and interviewing other people.
Speaking: anecdote SB page 89	Fluency practice	Talking about the most positive or negative person they know.
Language for Life SB page 90	Body idioms	Listening to a conversation and identifying phrases that are different. Matching useful phrases to those they've underlined. Then writing example sentences using the useful phrases. Writing and practicing a conversation using body idioms.
Life Skills SB page 90	Effective comunication	Listening to a podcast on how to improve the presentation and layout of documents. Analyzing documents and pointing out the positive features of a well laid out document.
Vocabulary Extra SB page 91	Metaphor	Looking at some common metaphors to describe people's emotions. Using these metaphors to describe personal experiences.

8 Attraction *Teacher's notes*

Warm up

Write the title of the unit on the board and ask the students to say what factors make people attractive. Is it physical beauty, personality, wealth, power, or something else? Do they think it's true that opposites attract, or that we tend to be attracted to people who are most like ourselves?

Listening & Vocabulary (SB page 82)

1

Groupwork. Put the students into small groups and ask them to discuss the questions. Ask them to make a group decision on the most handsome man and most beautiful woman, and encourage them to go into detail about what it is that makes them more attractive than other men and women. Then different groups present their ideas to the class.

2 2.14

- Ask the students to work individually to decide how to complete the collocations.
- Allow them to compare their answers in pairs before playing the recording for them to check. Then ask the students to discuss the opinions they heard and whether or not they agree with them.

ANSWERS:

a skin
b bone structure
c teeth
d eyes
e jaw
f eyes
g lips
h smile
i nose
j cheekbones
k eyebrows
l in the cheeks

2.14 **(I = Interviewer; W = Woman; M = Man)**

1
I: What do you think makes a face attractive?
W1: For a woman, smooth skin and good bone structure.
I: And for a man?
W1: Um, nice white teeth, sparkling eyes, and a square jaw. That's what I like, anyway.

2
I: What do you think makes a face attractive?
M1: Big eyes, full lips, and a big smile.
I: Like Beyoncé?
M1: Exactly.

3
I: What do you think makes a face attractive?
W2: It's probably easier to say what I don't like. On a man, I don't like a small nose – it doesn't have to be enormous, but a little turned-up nose on a man looks silly.
I: So you don't like Bruno Mars, then?
W2: Well, I like everything about him except his nose!

4
I: What do you think makes a face attractive?
M2: High cheekbones, especially on a woman. Like Jennifer Lawrence. She's my ideal woman. I love her arched eyebrows.

5
I: What do you think makes a face attractive?
W3: I love dimples.
I: Do you mean a dimple in the chin?
W3: Yeah, I do like that, but I meant dimples in the cheeks when somebody smiles – it's so cute.

Language note

Vocabulary: collocation

When describing *lips*, rather than using *thick*, *big*, or *fat*, which all sound negative, the strong collocation is *full*, which sounds positive.

3

Pairwork. Put the students into pairs and ask them to think about people they know with interesting faces. When they're ready, ask them to take turns describing these people to their partners. Encourage them to use as many of the collocations from Exercise 2 as they can. As they work, go around listening and helping where necessary. Encourage students who produce particularly good descriptions to repeat them for the class.

Reading (SB page 82)

1

- Go through the statements with the class and make sure everyone understands them. Explain that "Beauty is skin deep" is a saying which means that beauty is just superficial, on the surface of the skin. The saying also suggests that there is more to people than their appearance.
- Put the students into pairs and ask them to decide whether they agree with the statements or not. Ask them for their opinions on this before moving on to the next stage of the activity.
- Ask the students to read the article and mark the statements true or false according to the research reported in it.

> **ANSWERS:**
> **a** False
> **b** True
> **c** False
> **d** True
> **e** True

2

- Remind the students of the work they did on guessing the meaning of unknown words from context in Unit 5. Then ask them to underline any words and phrases in the article that they don't know and to try to figure out their likely meaning from the context.
- Get them to complete the glossary and add to it any other words that they underlined. Encourage them to try to write their own definitions before turning to a dictionary to check.

> **ANSWERS:**
> **a** zeitgeist
> **b** myriad
> **c** prevailing
> **d** plump
> **e** slim
> **f** curvaceous
> **g** biceps
> **h** six-pack
> **i** tangible
> **j** to be endowed with

Grammar (SB page 84)

Passive report structures

1

Ask the students to look at the two versions of each sentence and discuss the questions with the class. Focus the students' attention on the information and the examples in the margin.

> **ANSWERS:**
> **a** passive
> **b** passive
> **c** passive

Language notes

Grammar: passive report structures

- When reporting what people consider(ed) to be true, it's often easier to drop the "people," especially if you don't know or you don't care which people, and use a passive report structure. If you're writing or submitting a formal spoken report, it's more appropriate.
- The most common reporting verbs are: *say*, *think*, *consider*, *believe*, and *assume*.
- The two ways of presenting a passive report structure are:
  1) subject + *is/was/are/were* + past participle of reporting verb + infinitive, e.g. *Chocolate is thought to be bad for your skin.*
  2) *It* + *is/was* + past participle of reporting verb + *that* + subject phrase, e.g. *It's said that reading in a dim light can damage your eyes.*

2

Ask the students to work individually to put the words in the correct places in the sentences. Allow them to compare in pairs before checking with the class.

> **ANSWERS:**
> **a** Chocolate is thought to be bad for your skin.
> **b** It has been suggested that you should drink at least two liters of water a day.
> **c** It used to be assumed that carrots were good for your eyesight.
> **d** It is said that reading in a dim light can damage your eyes.
> **e** Shaving body hair is widely believed to make it grow back thicker and faster.
> **f** It is often said that we only use 10% of our brains.

3

- Ask the students to rewrite the statements in a more informal style. As they do this, go around checking to see that everyone is manipulating the structures correctly.

- Put the students into pairs and ask them to discuss whether people believe the same things in their country or countries.

> **ANSWERS:**
> **a** People think that chocolate is bad for your skin.
> **b** Some doctors have suggested that you should drink at least two liters of water a day.
> **c** People used to assume that carrots were good for your eyesight.
> **d** They say that reading in a dim light can damage your eyes.
> **e** Many people believe that shaving body hair will make it grow back thicker and faster.
> **f** They often say that we only use 10% of our brains.

Listening (SB page 84)

1 2.15

- Focus the students' attention on the pictures and ask them to discuss in pairs what kind of people they think they are. Read aloud the opinions and ask them to match each person with one of the opinions.
- Play the recording for the students to check their ideas.

> **ANSWERS:**
> **a** Rita
> **b** Michael
> **c** Jean

> 2.15 **(JO = Jean Oldham; RT = Rita Taylor; MH = Michael Hirst)**
>
> **JO:** Personally, I'm dead set against cosmetic surgery of any kind. I work for a women's magazine, so you can imagine how many beautiful models I've met. But I'm also in daily contact with women who are not physically perfect, and I have to say that the most beautiful women I know are not models – they are the intelligent, interesting women whose life experience shows on their faces. I believe that true beauty comes from within, and no amount of cosmetic surgery can give you that.
>
> **RT:** Yes, I agree with you, Jean, but not everybody has the confidence to let their inner beauty shine through. Cosmetic surgery can actually give people that confidence. I really don't think there's anything wrong with trying to improve on what nature has given us.
>
> **MH:** Ah, well, that's where I disagree with you, Rita. I think we should be grateful for what we have. The point is, it's selfish and indulgent of people to spend vast amounts of money on superficial improvements when there is so much poverty and sickness in the world.
>
> **RT:** Actually, it's not that expensive, you know, Michael. I mean, you could have your nose done for the price of a vacation, and quite frankly, cosmetic surgery can do more for you than a vacation, because the benefits last longer.
>
> **MH:** Are you saying I need a nose job?
>
> **RT:** No, of course not. I guess what I'm trying to say is that cosmetic surgery nowadays is almost as routine as going on vacation. Basically, it's here to stay, and I'm afraid you just have to accept it.
>
> **JO:** Well, I don't go along with that at all. Growing old is a natural part of life, and if you ask me, what we need to accept is that we can't look young forever.
>
> **RT:** Well, I would disagree with that, but let's leave it there.

2

- Ask the students to try to complete the extracts without listening to the recording again. Then play it for them to check their answers. Point out that the expressions they've completed are common ways of expressing strong opinions in discussions.
- Put the students into pairs and ask them to discuss whether or not they think cosmetic surgery is a good thing. Encourage them to use the highlighted expressions to give their opinions.

> **ANSWERS:**
> **a** have
> **b** believe
> **c** point
> **d** frankly
> **e** trying
> **f** ask

3

- Go through the topics in the box and make sure that everyone understands them. (Botox is a substance that can be injected under the skin to reduce wrinkles.)
- Give the students time to think about the topics and decide what their opinions are. Tell them that they can choose their own topics if they prefer. When they're ready, put them into pairs and ask them to take turns expressing their opinions on the topics they feel strongly about. Go around, offering help and encouragement. Ask any students who express their opinions particularly well to repeat them to the class.

Reading & Grammar (SB page 85)

have/get something done

1

- Explain that the woman in the pictures, Cindy Jackson, has had a makeover. Invite students to say why she might have had this makeover. Give students time to read the text and find out if they are right.
- Focus attention on the blanks in the text and ask the students to complete them with *have*, *had*, or *haven't*.
- Get students' reaction to the text and have a class discussion of the questions below the text.

ANSWERS:
Cindy had had her hair cut and colored, a new wardrobe, her teeth whitened and her makeup done by a professional.

1 had
2 had
3 had
4 had
5 had
6 have
7 haven't
8 had

The main change is that now she feels ten years younger, energetic, and hopeful.

2

Focus the students' attention on the two sentences and get them to identify that you use *have/get* + object + past participle to talk about things you get other people to do for you rather than things you do for yourself. Draw their attention to the further examples in the margin.

ANSWERS:
I cut my hair = I did it myself.
I had my hair done = Somebody else did my hair.

You use it when we're talking about services you ask (and usually pay) people to do for you.

Language note

Grammar: *have/get something done*
(See Student's Book page 146.)

3

- Ask the students to put the words in order to make sentences. Check answers with the class before asking them to use the sentences to make questions.
- Again, check answers with the class before moving on to the next stage of the activity.
- Put the students into pairs and ask them to take turns asking and answering their questions.

ANSWERS:
a I get my car serviced every six months.
b I had my house redecorated four years ago.
c I get my hair cut once a month.
d I had a burglar alarm installed.
e I had my blood pressure checked last month.
f I've never had my nails done.

a How often do you get your car serviced?
b When was the last time you had your house redecorated?
c How often do you get your hair cut?
d Have you ever had a burglar alarm installed?
e When was the last time you had your blood pressure checked?
f Have you ever had your nails done?

4

Pairwork. Go through the example question with the class, and then ask them to make questions with the other prompts and take turns asking and answering them. Point out that they can also use their own ideas if they wish. As they work, go around checking to see that they're using the target structures correctly.

5 Grammar Extra 8, Part 1

Ask the students to turn to Grammar Extra 8, Part 1 on page 146 of the Student's Book. Here they'll find an explanation of the grammar they've been studying and a further exercise to practice it.

> **ANSWERS:**
> **1**
> **a** Would you ever get your head shaved?
> **b** Would you ever have/get your teeth whitened?
> **c** Would you ever have/get your hair colored?
> **d** Would you ever have/get a tattoo done?
> **e** Would you ever have/get your legs waxed?
> **f** Would you ever have/get your ears pierced?
> **g** Would you ever have/get your teeth straightened?

Reading & Speaking (SB page 86)

1

Groupwork. Put the students into small groups. Ask them to discuss the questions and to be prepared to report back to the class on what they have decided.

2

- Ask the students if they have ever been a participant in a research project. Give them plenty of time to read the article and take in the information in it. As they note down their answers, go round checking and giving help where needed.

> **ANSWERS:**
> **a** Maria & Ally
> **b** Betty & Fernando
> **c** Max & Ally
> **d** Phillip & Reena

Vocabulary (SB page 86)

1

- Ask the students to look at all the words in the list, which all describe a person's character, and to decide whether they think they are usually positive or negative.
- Ask them to find the words in the article on page 87 and check their answers.

> **ANSWERS:**
> **a** Negative
> **b** Positive (sometimes negative)
> **c** Positive
> **d** Positive
> **e** Negative
> **f** Positive (sometimes negative)
> **g** Positive
> **h** Positive
> **i** Negative
> **j** Positive
> **k** Positive (sometimes negative)

Language notes

Vocabulary: describing character

- It's always important for your students to note whether an adjective carries a positive, negative, or neutral connotation. Sometimes a neutral word like *sensible* can be given a negative charge by preceding it with *too* (*too sensible* makes a person sound a little safe and a bit boring). Similarly, a positive word can be made negative by adding the prefix *over-* (*over-optimistic* makes a person sound almost gullible).
- The compound adjectives listed on this page all require a hyphen between their separate parts to show that the elements are connected to form one meaning. Other examples include: *small-minded, loud-mouthed*, and *big-headed.*

2

- Ask the students to find the words in the list in Exercise 1 that are closest in meaning to those in bold in the sentences.
- Check answers. Then put the students into pairs and ask them if they can identify with any of the sentences.

> **ANSWERS:**
> **a** sensitive; trustworthy
> **b** sensible
> **c** laid-back
> **d** stand-offish
> **e** open-minded
> **f** mature
> **g** enigmatic
> **h** down-to-earth
> **i** self-centered

Pronunciation (SB page 86)

1 2.16

- Focus the students' attention on the adjectives in the box and ask them to decide where the stress should be in each one. Encourage them to say the words out loud as they try to underline the stress so that they get a feel for what sounds right.
- Play the recording for the students to check their answers. Then play it again for them to listen and repeat. When they've done this chorally, ask for individual repetition of the words and make sure everyone is putting the stress in the correct place.

ANSWERS:

compatible	lively
flexible	mature
friendly	sad
generous	sensitive
happy	weak

2 2.17

- Point out that each of the adjectives in the box in Exercise 1 can be made into a noun by adding the suffixes *ity* or *ness*. Do the first one (*compatibility*) with the class as an example. Then ask them to change the remaining adjectives into nouns.
- Play the recording for them to check their answers and repeat the words.

ANSWERS:

compatibility	liveliness
flexibility	maturity
friendliness	sadness
generosity	sensitivity
happiness	weakness

3

- Play the recording again and ask the students to pay attention to the stress in the nouns. Ask if this is in a different place from where it was in the adjectives and if there's a difference between those ending in *ity* and those ending in *ness*.
- Play the recording once more. Ask for individual repetition of the adjectives and their nouns. Make sure everyone is putting the stress in the correct places.

ANSWERS:
ity = stress moves to syllable before the suffix
ness = no change in stress

Language notes

Pronunciation: word stress

- Adjectives that change to nouns ending in *ity* keep the stress on the third-to-last syllable, so *compatible* (□□□□) becomes *compatibility* (□□□□□□). The stress within the word changes, but the end pattern remains the same.
- Adjectives ending in *ness* keep the stress in the same place, so *happy* (□□) becomes *happiness* (□□□). The stress within the word stays in the same place even though an extra (unstressed) syllable is added to the end of the word.

Listening & Speaking (SB page 88)

1

Read the sayings to the class, or ask a student to read them. Ask the students to discuss the questions in pairs and report their answers to the class.

ANSWERS:

a *Possible answers:*
1. People who have similar outlooks are drawn to each other.
2. You can't change the way you are.
3. Something that looks valuable may not be.
4. Your actions will have consequences.
5. Take care that the things you want in life are really those that will benefit you rather than harm you.

b Answers may vary.

2 2.18

Point out the genie illustrated on the page. Make sure the students know what one is (a mythical creature that is supposed to be able to make your wishes come true). Ask them to listen to the radio show and note down how the "law of attraction" is like a genie, according to Dr. Hudson.

ANSWER:
It can give you whatever you want.

2.18 (P = Presenter; Dr.H = Dr. Hudson)

P: Now, you may or may not have read the best-selling self-help book *The Secret*, but almost two million people have, and the movie version on DVD has sold one and a half million copies to date. To tell us what all the fuss is about, we have with us in the studio today psychologist and expert in the "law of attraction," Dr. Rick Hudson. Welcome.

Dr.H: Thank you - I'm pleased to be here.

P: Dr. Hudson, *The Secret* is based on the "law of attraction," the idea that like attracts like. This isn't a new phenomenon, is it?

Dr.H: No, no, not at all. The theory behind the "law of attraction" has been around for ages. But it is the recent success of *The Secret* that has brought it to the attention of so many people around the world.

P: What exactly is the "law of attraction"?

D.H: Well, put simply, the "law of attraction" is all about positive thinking. We attract things we want and we also attract things we don't want. So, if you were the sort of person who was always cheerful and optimistic, you would give off good vibrations, and these good vibes would in turn attract positive energy, and good things would happen to you. Similarly, a stressed-out kind of person would put out stressed vibes, and they would attract more stress into their lives. Whatever you are thinking and feeling at any given time is basically your request to the universe for more of the same.

P: Hmm. So how can you apply this theory, this positive thinking, to your everyday life?

D.H: You can use it to make some very positive changes in your life. It depends what you want.

P: Where do I start?

D.H: Ha, ha. Well, let me give you a very simple example - OK, let's suppose you're on your way to the grocery store on a Saturday morning, so you're arriving pretty much at the same time as several hundred other shoppers! The one thing that would improve your life at that moment is a parking space. So you start focusing on that space. You visualize the ideal parking space, right near the entrance, and you imagine yourself swinging into the space as you arrive.

P: OK, I like that image.

D.H: And to make the positive vibrations really work for you, you need to imagine how you would feel if you already had that space.

P: I see.

D.H: Imagine that you already had that space - how would you be feeling?

P: Um, amazed?

D.H: Right, so you're still in your car on the way to the grocery store, but you're saying to yourself, "I'm so happy I found a space. I'm delighted and grateful that I found a parking space so close to the entrance." It works. Try it.

P: I must say, it sounds too good to be true. Suppose I really, really wanted a ten-million dollar house with a swimming pool - would I just think about it, and hey presto it would materialize?

D.H: Well, if you wanted to start living your life according to the "law of attraction," you'd have to learn a few simple techniques, and these are explained in *The Secret*. But basically, if that's what you really want, then yes, you can make it happen.

P: But don't you think it encourages people to be more materialistic? I mean, I don't need a house with a swimming pool. Isn't that just being plain greedy?

D.H: Listen, I'll give you another example. Imagine that a genie appeared in front of you and offered to grant your wishes. Would you ask for something small? Say a new bicycle? No. You'd be asking for bigger things. A business, a soulmate, a million dollars. The "law of attraction" is like a genie.

P: Hmm.

D.H: And here's why it's important to think big. There is so much that can be improved in the world. There is much more you can contribute. But you cannot do this by being mediocre. You owe it not just to yourself - but also to the world - to THINK BIG.

P: Well, thank you, Dr. Hudson.

3

- Give the students time to read the questions and the options before you play the recording again. This will give them a chance to identify the kind of information that they should be listening for.
- Check answers before putting the students into pairs and asking them to discuss whether they believe in the "Law of attraction" or not. Ask several pairs to report back to the class on their views.

ANSWERS:	
1 b	5 b
2 a	6 b
3 c	7 c
4 a	

Grammar (SB page 89)

Unreal conditional structures

1

- Remind the students that they studied unreal conditionals in Unit 3 and that the sentences they looked at had an *if*-clause and a result clause. Tell them that they're now going to look at how to talk about hypothetical situations without using *if*. Give the students time to read the questions and complete them with *would* or *were*.
- Check the answers with the class and then put the students into pairs and ask them to underline the words you can use instead of *if*. Tell them to try making similar questions starting with *if*, if this helps.
- Again, check answers with the class before moving on to the next stage of the activity. Draw their attention to the information in the margin and point out that unreal conditions without *if* follow the same structure as those with *if*: the *if*-clause uses the simple past and the result clause uses *would*.
- Give the students a few minutes to think about their own answers to the questions. When they've done this, ask them to compare their answers with their partner and see how similar they are.

ANSWERS:

a were; would
b were; would; would
c were; would
d would
e were; would
f were; would

Words you can use instead of *if*: *suppose, imagine, supposing, assuming*

Language note

Grammar: unreal conditional structures
(See Student's Book page 146.)

2

Pairwork. Ask the students to work in pairs to complete the questions. Check their questions before asking them to go around the class interviewing people. Ask them to keep a note of the replies and to report back to the class on what they found out.

3 Grammar Extra 8, Part 2

Ask the students to turn to Grammar Extra 8, Part 2 on page 146 of the Student's Book. Here they'll find an explanation of the grammar they've been studying and a further exercise to practice it.

ANSWERS:

2

a Supposing you could take a year off work, what would you do?
b Imagine you could have dinner with anyone in the world. Who would you choose?
c Assuming you were a millionaire, what would you spend most of your money on?
d Supposing someone was late for your first date, how long would you wait?
e Assuming your first date went well, how long would you wait before calling him/her again?
f Imagine that you had a different job. What do you think you'd have chosen to do?
g Supposing that you hadn't gone to bed until 3:00 a.m., how do you think you'd be feeling now?
h Imagine that you could change one aspect of your character. What would it be?

Speaking: anecdote (SB page 89)

For more information about how to set up, monitor, and repeat anecdotes, see pages xix to xx in the Introduction.

- Go through the instructions and the questions with the class. Make sure they understand that they can choose to talk about either a very positive person or a very negative person. Give the students a minute or two to decide who they're going to talk about. Then ask them to look at the questions and think about their answers to them. Allow them to make notes of what they're going to say and how they're going to say it, but discourage them from writing a paragraph that they can simply read aloud. Go around, monitoring and giving help where necessary.

- Pairwork. Put the students in pairs and ask them to take turns telling their partner about the most positive (or negative) person they know. Encourage them to ask each other follow-up questions to get further information. Then ask some pairs to report back to the class about what they found out.

Language for Life (SB page 90)

1 2.19

- Ask the students to read the conversation as they listen to the recording and underline eight phrases that are different.
- When checking answers, ask if anyone can remember what the speakers actually said.

ANSWERS TO EXERCISES 1 AND 2:

1 really busy (**e**)
2 say something to make you feel worse (**a**)
3 talk about it (**d**)
4 around here (**f**)
5 decided yet (**g**)
6 it was really expensive (**h**)
7 see how I feel at the time (**b**)
8 someone to talk to (**c**)

2.19 **(L = Laura; P = Phil)**

L: Hey, Phil, how are you doing?
P: Oh, hi, Laura – not too bad, thanks. How are you?
L: Oh, up to my eyes in work as usual. I'm on my way to my third meeting today. How's Mandy?
P: Oh, we broke up three weeks ago. She's on vacation with her new boyfriend.
L: Oh, no – trust me to put my foot in my mouth. I'm really sorry.
P: No, it's OK. I need to get it off my chest.
L: Who's her new boyfriend?
P: You wouldn't know him. He's not from this neck of the woods.
L: How did she meet him?
P: Through work, I think. He's one of those people who seems to be involved in a lot of things. He owns several companies, including the one Mandy was working for.
L: Oh, Phil, I don't know what to say.
P: Yeah – it's hard. I mean, we were supposed to be going on vacation together in a couple of weeks.
L: So, what are you going to do?
P: I don't know – I haven't made my mind up yet. It cost an arm and a leg, so I might go anyway, but I might not feel like it when the time comes. I don't know. I'll just have to play it by ear.
L: Look, Phil, I'm afraid I have to run – but if you need a shoulder to cry on, you know where to find me.
P: Thanks, Laura – I'll be fine.

2

- Pairwork. Ask the students to work together to match the useful phrases to the expressions they underlined in Exercise 1. Point out that these phrases are all idioms involving parts of the body.
- Play the recording for them to check their answers. Then ask them to choose at least three phrases and write example sentences using them. Put them in pairs to compare their sentences.

(See answers to Exercise 1.)

3

- Pairwork. Ask the students to work in pairs and to look in a dictionary to find six useful phrases using the body parts in the box. As they do this, go around giving help and making sure they choose suitable phrases. Remind them that these have to be worked into a conversation and must convey the appropriate meaning.
- Allow time for the pairs of students to practice their conversations and for each one to be performed for the class. You could ask the listening students to identify the body idioms used and to say what they think they mean.

Life Skills (SB page 90)

Layout of Reports and Essays

1 2.20

- Before listening to the podcast, brainstorm with students the characteristics of a well presented report or essay. The focus is on the layout of the document rather than the content. List students' do's and don'ts on the board.
- Listen to the podcast. Does the advice match the students' ideas?

ANSWERS:
1 The text is aligned to the left.
2 Only one font is used.
3 Heading and sub-heading have different sizes.
4 A neutral font is used.
5 Suitable spacing. Not too close, not too far.
6 Bullets points used.

2.20 (S = Stacey; JO = John Orr)

S: On today's podcast we have Corporate Communications expert John Orr talking to us about what we can do to improve the layout of documents such as reports to make them more attractive, more accessible, and easier to read.

JO: Thank you, Stacey. It is important to have well laid out documents, but this is much more than just aesthetics.
When a document has a neat and organized layout, it helps to clarify the writer's logic and the structure of the ideas being presented. Additionally, people tend to pay more attention to attractive documents. If you want your document read and to get positive results, pay attention to content AND layout. Finally, a document is a reflection of its writer. A neat, well organized layout says that the writer is professional and cares about his or her work. It leaves positive impression on anyone who reads it. Here are ten tips to help you improve the layout of your document.

1. Use no more than two fonts in a document, although one font is usually enough.
2. Use neutral fonts. Word processing programs offer many options, but stick to the neutral ones for a more professional looking document.
3. Use size 12 font for the main document, font size 16 for headings and font size 14 for subheadings.
4. Use color to your advantage in headings, subheadings, tables, and charts. Do not overdo color. Be consistent throughout the document.
5. Paragraphs should be suitably spaced within the paragraph and between paragraphs. If lines are too close together, the document is more difficult to read.
6. Align the text to the left.
7. Number the pages of longer documents.
8. Add a table of contents for longer documents.
9. Use charts, tables, and images, but don't overdo it.
10. Finally, use bullet points and numbered lists where appropriate.

I hope these tips are helpful. They have certainly come in useful in my own professional life, and I apply them to my everyday work.

S: Thank you, John. Join us next time for ....

2

Have students look at the text. It has an unsuitable layout for an academic or corporate setting. Have students rewrite the text so that it follows the advice given by the consultant.

Vocabulary Extra (SB page 91)

Metaphor

1

Ask the students to look at the sentences and match each one with one of the adjectives from the box.

ANSWERS:
a happy
b sad
c angry
d busy
e nervous
f losing your temper

2

Go through the instructions and the example with the class, and then ask the students to work individually to underline the correct words.

ANSWERS:
1 flared up
2 blew his top
3 snowed under
4 on top of the world
5 feels really down
6 strung out

3

Ask the students to match the emotions from Exercise 1 to the lists of words. They should then find example sentences from the dictionary boxes. Check answers and ask them to choose one phrase for each metaphor that they'd like to learn.

ANSWERS:
a busy
b nervous
c angry
d happy
e losing your temper
f sad

4

- Ask the students to work individually to make their choices. They should then compare their answers in pairs and check them in the metaphor boxes.
- Encourage the pairs to discuss whether they agree or not with the statements and to report back to the class.

ANSWERS:
a gloomy
b inundated
c let
d up; bright

5

Pairwork. Ask the students to take turns asking and answering the questions. Encourage them to report back to the class on what they found out.

6

Ask the students to look in their own dictionaries to find out what information they give on metaphors and how this is shown.

Further practice material

Need more classroom practice activities?

Photocopiable resource materials in the Teacher's Presentation Kit / Extra Resources

Need more tests?

Test Generator
Teacher's Presentation Kit / Extra Resources / Tests

Need more on important teaching concepts?

Key concepts in *American Inside Out Evolution* pages xxi-xxxvi

Need student self-study practice?

Workbook pages 32-35

Need more information and ideas?

American Inside Out Evolution website www.macmillan.com.br/americaninsideoutevolution

Need to check what your students can do by the end of this unit?

Self-evaluation checklists on pages xxxiv-xlvi

9 Genius *Overview*

Section	Aims	What the students are doing
Reading & Vocabulary SB page 92	Scanning; reading for detail Describing places	Naming people who are geniuses in various fields. Scanning an article to find the adjectives used to describe things. Explaining the connections between things in the article. Replacing words and phrases in sentences with ones used in the article.
Listening & Vocabulary SB page 94	Listening for detail Describing places	Listening to information about Stonehenge and answering questions. Matching synonyms. Then talking about the oldest building they've visited.
Grammar SB page 95	Past modals of deduction	Studying ways of talking about certainty and uncertainty. Completing sentences about the construction and purpose of ancient monuments. Then discussing theories about other ancient ruins.
Speaking: anecdote SB page 95	Fluency practice	Talking about their favorite historic place.
Listening & Grammar SB page 96	*look*, *seem*, and *appear* Listening for gist and detail	Discussing the story behind two paintings by Almeida Júnior. Then listening to a museum guide to compare descriptions. Matching sentences to the paintings. Finding examples of the use of *look*, *seem*, and *appear* in the audioscript.
Reading & Vocabulary SB page 97	Reading for detail Time expressions	Comparing events in Frida Kahlo's life with elements in her paintings. Matching time expressions with similar meaning. Writing about the life of a famous person.
Speaking & Listening SB page 98	Fluency practice Listening for specific information Reading for detail	Discussing and evaluating inventions. Listening to an interview and putting questions in order. Matching responses to questions. Completing a text with suitable words. Discussing the clockwork radio and appliances they would miss if there were no electricity.
Vocabulary & Pronunciation SB page 99	Collocations Word families	Matching verbs with the nouns they collocate with. Putting stages of production of a new invention into a logical order. Completing a table with words in the same family. Completing extracts from newspaper reports with appropriate collocations.
Language for Life SB page 100	Explaining how something works	Listening to a conversation and matching objects with functions. Completing useful phrases with *it*. Comparing written and spoken instructions for a coffee machine. Using informal language to explain how to use a machine or gadget.
Life Skills SB page 100	Self-Awareness	Looking more deeply into the meaning of the concept of 'genius'. Listening to an alternative idea of what a genius is. Thinking and writing about their own skills and contributions to society.
Writing Extra SB page 101	Narrative	Completing a text with time expressions. Choosing appropriate verb structures to complete a description. Writing a story about an innovation by expanding notes.
Writing WB page 39		Writing a story.

9 Genius *Teacher's notes*

Warm up

Write *a genius* on the board and ask the students what it means (someone who possesses exceptional mental or creative ability). Ask them for the names of a couple of people whom they consider to be geniuses and ask what these people have done to deserve the name *genius*.

Reading & Vocabulary (SB page 92)

1

- Pairwork. Put the students into pairs. Go through the categories with the class and ask them if they can think of someone (alive or dead) whom they regard as a genius for each of these categories.
- Ask the pairs to report back to the class on the names they've chosen and see how much agreement there is.

2

- Ask the students to look at the picture on page 93 and decide which words in the box they'd use to describe the City of Arts and Sciences. Draw their attention to the information about Santiago Calatrava in the margin.
- Tell the students to read the article and see if the words used in it match their choices. Find out if they like the buildings or not. Then ask them to classify the words as outlined in the instructions.

POSSIBLE ANSWERS:
a post-modern, space-age, important, contemporary, eccentric, sprawling
b important, urban
c post-industrial, sprawling

Cultural notes

Santiago Calatrava is a prolific architect, and his designs dot cities around the world. Below is a list of just a few:
The World Trade Center Transportation Hub, New York City – completed in 2016, this building is located at the site of original WTC which was the target for the September 11th 2001 attacks. This building has been controversial due to time and cost overruns.
Museum of Tomorrow, City of Rio de Janeiro – completed in 2015, this building is located on the waterfront. Its forty-five degree angle gives the impression that it is floating on the water.
Florida Polytechnic University, Lakeland, Florida – completed in 2014, Calatrava was responsible for designing the entire campus, which would give it a unified look. As in many of his designs, Calatrava integrated the features of the landscape (the lakes) into the design of the central building.
Turning Torso, Malmo, Sweden – completed in 2004, this building was the designer's first skyscraper and the first twisting skyscraper to ever be built.

3

Pairwork. Put the students into pairs. Ask them to try to remember what the connections are and to decide how they could explain them, before they look back at the text. Check answers by getting several pairs to give their explanations.

ANSWERS:
a Calatrava always had a relationship with art. He was taken to museums as a child and started art classes when he was eight years old.
b The City of Arts and Sciences integrates the natural landscape into its design.
c The government of Valencia had a vision to create an important museum which became the City of Arts and Sciences.
d The movie *Tomorrowland* featured the City of Arts and Sciences and some scenes were shot there.
e Santiago Calatrava also designed the Turning Torso, inspired by the human body.
f The City of Arts and Sciences lies on the dry bed of what was once the River Turia.

4

- Ask the students to look back through the article and find words and phrases with the same meaning as those underlined in the sentences.
- Check answers with the class before putting the students into pairs. Ask them to adapt each sentence so that it describes their own city or one they know well.

ANSWERS:
a expansive
b renowned
c bisect
d integrates
e iconic
f prolific
g is (also) controversial

Listening & Vocabulary (SB page 94)

1 2.21

- Pairwork. Focus attention on the pictures of Stonehenge and ask if anyone has visited the site (in England). Then put the students into pairs and ask them to read the questions and try to guess the correct answers.
- Play the recording for them to check.

ANSWERS:
1 a
2 c
3 b
4 c
5 b
6 a

2.21 **(OB = Oliver Bridge; RJ = Richard Jones)**

OB: It's a cold, gray morning. The sky is overcast and it's drizzling. For me, these are ideal conditions to visit the mysterious and ancient Stonehenge, my favorite place.
As a child, when I first visited the stone circle, it was the sense of mystery that fascinated me – what are the stones for? How did they get here, and what kinds of ceremonies and events went on here? As an adult, what I love about Stonehenge is that it's been standing there for 5,000 years – and it endures. I love the fact that after so many millennia, it remains such an enigmatic and enchanting place.
It's a little difficult to picture exactly how it was all that time ago, with only a few stones left and half of those fallen down. When it was complete, the stones would have been carefully laid out as a circle with a horseshoe in the center. Two types of stone were used – sarsen and bluestone. The huge upright stones are sarsens weighing up to forty tons each. Then the inner circle is made up of bluestones, and they weigh a mere four tons each. The bluestones are so-called because they turn blue when they get wet.
Stonehenge is, without a doubt, one of the greatest engineering achievements of pre-historic times. The stones were huge, and not a single one can be found locally. One can only marvel at the phenomenal effort involved in bringing the stones here.
I'm joined by Richard Jones, an expert in Stonehenge history, to tell us about the latest theories about how the stones were brought here, and why.
Richard, these huge upright stones, the sarsens – I suppose they were dragged across the land.

RJ: They would have been dragged, yes, from the Marlborough Downs, about twenty miles away to the north of here.

OB: And the bluestones, they were, they came from Wales, is that right?

RJ: From south-west Wales, from the sunny mountains of south-west Wales. Yes, a good 250 miles away from here.

OB: So there must have been some really powerful reason for them to situate it here.

RJ: Yes, there must have been a very good reason to bring them all the way here. It couldn't have been easy to get these stones in place – they didn't have the wheel at that time. In fact, it must have taken them years.

OB: But the reason why it's located here remains a mystery.

RJ: Absolutely. Something drew them to bring all these materials here, to this place. Why they brought them here, no idea. And you know, if you put twelve archaeologists in one room, you'll have twelve different theories – but we will never know for sure because Stonehenge was built before written history began. So we don't have any written evidence of a motive, a reason for why Stonehenge is here.

OB: All we can do is speculate. No one really knows what went on here, and I've got a feeling that Stonehenge will always keep some of its secrets.

2

- Go through the instructions with the class and make sure they understand that they have to find two synonyms for each underlined word or phrase.
- Play the recording again for the students to identify which word was actually used in the radio show.
- Put the students into pairs and ask them to tell each other about the oldest building they've ever visited. Encourage them to give as many details as possible. Tell the listening partner to ask follow-up questions in order to find out as much information as possible.

ANSWERS:
a drizzling; spitting
b endures; survives
c enigmatic; intriguing
alluring; enchanting
d just; a mere
e drew; inspired

The words underlined above are those actually used in the recording.

Grammar (SB page 95)

Past modals of deduction

1 2.22

- Tell the students that they're going to listen to five people talking about what they think Stonehenge was built for. Go through the list of suggestions with the class, and then play the recording and ask the students to decide how certain each speaker is. When checking answers, ask them for the reasons for their choices. Was it the speaker's tone of voice or the words they used that influenced their decision?
- Go through the information in the margin, and then ask the students to complete the sentences.

ANSWERS:
a almost certain
b almost certain
c uncertain
d uncertain
e uncertain

1 It must have happened.
2 It couldn't have happened.
3 It might have happened. / It may have happened. / It could have happened.

2.22

a
The big stones look like a doorway. The shape is very similar to those found in Japan at the entrance of some of our temples. I think it must have been a kind of temple, a religious place.

b
Well, apparently, the stones are aligned with the sun and the moon at certain times of the year – the solstices and the equinoxes. So I think it might have been a kind of prehistoric calendar. But it couldn't have only been a calendar. It was more important than that. I think Stonehenge must have been a place where people worshipped the Sun and the Moon.

c
I think it might have been a place where important ceremonies took place. It probably had a roof on it originally – if you think about it, it makes sense. It was obviously an important place, and it rains a lot around here.

d
We don't know, do we? It could have been a landing site for spacecraft from other planets, for all we know. Some people believe it was. Personally, I think it's just a bunch of stones in a field.

e
Well, it's a mystery, isn't it? Even the archaeologists can't agree. There's one group who have dug up bones, and they think they can prove that it must have been a cemetery. Then there's another group of archaeologists who think that the bluestones may have had special properties, and that's why they brought them all the way from Wales. Personally, I think it may have been a kind of healing place.

Language note

Grammar: past modals of deduction
(See Student's Book page 148.)

2

- Do the first one with the class as an example. Remind the students that they can use only two to five words including the word given to complete the second sentence. Ask them to complete the remaining sentences, and allow them to compare their answers in pairs before checking with the class.
- Put the students into pairs and ask them to discuss any other theories they know about the origin of the places mentioned, or other ancient monuments that they know about.

ANSWERS:
a might have been moved
b must have been transported
c could have involved
d may have been
e couldn't have come
f must have been built

Cultural notes

The Great Sphinx of Giza /ðə greɪt ˈsfɪŋks əv ˈgizə/
The sphinx is a mythological creature with a lion's body and a human head. The Sphinx at Giza dates back to the 3rd millennium B.C. and is the oldest sculpture in the world.
The Nile /ðə ˈnaɪl/
The Nile is the longest river in Africa and possibly the longest river in the world (6,650 km). It flows south to north through ten African countries (Burundi, Congo, Egypt, Eritrea, Ethiopia, Kenya, Rwanda, Sudan, Tanzania, and Uganda).
The Great Pyramid of Giza /ðə greɪt ˈpɪrəmɪd əv ˈgizə/
The pyramids at Giza were built 4,500 years ago. The Great Pyramid is the only one of the Seven Wonders of the World still standing.

The Nazca Lines /ðə ˈnæzkə ˈlaɪnz/
The Nazca Lines are a series of lines and images drawn in the soil in the Nazca Desert in Peru. The full force of the designs can be seen from the air. They're believed to have been drawn up to 2,500 years ago. Why the lines exist isn't known, but some speculate they were for religious purposes.
Easter Island /ˈistər ˈaɪlənd/
Easter Island is a Polynesian island in the south-eastern Pacific Ocean. It's famous for its huge statues (called "moai") and is a UNESCO World Heritage Site.
Machu Picchu /ˈmætʃu ˈpitʃu/
Machu Picchu is a pre-Columbian Inca ruin set on a high mountain ridge in Peru. It was built in about 1440 and was inhabited until the Spanish conquest of Peru in 1532. After that time it was largely forgotten about for centuries until it was rediscovered in 1911. It was designated a UNESCO World Heritage Site in 1983.

3 Grammar Extra 9 Part 1

Ask the students to turn to Grammar Extra 9 Part 1 on page 148 of the Student's Book. Here they'll find an explanation of the grammar they've been studying and a further exercise to practice it.

ANSWERS:
1
a Albert Einstein may have been born in Austria.
b US astronauts couldn't have seen the Great Wall of China from the Moon.
c Picasso must have produced more than 5,000 paintings in his lifetime.
d Shakespeare may/might not have died on his birthday.
e Mozart couldn't have been very well known when he died.
f Walt Disney must have won more Oscars than any other entertainer.
g Leonardo da Vinci could/may/might have had an affair with Mona Lisa.

Speaking: anecdote (SB page 95)

For more information about how to set up, monitor, and repeat anecdotes, see pages xix to xx in the Introduction.

- Go through the instructions and the questions with the class. Give the students a minute or two to decide which place they're going to talk about. Then ask them to look at the questions and think about their answers to them. Allow them to make notes of what they're going to say, but discourage them from writing a paragraph that they can simply read aloud.
- Pairwork. Put the students in pairs and ask them to take turns telling their partner about their favorite historic place. Encourage them to ask each other questions to get further information. Then ask some pairs to report back to the class.

Listening & Grammar (SB page 96)

look, seem, appear

Warm up

Groupwork. Ask the students to brainstorm all the words they know that have something to do with art. Write their suggestions on the board and leave them there as a vocabulary bank for them to use as they talk about their attitudes towards art.

1 2.23

- Pairwork. Put the students into pairs and ask them if they know of the painter Almeida Júnior and are familiar with his paintings. Then ask them to look closely at the paintings in the Student's Book and to discuss what they think the story might be behind them. Ask the students to say what they can see in each picture, whether they like the paintings, what they think the people in the paintings might be thinking or feeling, etc.
- Tell the students that they're going to listen to a museum guide describing the paintings. Ask them to listen and compare the ideas mentioned to their own.

2.23
This oil on canvas, *The Guitar Player*, was painted by Almeida Júnior in 1899. This painter was known for depicting the rural life of Brazilians in the 1900s. His work portrays the people as they were and it shows the simple and somehow sad life they led, as you can see by their looks in this picture: the woman is wearing simple clothes and the man is wearing a rustic hat, a checked shirt and white pants. He is playing a folk instrument. The setting is the window of what seems to be an old house as you can see by the uncovered walls. It looks like the end of a day's work, when people just get together to relax. The pinkish color of the wall and of the clothes looks as if they are lit by the sunset. The woman seems to be singing to a sad or nostalgic tune, while the man just appears to be laid back.
This other oil on canvas was painted in 1899 too. It is called *Longing*. It also portrays life of simple people as you can see by the walls and floor as well as the country hat in this picture. The woman by the window is wearing simple clothes and flat shoes. She looks like a widow, as she is wearing dark, plain clothes. She looks as though she is reading a letter or document that may have sad news or memories. She looks sad as you can see tears in her eyes.
Also, she seems to have suffocated feelings since she is covering her mouth with her shawl. Her

hair seems to be a bit disheveled which gives the impression that she has forgotten about herself. Almeida Júnior is famous for being a pioneer in regionalist paintings of naturalist style. He lived in the rural area for a long period of his life and seemed to know well the reality he portrayed. These two pieces were painted the year he was prematurely dead, stabbed by his cousin who had just found out he was having an affair with his cousin's wife.

2

- Ask students to match the sentence beginnings and endings. Then focus their attention on the information in the margin about *look*, *seem*, and *appear*.
- Check answers before asking the students to match the sentences with the paintings.

ANSWERS:
a 3 (She looks like a widow)
b 1 (She looks a bit nostalgic)
c 2 (She looks as if she has suffocated feelings)

3

Ask the students to turn to page 152 and read the audioscript as they listen to the recording again. Ask them to underline any sentences that include examples of *look*, *seem*, and *appear*. Check answers and make sure the students are aware of the various structures used with *look*, *seem*, and *appear*.

4 Grammar Extra 9, Part 2

Ask the students to turn to Grammar Extra 9, Part 2 on page 148 of the Student's Book. Here they'll find an explanation of the grammar they've been studying and a further exercise to practice it.

ANSWERS:
2 (Students' own answers.)

5

Ask the students to look at the paintings for 30 seconds and try to remember as many details as they can. When the 30 seconds are up, ask them to turn to *Additional Material* and answer as many questions as they can. Don't let them turn back to the paintings until they've answered all the questions. In a class feedback session, find out who got the most correct answers.

ANSWERS:
The Guitar Player, 1899
a The woman is wearing simple clothes.
b The man is wearing a rustic hat, a checked shirt and white pants.
c He is holding a folk instrument.
d It's a scarf.
e Checked blue shirt.
Longing, 1899
a She looks sad (as you can see tears in her eyes).
b The woman is wearing simple clothes and flat shoes. She looks like a widow, as she is wearing dark, plain clothes.
c She is holding a letter or document that may have sad news or memories.
d A simple living room.
e A country hat.

Reading & Vocabulary (SB page 97)

1

Focus attention on the text and the picture. Ask the students to read about Frida Kahlo's life and to discuss in pairs what aspects of her life they think are depicted in her paintings.

Cultural note

The Chicano Movement was a civil rights crusade in the 1960s which sought the empowerment of Mexican Americans in the United States, seeking land and worker rights, better education for children from their communities, political activism, and greater awareness of Mexican American history and culture.

2

- Focus attention on the underlined time expressions in the text. Go through the instructions with the class and make sure they understand that only one option in each pair is correct and has a similar meaning to the expression underlined in the text.
- Ask the students to work individually to identify the correct expressions. Allow them to compare in pairs before checking answers with the class.

ANSWERS:
a At the age of six
b After that
c During her life
d during her convalescence
e previously
f as soon as she returned
g while she was separated

Language note

Vocabulary: time expressions
These discourse markers provide us with a logical sequence to the text. There are several phrase types that can be adapted to suit individual circumstances and lengths of time (*while he/she/they was/were -ing*, *when he/she was* (age), *during/throughout his/her/their* (long-term event), etc.).

3

- Go through the instructions with the class and give them a few minutes to think about who they're going to write about and to decide what information they know about this person. As the students write their sentences, go around making sure they haven't named the person and that they're using time expressions from Exercise 2.

- Put the students into pairs. Ask them to take turns guessing who their partner's sentences describe.

Speaking & Listening (SB page 98)

1

- Groupwork. Focus the students' attention on the pictures of products invented in the last five hundred years. Ask them to decide on the order in which they were invented and to guess a date for each one.
- Ask the students to turn to *Additional Material* section to check their answers. Find out which group got closest to the correct order and dates. Then ask the students to remain in the same groups and to discuss the questions. Get them to report back to the class on their ideas.

ANSWERS:
1 f toothbrush (1498)
2 b toilet (1596)
3 d false teeth (1770)
4 a contact lens (1887)
5 e razor (1895)
6 c zipper (1913)

2 ▶ **2.24**

- Focus attention on the picture and the information. Ask the students to suggest circumstances in which a clockwork radio would be a good idea.
- Tell the students that they're going to listen to an interview with Trevor Baylis. Go through the questions with the class, and then ask them to listen and number the questions in the order they are asked.

ANSWERS:
The correct order: **d, e, b, f, a, c**

▶ **2.24 (I = Interviewer; TB = Trevor Baylis)**

I: Trevor, let me start by asking you what gave you the idea for the clockwork radio.

TB: Well, I was sitting where I am now looking at that television over there, and I was, um, actually watching a program about the spread of AIDS in Africa, and they said the only way they could stop this dreadful disease cutting its way through Africa was with the power of information and education. But there was a problem. Most of Africa doesn't have electricity. The only form of electricity available to them was in the form of batteries, which were horrendously expensive. And so I said to myself, hang on, hang on. Now, this is where dreams play an important part in everybody's life. Um, the beautiful thing about a dream is you can do anything you like in your dreams, right? Now why I am saying this to you is because I could see myself listening to some raunchy number by Dame Nellie Melba on my wind-up gramophone, mmm? And then I am thinking to myself, blimey, if you can get all that noise by dragging a rusty nail around a piece of old bakelite using a spring, surely there's enough power in that spring to drive a small dynamo which in turn will drive my radio, and so I was stirred enough to get off my backside and go to my shed, and actually find enough parts to actually start doing those first primitive experiments ...

I: And, um, how long did it take you to design a prototype from the idea?

TB: Well, from the actual, from the concept to having, er, the first in-a-box model out there, it would have taken me two to three months, I guess, so yes, it took about two or three months.

I: So you got, you got the prototype. How easy was it from that point on? How easy was it to find a backer and set up production?

TB: Well, first things first. I did know that there are these thieves about that will steal your idea. So I found a lady called Jackie Needle, a patent attorney, and I said to her, "Jackie, I want to write up a patent, can you help me?" So we did a search and couldn't find any clockwork radios of the kind that I had done, and she filed for a patent to me, for me, and therefore then I had a starting date, as it were. Now I knew that nobody pays you for a good idea, but they could pay you for that piece of paper, so then I went round every British company I could think of with a confidentiality agreement, and they all talked down to me. "Oh yes, I think we're, I think that we are working on something like this, aren't we, Johnny?" You know all that old sausage. Um, I mean it was so humiliating ... and in the end, quite frankly after about three or four years of this, I thought, I have had enough of this. Why do I need this? I was fifty-six or something when this happened. So I was given a chance through the BBC World Service to meet up with the guys from the BBC Tomorrow's World program, and they said, "Come on, we'll do the story."

I: So the whole thing got off the ground. How long was it then before the production of them started?

TB: Well, the important thing was funding. The Tomorrow's World program was seen by a fellow in South Africa, a chap from a company called Liberty Life. He came to my house here, and we sat out there, and he said, "Look, um, we can help you make this happen, providing we can share in its success." I said of course, and so we formed a company called Baygen, Baylis Generators, and he wrote a check for three-quarters of a million pounds whilst I was in this room.

I: And how many radios are produced each month?

TB: Well, I'm sure they might tell me differently, but I'm sure they must be doing 200,000 a month.

I: And finally, what advice would you give to someone who had a good idea?

TB: Don't go down the pub and tell everybody about it. That's the first thing, right? Get on to the Patent Office. Get their literature, and read all about it, right? Nobody pays you for a good idea, but they might pay you for a piece of paper which says you own that idea. But remember, somebody might already own that idea, so you must do a search first. There's no excuse afterwards.

Language note

TV program (British English) = *TV show* (American English)
blimey (British English) = *gosh* (American English)

Cultural note

The BBC program *Tomorrow's World*
A series on BBC that presented the latest technological developments likely to affect our day-to-day lives. It ran from 1965 until 2003.

3

- Ask the students to match the replies to the questions.
- Play the recording a second time for them to check their answers.

ANSWERS:
1 c
2 e
3 a
4 d
5 f
6 b

4

Pairwork. Ask the students to take turns telling each other all they can remember about the story of Trevor Baylis that they heard in the interview in the previous section. Then ask them to work together to complete the summary.

ANSWERS:
1 epidemic
2 spread
3 electricity
4 dream
5 prototype
6 patent
7 set
8 yourself

5

Do this as a class activity, but give them time to think of ideas to contribute to the discussion.

Vocabulary & Pronunciation (SB page 99)

1

Focus the students' attention on the collocations. Ask them to decide which verb in parentheses also goes with the noun to give a similar meaning. Allow the students to discuss their ideas in pairs or small groups and to use their dictionaries to check their answers.

ANSWERS:
a set up
b carry out
c come up with
d apply for
e begin
f develop
g conduct

2

Pairwork. Ask the students to discuss in pairs what they think is the most logical order for the stages in Exercise 1.
Get them to report back to the class on their decisions.

ANSWERS:
Probably: **c, b, f, g, d, a, e**

3 2.25

- Focus the students' attention on the table and explain that some words come in families, i.e. from the same root there can be one or more noun, adjective, and verb. Do the first line of the table with the class, eliciting the words *biology*, *biologist*, and *biological* and pointing out that the adjective collocates with the noun.
- Ask the students to complete the table and then to decide where the stress should go on each word. Encourage them to say the words aloud as they do this so that they get a feel for what sounds right. They should then practice saying the words.
- Play the recording for them to check their answers. Play it a second time for them to listen and repeat.

ANSWERS:

1 Noun (subject)	2 Noun (person)	3 Adjective	+ example collocations
a biology	biologist	biological	weapons
b chemistry	chemist	chemical	reactions / weapons
c economy/ economics	economist	economic	growth / research
d genetics	geneticist	genetic	engineering
e math	mathematician	mathematical	equations / research
f science	scientist	scientific	advances / research
g technology	technologist	technological	advances / research

Language notes

Pronunciation: word families

- As a general rule, the following endings belong to words that are stressed on the third-to-last syllable (if the word is three or more syllables long): *-logy / -logist, -ist, -ical* (*biology / biologist* □☐□□, *economist* □☐□□, *mathematical* □□☐□□).
- Words ending in *-ic(s)* are generally stressed on the penultimate syllable (*genetics* □☐□, *economic* □□☐□).

4

Tell the students to read the newspaper extracts and decide which adjective + noun collocation best fits in each blank. Allow them to compare answers in pairs before checking with the class.

ANSWERS:
1 mathematical equations
2 Scientific research
3 genetic engineering
4 economic growth
5 biological weapons
6 Technological advances
7 chemical reactions

5

Ask the students to look in their dictionaries and find other nouns that go for each of the adjectives in the table in Exercise 1. Then tell them to write an example sentence for five collocations that are new to them.

Language for Life (SB page 100)

1 2.26

- Focus attention on the picture and tell the students that they're going to listen to a conversation between these women. Explain that Brigit is going to stay at Alice's house while Alice is away. Go through the objects and functions with the class so that they know what to listen out for. Then play the recording and ask them to match the objects with the functions.
- Check answers with the class.

ANSWERS:
a 3
b 6
c 1
d 5
e 4
f 2

Brigit is surprised to learn that she has to look after Molly, the dog.

2.26 (A =Alice; B = Brigit)

A: Oh, I'm so glad you can stay here while we're away and keep an eye on the place.
B: No problem. It'll be nice to have a change of scenery for a couple of weeks.
A: Now, there are a few things I need to tell you. Did you get the keys in the mail?
B: Yes, I have them here.
A: OK, to open the front door, you need the small key.
B: OK.
A: You need to turn it twice counter-clockwise.
B: OK. And I guess the big key is for the back door?
A: Exactly. Now, if you need the heating on, you just need to turn up the thermostat.
B: OK, and where do I do that?
A: There's a dial in the hallway, between the sitting room and the kitchen. Just turn it until it clicks.
B: OK.
A: And then make sure you turn it down again before you go to bed.
B: Of course.
A: OK - the TV's in the living room, and you use the silver remote control to turn it on and off, and the smaller black one for changing the channel. Do you think you'll watch a DVD?
B: Er, no, it's OK.
A: Now, what else? The smoke alarms are always going off in our house. The best thing to do is to have the fan on when you're cooking - just press the red button above the stove to turn it on. You can't miss it. And if the smoke alarm goes off, just stand under it and wave your arms.
B: OK. Is there anything else?
A: Oh, yes, I know what I haven't told you. Do you like coffee?
B: Yes, I love it.
A: Well, there's a coffee machine next to the stove. It's very easy to use. Basically, plug it in at the wall, and the on/off switch is on the back of the machine. Then you put a filter into the filter holder and put the coffee into the filter. Put water into the thing above it, and make sure the lid's on tight. Then put a cup under the place where the coffee comes out.

The machine will warm the water up to the right temperature, so you just have to wait a few seconds. When the cup's full, take it out and your coffee's ready. Anyway, I'll leave you the instructions.

B: Oh, good, thanks.

A: That's it then. Oh, and Molly needs a walk twice a day, and don't forget to let her out before you go to bed – we wouldn't want her to have an accident.

B: Molly? You didn't mention ...

A: Oh, didn't I? She's no trouble, are you? Yes ... oh yes ... you're good ... down girl, down.

2

- Go through the example with the class, and then ask the students to decide where to insert *it* in each sentence.
- Ask the students to decide what *it* refers.

ANSWERS:

a You need to turn it twice counter-clockwise.
b You turn it until it clicks.
c Make sure you turn it down again.
d You use the silver remote control to turn it on and off.
e Press the red button above the stove to turn it on.
f Plug it in at the wall.
g Put water into the thing above it.

a The front door key
b The dial for the thermostat
c The thermostat
d The TV
e The stove fan
f The coffee machine
g The coffee filter

3

Ask the students which they think is likely to be in more formal language, the written instructions or Alice's spoken instructions. Ask them to read both texts and underline the formal equivalents of the highlighted words and phrases.

Spoken	Written
put	insert
put	place
put; the thing above it	pour; the water tank
make sure; on tight	ensure; secure
put	place
the place where the coffee comes out	the spout
warm the water up	heat the water
right	correct
take it out	remove it

4

- Give the students time to decide which machine or gadget they're going to talk about. Allow them to make brief notes if they wish, but don't allow them to write full sentences to read aloud.
- Put the students into pairs and ask them to take turns giving their spoken instructions. Ask the listening partner each time to say whether they'd now feel confident about using the machine or gadget.

Life Skills (SB page 100)

Knowing Yourself Better

1 2.27

Students will listen to a definition of a genius. Walk around the classroom to check if the students agree or not with the definition and why.

2.27
In this unit we have seen examples of artists and inventors who can be considered geniuses. A genius is defined in the Macmillan online dictionary as "someone who is much more intelligent or skillful than other people." More than that, however, true geniuses are people who use their gifts to present solutions to problems or enhance people's lives in some way. Listen to the profile of Uzo and find out how she found solutions to everyday problems and enhanced people's lives.

2 2.28

- Have students reflect on what they have listened to in the unit and brainstorm characteristics of a genius. Put these ideas up on the board.
- Students will listen a short text about Uzo, a young woman who has used her knowledge and skills to train other women and create jobs. Discuss students' responses to the questions. Compare Uzo to the other people discussed in the unit. Do they share any characteristics?

POSSIBLE ANSWER:
Uzo turned her hobby and skills into a source of income for other young women who needed a job. By providing jobs and recycling scraps to make useful and beautiful things, she's enhancing the lives of the people in her home town and helping the environment.

2.28
Uzo from Lagos, Nigeria has always loved sewing and making things with her hands. She grew up in her father's tailor shop, where she would use the scraps first to make clothes for her dolls, then bags and other accessories for herself and her friends. By the time she was a teenager, she had a whole list of things she was making from scraps. Back in her home town after graduating from university, she saw many young women out of work and with dim prospects for the future. She decided to gather scraps from all over town and started teaching the women the techniques she had developed

over the years. Soon they were making bags, clothes, and hats for sale locally and regionally. Uzo took a simple idea and used her skills to create jobs and bring hope to dozens of women in her home town.

3

Have students think about their own skills and abilities and how they can use these to benefit others. Students can write their thoughts down.

Writing Extra (SB page 101)

Narrative

1

- Focus the students' attention on the first text and get them to identify the illustration (a pad of Post-it® notes). Ask them to read the text and complete it with the time expressions from the box.
- Check answers with the class and then elicit their reactions to the text. Did they know of the origins of the Post-it® note? Do they think that many inventions are basically very simple ideas or come from things that were initially regarded as failures?

ANSWERS:
1 In 1977
2 Each Sunday
3 One Sunday
4 a few months earlier
5 The following day

2

Tell the students that they're going to read about another invention that was discovered almost by accident. Ask them to read the article and choose the most appropriate verb structures. When they've finished, ask them to compare their answers with a partner. Then check with the class.

ANSWERS:
1 was working
2 felt
3 had been affected
4 had heard
5 had been installed

3

- Focus attention on the notes and the picture of Mark Zuckerberg, the founder of Facebook®. Ask the students whether they use Facebook and if they know anything about its origins. Ask them to read the notes, and explain anything they don't understand.
- Go through the outline with the class and then ask them to use it to write an article about how Zuckerberg developed Facebook.

POSSIBLE ANSWER:
Mark Zuckerberg founded Facebook® while studying psychology at Harvard University. He had already developed a number of social-networking sites for fellow students, including Facemash, a site for rating people's attractiveness.

In February 2004 he launched "The Facebook." Within 24 hours, 1,200 students had signed up, and after one month, half the student population of Harvard had set up profiles on the site.
The site became "Facebook" in August 2005 when Zuckerberg purchased the name "facebook.com" for $200,000. Previously the site was only available to college students, but since September 2006 it's been available to anyone over thirteen.
In 2007, rumors that Prince William had signed up circulated, but this was not true. In 2008, four years after three Harvard classmates accused Zuckerberg of stealing the idea for Facebook®, he settled out of court.
Today, Zuckerberg is one of the youngest billionaires in the world.
In 2010, a movie about how Facebook started called *The Social Network* came out. Facebook grew in 2012 with the purchase of Instagram, and the social network reached 1 billion active users per month from around the world. There was further growth in 2014 with the purchase of WhatsApp. There are currently 2 billion monthly active users, who spend around twenty minutes on Facebook each visit.

Cultural note

Harvard University /ˈhɑrvɜrd junɪˈvɜrsəti/
A private college in Massachusetts that was founded in 1636, making it the oldest college of its kind in the USA. Only excellent students or members of the social elite are considered as students.

Writing

Workbook page 39

Writing a story
Narrative tenses
Use of pronouns
Lexical variety: nouns

Further practice material

Need more classroom practice activities?

Photocopiable resource materials in the Teacher's Presentation Kit / Extra Resources

Need more tests?

Test Generator
Teacher's Presentation Kit / Extra Resources / Tests

Need more on important teaching concepts?

Key concepts in *American Inside Out Evolution* pages xxi-xxxvi

Need student self-study practice?

Workbook pages 36-39

Need more information and ideas?

American Inside Out Evolution website www.macmillan.com.br/americaninsideoutevolution

Need to check what your students can do by the end of this unit?

Self-evaluation checklists on pages xxxix-xlvi

Review C *Teacher's notes*

These exercises act as a check of the grammar and vocabulary that the students have learned in Units 7–9. Use them to find any problems that students are having, or anything that they haven't understood and that will need further work.

Grammar (SB page 102)

Remind the students of the grammar explanations they read and the exercises they did in the Grammar Extra on pages 146 to 149.

1

This exercise reviews reporting verbs from Unit 7. Remind the students of the two different patterns: with the hearer as direct object and where the hearer isn't the direct object.

ANSWERS:
1 announced
2 assure you
3 confirm
4 admit
5 inform you
6 explain
7 suggest

2

This exercise reviews past modals of obligation from Unit 7.

ANSWERS:
1 need 2 had 3 allowed 4 didn't
5 should 6 should

3

This exercise reviews articles from Unit 7. Check answers with the class before asking the students to say which of the sentences are true for them.

ANSWERS:
a – b an c the

4

This exercise reviews passive reporting structures from Unit 8.

ANSWERS:
a The rate of inflation is expected to rise sharply.
b It is thought the President will resign soon.
c It is said that the world's climate will become more extreme.
d Vast oil reserves are thought to exist under the Arctic ice cap.

5

This exercise reviews unreal conditionals from Unit 8. Check answers with the class before asking the students to answer the questions for themselves and then compare with a partner.

ANSWERS:
a If you won $10 million, would you keep it all?
b Supposing you could be someone famous, who would it be?
c Imagine you were able to do your dream job. What would you do?
d Assuming time were no object, what new skill would you like to learn?

6

This exercise reviews past modals of deduction from Unit 9.

POSSIBLE ANSWERS:
a Amy might have woken up late.
b Will might have had too much to drink last night.
c Daniela must have gone out.
d Kenji must have had an accident.

7

This exercise reviews *looks, looks like, looks as if/ though*, and *seems to be* from Unit 9. Remind the students that they may have to change some of the forms. Check answers with the class. Then ask the students to decide which sentences are true for them and to discuss them with a partner.

ANSWERS:
a looks
b looked like
c though
d seemed
e as if
f to be

Vocabulary (SB page 103)

1

This exercise reviews word formation from Unit 7.

ANSWERS:
a bullish
b cheerful
c endless
d foolish
e homeless
f relentless
g selfish
h stressful
i tearful

2

This exercise reviews word formation from Unit 7.

dis-	il-	im-
dishonest	illegal	immature
disloyal	illegible	immoral
disobedient	illiterate	impatient
dissatisfied	illogical	impolite
in-	**ir-**	**un-**
inadequate	irrational	unadventurous
inappropriate	irrelevant	undivided
incapable	irresistible	unusual
indecisive	irresponsible	unwilling

3

This exercise reviews the words to describe personal appearance from Unit 8. Check answers with the class before putting the students into pairs to discuss which features they think make a person attractive.

ANSWERS:
1 mouth **2** lips **3** cheekbones **4** skin
5 teeth **6** eyes **7** dimples **8** jaw

4

This exercise reviews useful adjectives for describing a person's character from Unit 8. Check answers, and then ask the students to work individually to choose three adjectives to describe themselves. They should then compare their choices with a partner.

ANSWERS:
a 2 **b** 5 **c** 8 **d** 10 **e** 11 **f** 3
g 7 **h** 4 **i** 1 **j** 6 **k** 9

5

This exercise reviews time expressions from Unit 9. Ask the students if they've seen any movies starring Audrey Hepburn. They may know *Breakfast at Tiffany's*.

ANSWERS:
1 When **2** During **3** After **4** While
5 Soon **6** As **7** Barely

Pronunciation (SB page 103)

1

Remind the students that the boxes show the syllables of a word and the large boxes indicate the stressed syllables. Here they are being asked to classify words according to how many syllables they have and where the main stress falls. Encourage them to say each word aloud to get a feeling for what sounds right.

2 2.29

Ask the students to underline the stressed syllable in each word. Then play the recording for them to check their answers. Play it a second time for them to listen and repeat.

ANSWERS:
1 and 2

A: □□	B: □□□	C: □□□
drizzle	attractive	company
lively	cosmetics	genuine
science	encourage	qualities
urban	meander	traveler

Further practice material

Need more classroom practice activities?

Photocopiable resource materials in the Teacher's Presentation Kit / Extra Resources

Need more tests?

Test Generator
Teacher's Presentation Kit / Extra Resources / Tests

Need more on important teaching concepts?

Key concepts in *American Inside Out Evolution* pages xxi-xxxvi

Need more information and ideas?

American Inside Out Evolution website www.macmillan.com.br/americaninsideoutevolution

Before the next lesson

Ask the students to bring some advertisements from magazines and newspapers to the next lesson. Alternatively, bring in a selection yourself.

10 Sell *Overview*

Section	Aims	What the students are doing
Speaking & Vocabulary SB page 104	*see* and *look at*	Discussing logos and branded goods. Underling the correct phrases to complete a description.
Listening & Vocabulary SB page 105	Listening for gist	Listening to a marketing executive and a school principal talking about children and advertising. Then matching opinions to speakers.
Reading & Vocabulary SB page 106	Reading for gist and detail Sales and marketing collocations	Reading about trends in television advertising and matching people to their opinions. Answering comprehension questions. Completing a glossary with words and phrases from the text.
Grammar SB page 106	Relative clauses	Studying the functions and punctuation of relative clauses. Matching sentences with suitable follow-ups. Studying relative clauses and relative pronouns.
Listening & Speaking SB page 108	Listening for gist and for detail Fluency practice - agreeing and disagreeing	Discussing celebrity magazines. Listening to a radio show and explaining the issues discussed. Reading sentences from the listening and identifying who said what. Then replacing highlighted words with what was actually said. Categorizing phrases used by the speakers according to their function.
Grammar SB page 109	Emphasis (cleft sentences)	Changing emphasis by using cleft sentences. Correcting statements about celebrities using cleft sentences.
Pronunciation SB page 109	Stress in cleft sentences	Practicing stress in cleft sentences.
Reading & Vocabulary SB page 110	Reading for detail	Reading a text about product placement in the *Iron Man* movies. Replacing missing sentences in the text. Deciding what words and numbers in the text refer to. Talking about a favorite movie character.
Speaking: anecdote SB page 111	Fluency practice	Talking about a blockbuster movie they've seen.
Language for Life SB page 112	Using emotive language	Listening to people talking about going to see a movie and identifying which movie it is. Completing useful phrases for describing people's feelings. Then identifying incorrect collocations. Listening to people and identifying their general reaction to a movie. Using the useful phrases to discuss the worst movies, TV shows, concerts, etc. that they've seen recently.
Life Skills SB page 112	Selling	Listening to a persuasive presentation and noticing features. Selling items using persuasive language.
Vocabulary Extra SB page 113	Collocations	Identifying collocations and categorizing them. Rewriting a text using alternative collocations. Studying noun-verb collocations and noun-adjective collocations.

10 Sell *Teacher's notes*

Warm up

Ask the students to form groups to discuss the advertisements that they were asked to bring to class at the end of the previous lesson and decide who the advertisers are trying to persuade to buy their product (children, adults, women, men, etc.) and how they're doing it (e.g. by suggesting that you'll be more attractive, socially successful, etc. if you buy it).

Speaking & Vocabulary (SB page 104)

1

Pairwork. Ask the students to look at the five sets of logos, identify the companies that own them, and decide which is the correct one in each case. They can check their answers in the *Additional Material* section.

ANSWERS:
1 b (Starbucks) **2 b** (Nike) **3 a** (Apple) **4 c** (Adidas) **5 c** (McDonald's)

2

- Pairwork. Ask the students to discuss the questions and try drawing brands for their partners to identify.
- In a class feedback session, display the various logos that the students have drawn and see if the rest of the class can identify them.

3

- Focus the students' attention on the different ways of saying *look* and *see*. (See Language note below.)
- Ask the students to look at the words and expressions in the box, to decide if they are more like *look* or *see*, and to write them in the correct column. Allow students to compare answers in pairs before checking with the class.

ANSWERS:
Look: glance, eye, stare, gaze
See: notice, catch sight of, spot, make out

Language notes

Vocabulary: *look at* and *see*

- The verbs *look at*, *gaze at*, *stare at*, *glance at*, and *eye* all suggest the action is deliberate.
- The verbs *see*, *spot*, *make out*, *notice*, and *catch sight of* all suggest a more random, unpremeditated event.

4

- Ask the students to choose the right words to complete the description. Allow them to compare answers in pairs before checking with the class.
- Encourage the students to give their reactions to the text and then to discuss with a partner their own attitude towards brands and designer labels.

ANSWERS:
1 gazing at
2 eyeing
3 spot
4 stare at
5 gaze at me
6 noticed
7 catch sight of

Listening & Vocabulary (SB page 105)

1 2.30-2.31

- Focus the students' attention on the pictures and point out that Joe is a marketing executive and Sally a school principal. Tell them that they're going to hear Joe and Sally giving their opinions about children and advertising. Go through the statements with the class, making sure they understand all of them, and then ask them to predict which person made each statement.
- Play the recording and ask the students to listen and check their answers. Check answers with the class before putting the students into pairs to discuss whether or not they agree with the statements. Encourage them to report back to the class on their opinions, giving their reasons.

ANSWERS:

a Sally	**b** Joe	**c** Sally	**d** Joe
e Joe	**f** Sally		

2.30

Joe Smedley

Children are much easier to reach with advertising than adults are - they like it, and they pick up on it really fast. So, it's the advertiser's job to capitalize on this.

We have a term, "pester-power," which means the marketing potential of children nagging their parents to spend money. And I'm not just talking about toys here - our aim is getting children to pester parents to buy something for the whole family, like a vacation or a car. What we try to do is to produce advertisements that

appeal to both children and adults.
Another key concept for advertisers is peer pressure. Children want what their friends have - playground credibility is very important. In other words, brands give children a sense of identity and help them fit in with a peer group. So you can see children are a very important market for us, and in return, we like to promote education. This is something that's already happening across America. Companies donate free computers, and in exchange they can advertise their brands on book covers and posters. I think it's fantastic - the kids benefit, and the companies get brand loyalty from a very early age.
I'd love to be a child today. They really know what they want, and they have so many more choices. Advertisers respect children's opinions.

2.31

Sally McIlveen

Basically, children are being brainwashed by all the advertising that goes on around them. Quite honestly, if the children in my school remembered any of their schoolwork as well as they remember the advertising jingles they hear on TV, my job would be a pleasure.
Usually the students at our school wear uniforms, but Friday is a non-uniform day, and that's when you really see the power of advertising. The kids are dressed from head to toe in labels, mainly sports gear like Adidas®, Nike™, and that kind of thing. And they all look the same!
There's a great deal of pressure on parents to buy children all these labels and gadgets, and I feel so sorry for the families who don't have much money because the pressure is just the same.
I really believe it's time the government put a stop to all this aggressive TV advertising.
Some schools are actually being subsidized by companies like McDonald's™ and Pepsi®. OK, the school gets free equipment from these big companies, but then the children have to add up burgers or multiply cans of Pepsi in their math class. It's terrible to think that the schools end up promoting a product that's not even good for the children.
What I think is really sad is that children are being forced to be consumers from such an early age. I don't think all this choice is liberating for children - it just means that they're encouraged to be materialistic instead of focusing on more important basic values such as kindness and respect for others.

2

- Pairwork. Put the students in pairs and tell them who will be Student A and who will be Student B. Then ask them to turn to their respective pages and to follow the instructions there.
- Ask each student to find a word from the box that collocates with each list, using their dictionaries if necessary. Then tell them to check their answers with their partner.
- Ask the students to write example sentences for six of the collocations from the list.

ANSWERS:
Student A: a consumer **b** price **c** advertising
Student B: a sales **b** brand **c** market

Extra activity

Ask the students who have children themselves if their children pester them to buy certain brands. If they don't, ask if they pestered their own parents when they were children to buy things for them.

Reading & Vocabulary (SB page 106)

1

- Focus attention on the picture on page 107 and the title of the text. Explain that the article is from an online magazine about technology.
- Go through the questions and ask the students to give their ideas. Then ask them to read the first paragraph of the article on page 107 to check their answers.
- Give the students time to skim the whole article (reading for gist) and ask them to match the people interviewed to their opinion. Check answers as a class.

ANSWERS:
a 2 **b** 1 **c** 3

Cultural note

Super Bowl /ˈsuːpər bəʊl/ The Super Bowl is the championship game and trophy for the American Football *National Football League* (NFL). It is a major sporting event in the USA and takes place in early February.

2

Individual work. Ask the students to read the text again and to answer the questions. Ask students to check their answers in pairs before checking the answers with the class.

ANSWERS:
a People used to change channels, now they can skip ads.
b Cord cutters are no longer watching cable television.
c Shorter commercials, sponsored segments, split screen.

d People prefer to watch sports live (while it is happening).
e If the game is a blowout, people might stop watching before the end of the game.
f Although they used to be very powerful, they are now going extinct.
g Targeted ads reach a specific audience and might be more interactive.
h We are exposed to 3000-5000 ads per day (according to Google).

3

- Focus the students' attention on the highlighted words in the article. Ask them to discuss with a partner what they think they might mean.
- Ask the students to use the highlighted words to complete the glossary at the bottom of the article.

ANSWERS:
a browser
b overlook
c scramble
d intrusive
e decline
f split screen
g tune out
h air
i phenomenon
j insert
k cater

4

- Groupwork. Put students into small groups. Tell them that they're going to create their own car commercial. Ask them to go to *Additional Material* section and follow the instructions.
- Allow the students plenty of time to discuss the questions and make notes of their answers before asking them to compare their ideas with other groups.

Grammar (SB page 106)

Relative clauses

1

- Focus the students' attention on the examples in the margin and point out that the expressions in bold are relative clauses. Then go through the instructions and ask the students to look at the sentences specified in the article and underline the relative clauses in them. Ask them to work in pairs and to choose the description that best defines the function of each of these relative clauses.
- Check answers with the class and make sure that everyone understands the concept of defining and non-defining relative clauses. Ask them to look at the punctuation and to say what punctuation mark is used to show that a relative clause in non-defining.

ANSWERS:
In fact, there is even a name for the current generation who have given up on cable TV … - (TYPE 2)
Although it's difficult to measure, we actually believe more people might be watching TV these days than ever before, which is encouraging … - (TYPE 1)
Even a few years ago, you could rely on big network shows, which aired every week, to have huge viewing numbers all year round. - (TYPE 3)

Language note

Vocabulary: relative clauses
(See Student's Book page 148.)

2

Pairwork. Working in the same pairs, the students look at the pairs of sentences and identify the most suitable follow-up for each sentence.

ANSWERS:
a 1 **b** 2 **c** 2 **d** 1 **e** 2 **f** 1 **g** 1 **h** 2

3

- Focus the students' attention on the main sentences in Exercise 2 and the list of types of relative clause in Exercise 1. Get the class to identify the type of relative clause that each sentence contains.
- Discuss which of the relative pronouns cannot be used with non-defining relative clauses.

ANSWERS:
a
a TYPE 2 (defining)
b TYPE 1 (non-defining)
c TYPE 3 (non-defining)
d TYPE 1 (non-defining)
e TYPE 2 (defining)
f TYPE 1 (non-defining)
g TYPE 2 (defining)
h TYPE 3 (non-defining)

b that
c which

4 Grammar Extra 10, Part 1

Ask the students to turn to Grammar Extra 10, Part 1 on page 148 of the Student's Book. Here they'll find an explanation of the grammar they've been studying and further exercises to practice it.

ANSWERS:

1

a a job that you are interested in ~~it~~
b a bank account that never runs out ~~it~~
c a boss who you get on with ~~him~~
d a car that never breaks down ~~it~~
e a government that you voted for ~~them~~
f a friend who never lets you down ~~she~~
g a home that you are happy in ~~there~~
h a partner who you are in love with ~~her~~

2

a He bought me an expensive dress, which I didn't really like.
b Adam, who is almost never late, turned up at 10:30 this morning.
c That woman, who looks like my sister, works in our store.
d Mike's father, who lives in San Francisco, is in advertising.
e There's an elevator in the building, which you can use to go to the top floor.
f Ellen got me a really nice jacket, which was a complete surprise.

Listening & Speaking (SB page 108)

1

Go through the questions with the class, and then ask the students to discuss them in pairs. Encourage them to report back to the class on their discussion.

2 ▶ **2.32**

- Ask the students if they believe everything they read in the newspapers. If they don't, ask them for examples of things they've read in a newspaper that they either didn't believe or that subsequently turned out not to be true. Ask the students if they think all newspapers are equally reliable.
- Go through the instructions with the class and put the students into pairs. Play the recording and ask them to explain to each other why the actress isn't happy with the magazine editor.
- Check the answers with the class and then ask the students to say who they sympathize with most and why they sympathize with a particular person. Then have a class vote to find out who gets the most sympathy.

ANSWERS:
The magazine said that Shelley and her co-star had had breakfast together. The co-star is married to a good friend of Shelley's. Shelley's co-star's wife is filing for divorce.

▶ **2.32 (P = Presenter; S = Shelley Russell; J = Jim Falmer)**

P: Good evening and welcome to *Talkback*. Recently, the popular press has been under fire yet again, this time for their apparent disregard for truth and accuracy.
In the studio tonight we would like to welcome Shelley Russell, Oscar®-winning actress, and Jim Falmer, editor of *Celebrity Lives* Magazine.
Shelley Russell, let's start with you. Do you think there should be greater restrictions placed on the press and the stories they print?

S: Yes, absolutely. I can't open a magazine without reading stories full of false information about myself or people I know. It's getting ...

J: Sorry, but I can't believe that you're actually complaining about free publicity. I mean, I remember, Shelley, before you were famous, you were begging us to write features about you ... anything ...

S: If you would just let me finish – of course the press have been important. I'm an actress, and I understand the power of the press. But the thing is, I rarely seem to read anything true about myself these days. Take last week – your magazine wrote this story about me and my co-star, who, incidentally, happens to be married to a very good friend of mine, having breakfast together.

J: Oh, that. That was ... well, that was just some fun. I don't think you should take that too seriously.

S: Oh, really! You don't think that it's at all serious that my co-star's children woke up to the headline: SHELLEY AND SHAUN'S EARLY MORNING ROMANCE or that his wife is now filing for a divorce ...

J: Look, I don't know whether ...

S: Anyway, to get back to what I was saying ... The point I'm trying to make here is that famous people have families with feelings. I am sick of the popular press making up stories just so that they can splash sensational headlines across the front page and sell more magazines – it's irresponsible and it messes up people's lives.

J: Look, Shelley, you're just angry about that particular article because the pictures we printed of you weren't very flattering. Anyway, we made a public apology and said that there'd been some inaccuracies in the article.

S: Yes, but what you didn't say what the inaccuracies were, so ...

P: If I could just come in here, I think we need to address the root of the problem. Jim, why do certain magazines continue to print these stories when it's obvious that they are not true?

S: To increase circulation and make more money.
J: If you would let me answer the question – I think we have to look at the relationship between fame, the public, and the press. The public is fascinated by fame and scandal, and they love to read about their favorite stars. The problem is, it's not always clear what's true and what isn't. I mean, if a magazine prints something scandalous or embarrassing about a famous person, they're bound to deny it, but that doesn't mean it's not true.
S: Are you trying to say ...?
J: No smoke without fire, if you ask me.
P: Well, I'm sorry to interrupt you, but we'll carry on after this short break for some travel news ...

3

- Ask the students to read the sentences. Allow them to work with a partner to decide who said each one and note this down.
- Tell students to choose words from the box to replace the highlighted words in sentences ***a–f***. Then play the recording again for students to check their answers.

ANSWERS:
a P – under fire; disregard
b E – begging; features
c C – incidentally
d C – splash
e P – root
f E – scandalous; 're bound to

4

Ask students to complete the phrases with the words in the box. You could play the recording as they work to help them. Then play it for them to check their answers.

ANSWERS:
a but **b** finish **c** is **d** saying
e is **f** was **g** here **h** question
i is **j** but

Language note

Vocabulary: spoken discourse markers
These discourse markers are very common in (heated) discussions. In a normal conversation, people wait for the speaker to signal he/she has finished speaking before the next one starts. In a discussion like this, all parties are constantly trying to interrupt the speaker to get their point across, and the speaker has to defend his/her territory by using some of the devices here (e.g. *If you would just let me finish ...*) or by raising his/her voice just enough so that it shows he/she hasn't finished making his/her point.

5

Write the headings on the board and ask the students to say which column to write the phrases in. Don't erase the board before the next exercise.

ANSWERS:
Interrupting:
Sorry, but ...
If I could just come in here ...
I'm sorry to interrupt you, but ...
Responding to an interruption:
If you would just let me finish ...
Anyway, to get back to what I was saying ...
The point I'm trying to make here is ...
What you didn't say was ...
If you would let me answer the question ...
Introducing a point:
But the thing is ...
The problem is ...

6

Groupwork. Put the students into groups and ask them to discuss the statements. Tell them to look at the board and use the phrases in their discussions. Encourage the groups to report back to the class on their ideas.

Grammar (SB page 109)

Emphasis (cleft sentences)

1

Pairwork. Focus attention on the sentences in the margin. Then read aloud the two sentences in the exercise. Ask the students to discuss in pairs how the emphasis changes in sentence B. Check their answers, and then ask them if they can remember which sentence Shelley Russell used in the listening.

ANSWERS:
The speaker uses *what ... was* to emphasize the object of the sentence.
She used sentence B.

Language note

Pronunciation: emphasis (cleft sentences)
(See Student's Book page 148.)

2

- Do the first one with the class as an example, and then ask the students to work individually to change the emphasis of the remaining sentences by using the sentence beginnings provided. As they work, go around giving extra help where needed.
- Check answers with the class before asking the students to say whether or not the sentences are true for them.

ANSWERS:

a What I don't understand is why I never seem to have any money.
b The thing I like about weekends is (that) I can go shopping with my friends.
c What really annoys me is people who only talk about money.
d What I really feel like doing tonight is going to the movies.
e The thing I hate about the winter is (that) it gets dark so early.
f What I'd really like to do in the future is live and work abroad.

3

- Ask the students to read and discuss the statements in pairs. Tell them to decide which one of them is true. Allow them to compare notes with another pair before checking with the class.
- Ask the students to stay in the same pairs and to correct the false statements using the information in the box and the sentence beginnings given.

ANSWERS:

Statement **c** is correct.

a It wasn't Barack Obama who was the Democratic candidate, it was Hillary Clinton.
b It wasn't Benedict Cumberbatch who replaced Pierce Brosnan as James Bond, it was Daniel Craig.
c -
d It wasn't Stephenie Meyer who wrote the *Harry Potter* series, it was J.K. Rowling.
e It isn't Brad Pitt who plays Captain Jack Sparrow in *Pirates of the Caribbean*, it's Johnny Depp.
f It isn't Shakira who is married to Javier Bardem, it's Penélope Cruz.

Cultural Notes

Barack Obama /bəˈrɑːk oʊˈbɑːmə/ (born 1961) Barack Obama was the 44th President of the United States. He first became President on January 20, 2009, and was re-elected on November 6, 20012. He was the first African American president of the USA.

Hillary Clinton /ˈhɪləri ˈklɪntən/ (born 1947) Hillary Clinton is an American politician. She was the Democratic Presidential candidate for the 2016 election, eventually losing out to Donald Trump. She was the Secretary of State from 2009-2013. Her husband is former US president Bill Clinton.

Benedict Cumberbatch /ˈbɛnədɪkt ˈkʌmbəbætʃ/ (born 1976) Benedict Cumberbatch is a British actor. He is best known for his role as Sherlock Holmes on the British television series, and for his movie roles in *12 Years a Slave*, *The Imitation Game*, and *Doctor Strange*. He received an Academy Award nomination for *The Imitation Game*.

Pierce Brosnan /ˈpɪrs ˈbrɑznən/ (born 1953) Pierce Brosnan is an Irish actor, movie producer, and environmentalist. He was the fifth James Bond and acted in the role for four of the movies. Other movies he has starred in include *Dante's Peak*, *The Thomas Crown Affair*, and the musical *Mamma Mia!*

Stephenie Meyer /ˈstɛfəni ˈmaɪ.ər/ (born 1973) Stephenie Meyer is an American novelist best known for her vampire series, *Twilight*, which have sold over 100 million copies. This series was turned into a popular movie franchise.

J.K. Rowling /ˈdʒeɪ ˈkeɪ ˈroʊlɪŋ/ (born 1965) J.K. Rowling is a British author famous for her fantasy book series, *Harry Potter*, which have sold over 400 million copies. This series was turned into a popular movie franchise starring Daniel Radcliffe.

Brad Pitt /ˈbræd ˈpɪt/ (born 1963) Brad Pitt is an American actor who shot to fame in 1991 in the movie *Thelma and Louise*. Other movies he's starred in include *Seven*, *Fight Club*, and *Ocean's Eleven*. He was married to the actress Jennifer Aniston (2000- 2005) and Angelina Jolie (2014-2016). He and Angelina Jolie have three biological children and three adopted children.

Johnny Depp /ˈdʒɑni ˈdep/ (born 1963) Johnny Depp's movie debut was in *Nightmare on Elm Street* (1984). Six years later, he starred in the movie *Edward Scissorhands*. His most popular movies to date are probably the *Pirates of the Caribbean* movies in which he plays the role of Captain Jack Sparrow. His other movies include *Sleepy Hollow*, *Chocolat*, and *Sweeney Todd: The Demon Barber of Fleet Street*.

Katie Holmes /ˈkeɪt houms/ (born 1978) Katie Holmes is an American actress. She became famous on the TV show *Dawson's Creek* and later acted in movies including *Batman Begins* and *Logan Lucky*. She was married to Tom Cruise from 2006–2012 and received a lot of media attention.

Tom Cruise /ˈtɒm ˈkruːz/ (born 1962) Tom Cruise is an American actor. His most popular movies to date are probably *Top Gun*, *A Few Good Men*, *Jerry Maguire*, and the *Mission Impossible* franchise. He has been nominated for three Academy Awards. Cruise has been married three times including to actress Nicole Kidman (1990–2001) and actress Katie Holmes (2006–2012).

Emma Stone /ˈemə ˈstoʊn/ (born 1988) Emma Stone is an Academy Award-winning American actress famous for her roles in the movies *The Amazing Spider-Man*, *Birdman*, and *La La Land*.

Shakira /ʃəˈkiːrə/ (born 1977)
Shakira is a Colombian singer and songwriter. She is married to Spanish soccer player Gerard Piqué with whom she has two children.

Javier Bardem [xaˈβjer βarˈðen] (born 1969)
Javier Bardem is a Spanish actor. He is the first Spanish actor to be nominated for an Oscar (Best Actor, 2000, for *Before Night Falls*), as well as the first Spaniard to win one. He married Penélope Cruz in 2010 and they have two children.

4 Grammar Extra 10, Part 2

Ask the students to turn to Grammar Extra 10, Part 2 on page 148 of the Student's Book. Here they'll find an explanation of the grammar they've been studying and further exercises to practice it.

ANSWERS:

3

- **a** What I love about my country is the fantastic weather.
- **b** The thing I like most in a person is their sense of humor.
- **c** What I enjoy most is playing tennis.
- **d** The thing I hate most about studying English is the tests.
- **e** What we all most need in life is a stress-free job.
- **f** What I don't understand is why I never have enough free time.

4

- **a** It was in Mexico City that he met his wife.
- **b** It was only when he called that I understood how serious it was.
- **c** It was you that broke that cup, not Ian.
- **d** It was Ben that stole the cake, not Amy.
- **e** It was money that he wanted, not love.
- **f** It is the computer that Stacey spends all her time on, not the telephone.

Pronunciation (SB page 109)

1 2.33

- Read the instructions with the class. Ask them to read the sentences and decide which words are most likely to be stressed. Point out the underlining and the pause marks in the example. Ask the students to do the same for the remaining sentences. Encourage them to say the sentences aloud as they do this, so that they get a feel for what sounds right.
- Play the recording for them to listen and check their answers. Then play it again for them to repeat the sentences. When they've done this chorally, ask for individual repetition.

ANSWERS:

- **a** What I love about Peter // is his great sense of humor.
- **b** The thing I can't stand about this country // is the weather.
- **c** What I really hate about my job // is having to work on weekends.
- **d** What I find annoying about politicians // is that they never give a straight answer.
- **e** The thing I find most difficult about English // is the spelling.
- **f** What I would really like to do // is to take a year off.

Language note

Pronunciation: emphatic stress
English is a stress-timed language, so you would commonly stress the most important words in the sentence – the words that carry the meaning. In a typical sentence, this would mean stressing several nouns and a verb or two.

2

Pairwork. Ask the students to take turns finishing the sentences and giving their opinions.

Reading & Vocabulary (SB page 110)

1

- Ask the students which, if any, of the *Iron Man* movies they've seen. Put them in pairs and ask them to discuss the questions before they read the article and to note down their answers. Then ask them to report back to the class on how many of their ideas were mentioned.
- Ask the students for their reactions to the article. Are they aware of product placement in movies? Do they find it annoying or distracting?

ANSWERS:

- **a** Action movies, international audiences (particularly young people)
- **b** Robert Downey Jr. (Tony Stark), Gwyneth Paltrow (Pepper Potts). *Others*: Don Cheadle, Jon Favreau, Scarlett Johansson
- **c** Audi, Burger King, Dr Pepper, Yili milk

Cultural notes

Robert Downey Jr. /ˈrɒbə(r)t ˈdaʊni ˈdʒuːniər/ (born 1965)
Robert Downey Jr. is an American actor. He became famous as a young man in moves such as *Weird Science* and was nominated for an Academy Award for *Chaplin* in 1992. He is known for his characters in blockbuster movies, especially Iron Man and Sherlock Holmes.

Gwyneth Paltrow /ˈgwɪnɪθ ˈpæltroʊ/ (born 1972)
Gwyneth Paltrow is an American actress. She won the Academy Award in 1998 for *Shakespeare in Love* and her other movies include *Seven*, *Sliding Doors*, *Proof*, and the *Iron Man* series. She is also the owner of a lifestyle company, *Goop*, and a cookbook author.

2

Go through the instructions with the class and ask them to decide which sentences go in which blanks. Remind them that one sentence doesn't fit anywhere. As they work, go around giving help where needed and pointing out features such as time references and pronouns, which can help them decide.

ANSWERS:
1 d **2** a **3** g **4** b **5** e **6** f

3

Go through the instructions with the class and ask them to decide what each number or word refers to. Do the first one together as an example and ask them where in the text they found this information. Remind students not to write full sentences, just notes. Ask students to check answers in pairs before checking answers with the class.

ANSWERS:
621 million – *Iron Man* box office total
Yili – Chinese milk drink
1964 – Year *Goldfinger* was released
Pepper Potts – Tony Stark's assistant
70 million – Profit from product placement in *Die Another Day*
R8 – Tony Stark's car type
Robert Downey Jr. – *Iron Man* actor
BMW – Tom Cruise's car in *Mission Impossible*

4

Put the students into pairs and ask them to discuss their favorite movie characters.

Speaking: anecdote (SB page 111)

For more information about how to set up, monitor, and repeat anecdotes, see pages xix to xx in the Introduction.

- Go through the instructions and the questions with the class. Give the students a minute or two to decide which movie they're going to talk about. Then ask them to look at the questions and think about their answers to them. Allow them to make notes of what they're going to say and how they're going to say it, but discourage them from writing a paragraph that they can simply read aloud. Go around, monitoring and giving help where necessary.
- Put the students in pairs and ask them to take turns telling their partner about a movie they've seen. Encourage them to ask each other follow-up questions to get further information. Then ask some pairs to report back to the class about what they found out.

Language for Life (SB page 112)

1 2.34

- Focus the students' attention on the illustrations, which show posters for a variety of different movie genres. Ask them which type of movie they'd choose to go and see.
- Explain that all the people they're going to hear are about to see one of these types of movies. Ask them to listen to the recording and say which one it is.

ANSWER:
d *The Slime*

2.34 (I = Interviewer; G1 = Girl 1; B1 = Boy 1; B2 = Boy 2; G2 = Girl 2; G3 = Girl 3; B3 = Boy 3)

1
I: Excuse me. Do you mind if I ask you how you feel about seeing this movie?
G1: Pretty nervous, actually. I don't know what to expect, but I think I'm going to be scared.

2
I: Excuse me – are you feeling nervous about seeing this movie?
B1: Yeah, a little uneasy, I must admit ... but I brought my girlfriend, so I can hold her hand if I get scared.

3
I: How do you feel about seeing this movie?
B2: I'm looking forward to being scared to death.

4
I: What are you expecting from this movie?
G2: To be scared stiff – hopefully.

5
I: Do you think you're going to enjoy seeing this movie?
G3: Um, no – I don't think "enjoy" is the right word. But I've heard so much about it that I can't wait to find out what it's all about. In fact, I feel pretty apprehensive, but I love horror movies, and this one sounds like it's going to be really scary.

6
I: Any expectations?
B3: Well, I've been visiting the website for a while now, and I'm really looking forward to finding out what happens. I expect it to be absolutely terrifying!

2

- Ask the students to underline the words they think match what the speakers said.
- Play the recording again for the students to listen and check their answers.
- Go through the instructions and make sure that the students understand that, of the two remaining options in each phrase, one doesn't form a common collocation. This is the one they should cross out. They should check the other.

> **ANSWERS:**
> 1 "Pretty/ ~~Totally~~ / Extremely ✓ nervous, actually."
> 2 "Yeah, distinctly ✓ / ~~utterly~~ / a little uneasy, I must admit."
> 3 "I'm looking forward to being scared / ~~nervous~~ / bored ✓ to death."
> 4 "To be scared / ~~afraid~~ / bored ✓ stiff - hopefully."
> 5 "I feel ~~completely~~ / terribly ✓ / pretty apprehensive."
> 6 "I expect it to be absolutely / quite ✓ / ~~very~~ terrifying."

3

Explain the difference between gradable adjectives and absolute adjectives (see Language notes). Ask the students to look at the sentence frames and decide which adjectives go with which and how the meaning of *pretty* changes in the two frames.

> **ANSWERS:**
> **A:** boring, disappointing, entertaining, funny, good, interesting
> **B:** amazing, awesome, awful, extraordinary, ridiculous, spectacular

Language notes

Vocabulary: gradable and absolute adjectives

awful bad good fantastic

- The two adjectives in the center (*bad, good*) can be graded, e.g. *it was pretty good; it was very good.* Words that go with gradable adjectives are: *very, extremely, terribly, a little, a bit.*
- The two adjectives on either end (*awful, fantastic*) are extreme and cannot be graded, e.g. ~~*very awful*~~, ~~*a little awful*~~. Words that go with absolute adjectives are: *absolutely, totally, utterly, completely, thoroughly.*
- The adverb *pretty* can be used with both groups, but means "fairly" when used with gradable adjectives, and "very" when used with absolute adjectives.

4 ▶ 2.35

Play the recording, asking the students to listen and say what the general reaction to the movie was.

> **ANSWER:**
> Negative

▶ 2.35 (I = Interviewer; G1 = Girl 1; B1 = Boy 1; B2 = Boy 2; G2 = Girl 2; G3 = Girl 3; B3 = Boy 3)

1
I: So, how was it for you?
G1: Extremely disappointing. I wasn't the least bit scared, and you know from the start that everybody dies, so there's no suspense. Anyway, the characters are so annoying that I felt like killing them myself. It does not live up to the hype.

2
I: What did you think of it?
B1: Absolute garbage. My girlfriend fell asleep, and I spent the last half of the movie with my eyes shut - not because it was scary - but because the camera angles made me feel sick. Don't see it if you suffer from motion sickness. In fact, just don't see it.

3
I: So were you scared to death?
B2: No way. After all the hype, it was a massive letdown.

4
I: What did you think?
G2: Over-hyped nonsense. I spent most of the time waiting for something to happen. I feel completely disillusioned.

5
I: Did the movie live up to your expectations?
G3: No, it didn't. I don't think I've ever been so bored in my entire life, and I still don't have a clue what it's about. In fact, there's no story to speak of. This movie is a perfect example of hype over substance.

6
I: Your verdict?
B3: A total waste of time. I was bored out of my mind. The website was much more entertaining than the movie.

Life Skills (SB page 112)

Persuading Others

1

Ask students if they have ever sold anything, and if so, what it was and how they did it. Elicit what can be sold other than items (ideas, yourself, etc.). Go through the instructions with the class and clarify *persuasive* if necessary (good at making people agree to do or believe what you want them to). Listen to recording and then check answers as a class. Allow the students time to discuss how Eric did these things and refer to the Audioscript if necessary.

2.36

Eric: ... now that you've seen our sales figures and all that we offer, let me ask you - do you want to be a part of the footwear revolution? With our innovative business model, 10% of all the profits will go to charity to help provide shoes to children in need. In the past year alone, we've provided over 10,000 pairs of sneakers to children who would otherwise have none. Just imagine the real effect that your contribution could have to increasing this number. If you know that you can make a profit and improve the lives of others, then what's stopping you? And with our locally-produced materials and manufacturing, you will also be supporting the local economy.
I truly believe that with our passion and your investment, we can join forces to build a new kind of shoe company, one that is on the cutting edge of style, while maintaining our core company beliefs. Now, don't you think that is a goal worth pursuing?
I'm sure that you want to know more, so let's open up this meeting for questions ...

ANSWERS:
- asks questions to involve the listener
- gives examples and evidence
- uses descriptive words to add more detail
- shows the logic of what he is saying
- describes what the benefits would be
- gives the listener an emotional reason to care

2

Pairwork. Go through the instructions with the class and encourage the students to be creative in their selections. Allow students time to make notes before speaking. Monitor while students complete the task and makes notes of any examples of appropriate persuasive language. For feedback, elicit from some students what their partner tried to sell them and if they were successful. Highlight and praise any appropriate persuasive language that was noted during monitoring.

Vocabulary Extra (SB page 113)

Collocations

1

- Pairwork. Ask the students to read the text and identify the collocations. Ask them to match them to the categories listed below the text.
- Ask the students to check their answers in the dictionary extracts and to find and add more collocations to the categories.

ANSWERS:
a extremely important
b important aspect, useful information, informed decisions, practical suggestions
c cause problems
d difficulties arise
e soon realize

2

Go through the instructions and the example with the class, and then ask the students to work individually to rewrite the text.

ANSWERS:
Recognizing and using collocations is a particularly important part of learning a language. Learners quickly realize that particular words regularly and naturally combine with each other. However, deciding which words go with which can cause confusion. Occasionally, problems arise when the wrong word is used. Fortunately, good dictionaries provide further information to help learners make strategic decisions. This page offers some helpful suggestions.

3

- Ask the students to look at the dictionary extracts for *problem* and *decision* and to focus first on the verb collocates. Go through the examples with the class and ask them to divide the other verb collocates into the two meaning groups for each word.
- Ask the students to choose two verb collocates for each noun that are new to them and which they think would be useful to learn. Get them to write a definition and an example sentence for each one, using a dictionary if necessary.

ANSWERS:
problem
have: encounter, experience, face
solve: address, overcome, resolve, tackle
decision
make: arrive at, come to, reach, take
reject: overrule, overturn, quash, reconsider, rescind, reverse

4

Go through the instructions and the example with the class, and ask them to match the other adjective collocates with their meanings.

ANSWERS:
information
a accurate information
b additional/further information
c confidential/inside information
d relevant information

decision
a a tough decision
b a momentous decision
c an informed decision
d a unanimous decision
e a strategic decision
f a controversial decision

5

Pairwork. Ask the students to look at the collocation boxes for *issue* and *problem* and to discuss in pairs how they could arrange the verb and adjective collocates in different groups according to similarity of meaning.

ANSWERS:
Verbs used with *issue*
address, confront, tackle *an issue*
consider, examine, explore, raise *an issue*
cloud, complicate, confuse *an issue*
dodge, duck, evade *an issue*
fudge *an issue*

Adjectives used with *issue*
contentious, controversial, divisive *issue*
important, key, major, pressing *issue*
sensitive, thorny *issue*
unresolved *issue*

Adjectives used with *problem*
big, fundamental, important, major, pressing, real, serious *problem*
insoluble, intractable *problem*

Verbs used with *problem*
address, alleviate, overcome, resolve, solve, tackle *a problem*
cause, create, pose *a problem*
encounter, experience, face *a problem*
compound, exacerbate *a problem*

6

Ask the students to look in their own dictionaries to find out how information about collocations is shown.

Further practice material

Need more classroom practice activities?

Photocopiable resource materials in the Teacher's Presentation Kit / Extra Resources

Need more tests?

Test Generator
Teacher's Presentation Kit / Extra Resources / Tests

Need more on important teaching concepts?

Key concepts in *American Inside Out Evolution* pages xxi-xxxvi

Need student self-study practice?

Workbook pages 40-43

Need more information and ideas?

American Inside Out Evolution website www.macmillan.com.br/americaninsideoutevolution

Need to check what your students can do by the end of this unit?

Self-evaluation checklists on pages xxxiv-xlvi

11 Student *Overview*

Section	Aims	What the students are doing
Vocabulary & Reading SB page 114	Education; *is likely to / is expected to* Reading for gist and detail	Talking about the qualities of good teachers and students. Matching beginnings and endings of questions about education. Reading an article about student versus teacher perspective. Studying the language of predictions.
Pronunciation SB page 116	Abbreviations	Practicing the pronunciation of common abbreviations. Figuring out what abbreviations stand for.
Speaking: anecdote SB page 116	Fluency practice	Talking about their favorite or least favorite teacher at school.
Listening & Vocabulary SB page 116	Listening for gist	Talking about appropriate ages for taking responsibility for your life. Listening to parents who are worried about their daughter's future plans. Choosing the appropriate word to complete extracts from the interview. Completing statements and saying whether they agree with them.
Reading & Grammar SB page 117	Reading for detail Future forms	Reading an interview and choosing the most appropriate future forms.
Grammar SB page 118	Future forms and future time clauses	Completing a table with future forms. Identifying main and subordinate clauses. Completing sentences about the future.
Reading & Vocabulary SB page 119	Reading for gist and detail	Discussing outdoor sports. Reading an article about students who go hiking. Matching words to definitions.
Reading SB page 120	Exaggerated language	Choosing a favorite backpacker's story.
Vocabulary SB page 121	Exaggerated language	Identifying exaggerated language. Rewriting a story to make it more dramatic. Matching exaggerated expressions with their meanings.
Speaking SB page 121	Fluency practice	Preparing a dramatic story from prompts and telling the story to other students.
Language for Life SB page 122	Diplomatic language (making negative characteristics sound positive)	Putting questions from an interview into a logical order. Reading advice about job interviews and suggesting ways in which a candidate could improve his skills. Matching model answers to questions. Writing and practicing job interviews.
Life Skills SB page 122	Getting Organized	Reading tips to avoid a full email inbox. Discussing strategies to organize online habits.
Writing Extra SB page 123	Résumé and application email	Categorizing tips for writing a résumé under the headings DO and DON'T. Reading a résumé and identifying what is wrong with it. Making improvements to the résumé. Identifying the inappropriate parts of an application email.
Writing WB page 47		Writing a job application email.

11 Student *Teacher's notes*

Warm up

Ask the students to write down five subjects and five sports they did in school, then number each subject and sport from 1 to 5 according to how good/bad they were at it (1 = very bad; 5 = very good). Put them into pairs and ask them to tell each other about their performance in these subjects and sports. For example: *I was really good at math, but I was lousy in history.*

Vocabulary & Reading (SB page 114)

1

- Pairwork. Ask the students to think about what makes a good teacher and to write a list of qualities. Allow them to compare their lists with other pairs and then try to produce a class list of the three most important qualities.
- Do the same to produce a list of the qualities that make a good student.

2

- Do the first one as an example with the class. Then ask the students to match up the remaining questions.
- Ask the students to compare their answers in pairs before checking with the class. Allow them time to think about their answers to the questions, then discuss them in pairs.

ANSWERS:
a 8
b 1
c 4
d 6
e 3
f 7
g 2
h 5

3

- Go through the questions with the class first so that they know what information to look out for. Give them plenty of time to read the text and find the answers.
- When you've checked the answers, ask the students to read the article again and underline the expressions from Exercise 2 that are used in it. Point out that four of the expressions aren't used. Ask them to identify which ones.

ANSWERS:
a Lazy, undisciplined, energetic.
b Because his teacher was sarcastic and critical.
c None of them.

Get a bank loan
Go on to higher education
Learn by heart
Apply to college

4

- Go through the underlined structures with the class first and make sure they understand that these are used to make predictions about the likelihood of something happening. Give them plenty of time to read the text and find matching expressions.
- Encourage the students to use the expressions in sentences of their own.

ANSWERS:
He is bound to make an impact.
He is unlikely to go anywhere.
He is not expected to have trouble.

Language note

Vocabulary: *is likely to / is bound to / is expected to*
If you say *(something) is expected to (happen)*, you're referring to the expectations of your teacher / parents / boss / another, while if you say that *(something) is likely / bound to (happen)*, you are referring to the likelihood (possibility/ probability) based on individual factors.

5

- Ask the students to work individually to complete the predictions, and then allow them to compare their answers in pairs before checking with the class.
- Discuss with the class the likelihood of these things happening in their own country or countries. Encourage them to use the expressions they've just learned and to predict when these things might occur.
- Pairwork. Put the students into pairs. Ask them to discuss and write down three more predictions about the future of education in their country or countries. Then ask them to discuss their predictions with other pairs.

ANSWERS:
a are expected
b are likely to
c is highly unlikely
d are likely to
e are bound to

Pronunciation (SB page 116)

1 2.37

- Explain the difference between abbreviations and acronyms. (See the following Language note.)
- Focus attention on the list and ask the students to think about which ones are acronyms. Then play the recording for them to listen and repeat. Ask them to check the ones that can be pronounced as words.
- Play the recording again for them to underline the stressed letters in those which aren't acronyms.

ANSWERS:
1 AIDS ✓
2 B.S.
3 FAQ
4 MBA
5 NATO ✓
6 OPEC ✓
7 PhD
8 PIN ✓
9 UNICEF ✓
10 IRS

Language note

Pronunciation: abbreviations and acronyms
Abbreviations and acronyms both use letters to represent words, but acronyms can be pronounced like words, e.g. AIDS, NATO, OPEC, PIN, and UNICEF.

2 2.38

- Pairwork. Ask the students to work together to decide what the abbreviations stand for. Ask them to highlight those that are connected with education.
- Play the recording for them to check their answers. Then ask what the equivalent abbreviations are in their own language or languages.

ANSWERS:
1 Acquired Immune Deficiency Syndrome
2 Bachelor of Science
3 Frequently Asked Questions
4 Master of Business Administration
5 North Atlantic Treaty Organization
6 Organization of Petroleum Exporting Countries
7 Doctor of Philosophy
8 Personal Identification Number
9 United Nations International Children's Emergency Fund
10 Internal Revenue Service

Abbreviations that have something to do with education are:
B.S. MBA PhD

2.38
1 Acquired Immune Deficiency Syndrome
2 Bachelor of Science
3 Frequently Asked Questions
4 Master of Business Administration
5 North Atlantic Treaty Organization
6 Organization of Petroleum Exporting Countries
7 Doctor of Philosophy
8 Personal Identification Number
9 United Nations International Children's Emergency Fund
10 Internal Revenue Service

Cultural notes

Degrees: B.S., MBA, PhD
A B.S. is an academic degree taken in math and science subjects; an MBA is a Master's degree in business administration; and a PhD is an advanced degree recognized in many countries.
Organizations: NATO /ˈneɪtoʊ/, **UNICEF** /ˈjunɪsef/, **OPEC** /ˈoʊpek/
NATO is an international military alliance formed in 1949; UNICEF is an organization that provides emergency food and healthcare to children in conflict situations around the world; OPEC is a group of twelve oil-producing countries that have formed an economic alliance.

Speaking: anecdote (SB page 116)

For more information about how to set up, monitor, and repeat anecdotes, see pages xix to xx in the Introduction.

- Go through the instructions and the questions with the class. Give the students a minute or two to decide which teacher they're going to talk about. Then ask them to look at the questions and think about their answers to them. Allow them to make notes of what they're going to say and how they're going to say it, but discourage them from writing a paragraph that they can simply read aloud. Go around, monitoring and giving help where necessary.
- Put the students in pairs and ask them to take turns telling their partner about their favorite or least favorite teacher at school. Encourage them to ask each other follow-up questions to get further information. Then ask some pairs to report back to the class about what they found out.

Listening & Vocabulary (SB page 116)

1

Groupwork. Go through the questions with the class, and then ask them to discuss them in small groups. Get each group to report back to the class on what they decided.

2 2.39

- Go through the sentences with the class before playing the recording, so that they know what information to look out for.
- You may need to play the recording again to give the students a chance to decide which is the best summary.

ANSWERS:
b They think Serena should graduate from college before she tries to become a rock star.

2.39 (I = Interviewer; Mrs. B = Mrs. Benitez; Mr. B = Mr. Benitez)

I: What is Serena going to do when she graduates from high school?
Mrs. B: Until a few months ago, she was going to go to college, but she's changed her mind. Now she figures she's going to make it in the music world.
I: And how do you feel about that?
Mrs. B: We think she's making an enormous mistake.
I: But surely she can go back to her studies if her music career fails.
Mrs. B: That's true, but once she gets a taste of freedom, she'll find it harder to go back to college. I just think it's such a waste – four years from now, she'll have graduated and she'll still be young enough to try out the music business. At least if it doesn't work out, she'll have a qualification behind her.
I: Have you discussed this with her?
Mrs. B: Of course, but she's made up her mind. We're just hoping that she'll get it out of her system and then come to her senses and go back to her studies. When I graduated from high school, I didn't go to college, and I've regretted it ever since. I just don't want her to make the same mistake I did.
I: Will you support her while she's trying to be a rock star?
Mr. B: You mean financially? No. She won't be living at home, and we can't afford to pay for her to live in Los Angeles, so it's up to her to make it work.

3

Encourage the students to think back to what they heard and try to decide which is the correct alternative in each extract. When they've done as many as they can, play the recording for them to check their answers.

ANSWERS:

a make	**d** system
b taste	**e** senses
c behind	**f** up

Language note

Vocabulary: colloquial expressions
Note that the only words that change within these fixed phrases are the object pronouns (*me*, *you*, *him/her*, etc.) and the possessive adjectives (*my*, *your*, *his/her*, etc.). For example: *She might as well get it out of* ***her*** *system*; *It's up to* ***them***; *He needs to come to* ***his*** *senses.*

4

- Pairwork. Ask the students to work together to use the expressions from Exercise 3 to complete the statements appropriately. Remind them that they'll need to make some changes.
- Check answers with the class before giving the students time to think about whether or not they agree with the statements. Then discuss this as a class, encouraging the students to give reasons for their opinions and to say whether they think their parents would agree with them.

ANSWERS:
a get it out of your system
b a taste of freedom
c behind you
d make it
e up to you

Reading & Grammar (SB page 117)

1

Pairwork. Focus attention on the picture. Point out that this is Serena, the girl in the listening. Ask students to work with a partner and use the context to choose and underline the most appropriate future forms in the conversation.

ANSWERS:
1 exams start
2 I'm going to concentrate
3 I'm going to be
4 I'm going to find
5 I'm moving
6 you'll be able
7 we might have to
8 it's going to be
9 we'll have had
10 I'll be staying
11 I'll give
12 it'll be

2 2.40

Play the recording for the students to check their answers to Exercise 1. Then put them in pairs. Ask them to think about the question and then discuss their answers with their partner. Encourage the pairs to report back to the class.

2.40 (I = Interviewer; S = Serena)

I: You're graduating from high school soon, aren't you?

S: Yes, my exams start next week, but I'm not too worried about the results, because when I'm done with school I'm going to concentrate on my music career. I'm the lead singer in a band, and I don't need any qualifications to do that. I see my future very clearly - it's obvious that I've got what it takes to be successful. I'm going to be incredibly famous and fabulously rich.

I: So you've already got a contract then?

S: No, not yet. Actually, we don't have a manager yet, but the minute I've taken my last exam, I'm going to find a really good one.

I: So, do you intend to continue living at home?

S: No way. I'm moving to Los Angeles as soon as I graduate. L.A.'s where it all happens in the music industry.

I: Do you think you'll be able to live off your music right from the start?

S: Well, if we don't make it right away, we might have to get part-time jobs for a few months or something. I know it's going to be hard at first, but I bet you, by this time next year, we'll have had a single in the charts.

I: And where do you see yourself five years from now?

S: In five years, I'll be staying in the best hotels and won't be able to walk down the street without being recognized. In fact, I'll give you my autograph now if you like - it'll be worth a fortune in a few years!

Grammar (SB page 118)

Future forms and future time clauses

1

- Pairwork. Ask the students to complete the table with examples of different future forms from the interview with Serena on page 117. As they work, go around giving extra help where needed.
- Check answers with the class, going through the table and pointing out the various uses of the different forms.

ANSWERS:
- **a** Example 1: ... it'll be worth a fortune in a few years!
- **b** Example: ... we might have to get part-time jobs ...
- **c** *be going to*; Example 1: I'm going to concentrate on my music career.
- **d** Example: I'm moving to Los Angeles ...
- **e** Simple present
- **f** Example: I'll be staying in the best hotels ...
- **g** Future perfect

Language note

Grammar: future forms and future time clauses
(See Student's Book page 150.)

2

Focus attention on the sentences and ask a student or students to read them aloud. Go through the instructions and point out the underlining and circling in the example. Then ask the students to discuss and do the same for the three sentences.

ANSWERS:
- **a** ... (the minute I've taken my last exam), I'm going to find a really good one.
- **b** ... I'm moving to Los Angeles (as soon as I graduate).
- **c** ... (if we don't make it right away), we might have to get part-time jobs ...
- **1** The main clause
- **2** Simple present and present perfect (present progressive also possible)
- **3** When the subordinate clause comes before the main clause.

3

Ask the students to work individually to complete the sentences. Do the first one with the class as an example if you wish. Allow the students to compare their sentences in pairs before checking answers with the class.

ANSWERS:
- **a** fail; will kill
- **b** 'm going to grow; graduate
- **c** 'm never going to read; 've taken
- **d** 'll like; get
- **e** 's not / isn't coming out; 's done
- **f** finish; 'm going to set up

4

- Ask the students to work individually to complete the sentences. Remind them that these should be true.
- Put the students into pairs to compare and discuss their sentences. Ask them to report back to the class on any particularly interesting sentences.

5 Grammar Extra 11

Ask the students to turn to Grammar Extra 11 on page 150 of the Student's Book. Here they'll find an explanation of the grammar they've been studying and further exercises to practice it.

ANSWERS:

1
- **a** She might not pass the exam.
- **b** I've arranged to see the director at 3:00 p.m.
- **c** As soon as I've finished this test, I'm leaving.
- **d** I'm going to concentrate on my acting career.

- **e** By this time next week, the builders will have finished.
- **f** If you can't come with us, we won't go.
- **g** He's not coming out until he's finished his homework.
- **h** I think the team is going to win today.

2

Students' own answers.

Reading & Vocabulary (SB page 119)

1

Groupwork. Put the students into small groups and ask them to discuss the questions, then to report back to the class on their ideas.

2

- Ask the students to look at the picture and at the title of the article. Ask them what they think the article will be about and if they think they'd enjoy this kind of experience.
- Explain the expression *to take something with a grain of salt* (to be slightly wary about believing what someone says).

Cultural note

The **Appalachian Trail** is a marked hiking trail in the Eastern United States extending between Springer Mountain in Georgia and Mount Katahdin in Maine. The trail is about 2,200 miles long. More than 2 million people are said to take a hike on part of the trail every year. Thru-hikers attempt to hike the trail in its entirety in a single season. Most thru-hikers take between five and seven months. The average is a week or two shy of six months.

3

- Give the students time to look back through the text and find matching words and expressions.
- Check answers with the class before asking the students to say whether they know anyone who tends to exaggerate and embellish the stories they tell.

ANSWERS:

- **a** close shave
- **b** take it with a grain of salt
- **c** embellish
- **d** ordeal
- **e** cliff

Reading (SB page 120)

1

Go through the instructions with the class, making sure that everyone understands that these are two versions of the same hiking story. Ask the students to read both versions and decide which they prefer and why.

2

Pairwork. Ask the students to think about any situation that did not turn out well and tell their partners.

Vocabulary (SB page 121)

1

- Ask the students to read version 2 of Kenny's story on page 120 again. Point out that describing a stream as being raging rapids is an exaggeration. Ask them to find ten more examples of exaggerated language.
- Allow the students to compare notes in pairs before checking answers with the class.

ANSWERS:

Any ten of the following:
barked / snarled and snapped
some wet patches / a veritable swamp
woods / forest
walked / tramped
a bit of a scare / scaring me half to death
ran into / was attacked by
dirty / filthy and mud-splattered
wild dog / rabid wild dog
in a remote area / in the middle of nowhere
a little lost / hopelessly lost
hilly terrain / mountainous terrain
It was almost dark / It was pitch black
rather tiring / an exhausting brush with death
amusing / hysterical

Language note

Vocabulary: exaggerated expressions

The expressions in this section range from simple exaggeration (*dirty – filthy*) to hyperbole (*I was feeling sick – I was at death's door*). This is very common when spicing up a spoken story and, in some cases, has entered the common vocabulary; instead of saying *He was angry (about something)*, it's as common to say *He freaked out*. Other examples include: *I'm hungry = I'm starving*; *I'm thirsty = I'm parched*; *She cried a lot = She cried her eyes out*; *He was overweight = He weighed a ton*, etc.

2 ▶ 2.41

- Pairwork. Ask the students to read both versions of the second story. Point out that there's exaggerated language in both versions and they need to find this and combine elements of the story to make it as dramatic as possible.
- Play the recording for the students to compare with their stories.

> ▶ 2.41
> **Kenny's second story**
> "Last year I almost died when I contracted a nasty parasite. I made a huge newbie mistake of drinking water without treating it. Almost instantly, with miles and miles to go in my hike, I started to feel like I was going to die. My stomach was bubbling and boiling, and I vomited incessantly. I barely crawled into town, and they raced me to the hospital, where they pumped me full of meds. It took almost a year to recover."

3

- Ask the students to work individually to match the expressions with their meanings.
- Read the example sentence to the class, and then ask the students to choose three expressions from column A and use them in sentences of their own.
- Ask the students to compare their sentences in pairs or small groups. Then ask some of them to read their sentences to the class.

ANSWERS:	
a 3	**f** 7
b 9	**g** 2
c 4	**h** 5
d 10	**i** 8
e 1	**j** 6

Speaking (SB page 121)

1

Pairwork. Read the instructions to the class and point out that they can use their own ideas as well as the notes given. Ask the students to work together to devise their stories, and encourage them to make them as dramatic as possible.

> ### Language note
> **Vocabulary: linkers**
> These discourse markers provide cohesion in a text. This selection concentrates on: sequencing events (*To begin with, Then, Later*; others include: *After that, Next*); expressing attitude (*To my horror, Suddenly;* others include: *To my surprise, Naturally, Obviously*); and ending the story (*In the end, It turned out that;* others include: *Finally, At last*).

2

Put the pairs together to create small groups and ask them to tell their stories to each other.

Language for Life (SB page 122)

1 ▶ 2.42

- Focus the students' attention on the items ***a–g***. Ask the students to identify the situation (a young man being interviewed for a job).
- Put the students into pairs and tell them that they're going to hear the young man, Sam, being interviewed for a job. Ask them first to put the interview questions into what they think is the most logical order.
- Play the recording for them to check their answers. Then have a class discussion on whether or not Sam will get the job.

> **ANSWERS:**
> *Most logical order:* **e, f, c, b, g, d, a**

> ▶ 2.42 **(I = Interviewer; S = Sam)**
> **I:** Ah, come in. Sam, isn't it?
> **S:** Yes.
> **I:** Well, Sam, tell us a little about yourself.
> **S:** I'm 24, and I was born in Twin Falls, Idaho. I like baseball. In the winter, I go skiing, and, in the summer, I like sailing and windsurfing. Oh, and I'm a black belt in karate. Well, I say I'm a black belt. In fact, I'm a brown belt, but I'm taking my black belt in a few days, so ... um, anyway, I graduated last year, and now I'm looking forward to getting a job.
> **I:** OK. And why do you think you'd be right for a position in this company?
> **S:** Oh, well, uh, I'm interested in what your company does. Um, I haven't really thought about it.
> **I:** In your opinion, what are your greatest strengths?
> **S:** I'm outgoing and friendly, so I get along well with people.
> **I:** What would you say your weaknesses are?
> **S:** My weaknesses? I can't think of any. Ha ha. Oh, I know – I tend to be at my best in the afternoon. Mornings are tricky.
> **I:** OK. And what are your long-term objectives?
> **S:** To be the best I can – and to make a lot of money.
> **I:** What would you like to be doing five years from now?
> **S:** Lying on a beach in the Caribbean! Ha ha.
> **I:** Do you have any questions you'd like to ask us?
> **S:** Uh, no. I'm fine.
> **I:** OK, well, we'll be in touch.

2

- Ask the students to read the advice on how to do well in a job interview.
- Discuss with the class how Sam could have improved his interview skills. Play the recording again, if necessary.

> **ANSWERS:**
> He shouldn't have rambled about his achievements in sports.
> He shouldn't have suggested that he didn't have any weaknesses.
> He should have been more enthusiastic (not implying he didn't work well in the morning), and he should have found out about the company to give the impression of being interested in the job.
> He should have prepared for the interview better, including preparing his own questions to ask.

3 2.43

- Ask the students to match the model answers to the questions. Allow them to compare answers in pairs.
- Tell them that they're going to hear another interview and that they should listen and check their answers. When they've done this, ask them which of the highlighted phrases could be used in other interview contexts.

> **ANSWERS:**
> **1 b**
> **2 e**
> **3 c**
> **4 f**
> **5 d**
> **6 a**
> **7 g**
> All of them could be used in other contexts.

> **2.43 (I = Interviewer; L = Layla)**
> **I:** Ah, come in. Layla, isn't it?
> **L:** Yes, that's right.
> **I:** Well, Layla, tell us a little about yourself.
> **L:** OK. I graduated from college last year, and then spent four months traveling in South America. That was a great experience, but now I'm ready to embark on my career, and I'm very interested in working for a company like yours.
> **I:** OK. And why do you think you'd be right for a position in this company?
> **L:** Well, I've always been interested in working in the media. I think I'm well suited to this kind of work because I work well under pressure. I don't have much experience yet, but anything I don't know, I'm willing to learn.
> **I:** In your opinion, what are your greatest strengths?
> **L:** I'm highly motivated and conscientious. I'm a team player, but equally I can work on my own.
> **I:** What would you say your weaknesses are?
> **L:** I would say my greatest weakness has been my lack of proper planning in the past. However, since I've come to recognize that weakness, I've taken steps to correct it.
> **I:** OK. And what are your long-term objectives?
> **L:** I'd like to gain some experience in this field for a few years, and then decide which area I want to specialize in.
> **I:** What would you like to be doing five years from now?
> **L:** Ideally, I'd like to be managing my own team.
> **I:** Do you have any questions you'd like to ask us?
> **L:** Yes, I'd like to know a little about the training opportunities in this job.
> **I:** Yes, that's a good question. We believe in on-going training here, and we provide regular opportunities for our staff to attend relevant courses.
> **L:** Oh, that sounds great.
> **I:** OK, well, thank you for coming in, Layla. We'll be in touch.

4

- Pairwork. Go through the jobs with the class and make sure everyone understands them. Then put the students into pairs to write an interview for one of the jobs (remind them that they can use their own idea for the job if they wish). Try to make sure that several pairs choose each option. Go around, helping with vocabulary where needed and making sure that the students use the highlighted useful phrases from Exercise 3 in their interviews.
- Ask the students to practice their interviews. Ask a few confident pairs to perform theirs for the class.

Life Skills (SB page 122)

Getting a Handle on Your Email

- Ask students how many emails they receive in a typical day and if they tend to communicate more by phone, email, messaging, or in person.
- Give the students time to read the text and discuss their email habits and if they found the advice useful.
- Have students work in groups. Assign the groups one of the items in the list (or elicit other habits), and have them report back to the class.
- Discuss whether students feel like they spend too much time online, and what they can do about it generally.

Writing Extra (SB page 123)

Résumé and application email

1

- Make sure that the students understand what a résumé is (an account of a person's education, qualifications, job experiences, skills, and interests, which is used when making a job application). Focus their attention on the list of tips and tell them to decide which are things you should do and which are things you should not do when writing your résumé.
- Check answers with the class and see if anyone has any other tips.

> **ANSWERS:**
> **DO:**
> **a** be honest
> **d** use a clear layout
> **e** use bold and italic for headings
> **f** include dates
> **g** check for spelling and typing errors
>
> **DON'T:**
> **b** mention your bad points and failures
> **c** try to be amusing
> **h** use family or friends as references

2

- Ask the students to work individually to read Brad Arnoldson's résumé and to use the tips in Exercise 1 to identify the places where Brad has gone wrong.
- When they've finished, ask them to compare their answers with a partner.

> **ANSWERS:**
> - The résumé looks overly familiar and the layout is poor.
> - There are a number of spelling errors, e.g. *educasion*, *licence*, and typing errors, e.g. *compUter*.
> - No dates are included.
> - Brad has tried to be amusing with the funny email address, and the mention of blood donating as a "personal interest." This is inappropriate.
> - He has included his own mother as a reference.
> - The language is too informal.
> - He has attached a very informal picture.

3

- Pairwork. Go through the example with the class and point out that there are ways of making most things sound a lot better than they are without being dishonest.
- Put the students into pairs and ask them to look at the rest of the items under *Employment* and *Skills* in Brad's résumé and to think of ways to make them sound more formal and positive. When they've finished, ask them to turn to *Additional Material* section and read the improved version of Brad's résumé.

4

- Ask the students to read the email and then go back and cross out the parts that they think are inappropriate.
- Allow them to compare their answers in pairs before checking with the class.

> **ANSWER:**
> Brad's email with the inappropriate sections crossed out:
>
> ~~DO NOT DELETE!!!!!~~
> Dear Sir or Madam ~~or Ms~~:
> I am writing to apply for the position of summer camp counselor advertised ~~on your website~~ this week. As you can see from my ~~attached~~ résumé, I do not have a great deal of work experience and no experience whatsoever as a camp counselor. However, what I lack in experience I am willing to make up for in enthusiasm and hard work.
> Since I graduated from high school in June last year, I have been in continual employment. First of all, I worked as a sales clerk, where I learned a lot about the retail industry. ~~But it was my mother's store and we fought all the time, so I quit.~~ After that, I worked at a beach resort in Mexico, where I enjoyed working as part of a team and improved my spoken Spanish. ~~I quit because the pay was awful and I never had time to go scuba diving.~~ Through the variety of positions I have held, I have learned important interpersonal skills, improved my knowledge of Spanish, and have gained extensive computing skills. I feel the job you are offering will enable me to put these skills into practice.
> ~~As I'm unemployed right now~~, I can be available for an interview at your convenience.
> I look forward to hearing from you.
> Sincerely,
> ~~Brad Arnoldson~~ ☺
> Brad Arnoldson

Brad's email in a more appropriate form:

Dear Sir or Madam,
I am writing to apply for the position of summer camp counselor advertised in *The Times* this week. As you can see from my enclosed résumé, I do not have a great deal of work experience and no experience as a camp counselor.
However, what I lack in experience I am willing to make up for in enthusiasm and hard work.
Since I graduated from high school in June last year, I have been in continual employment. First of all I worked as a sales clerk where I learned a lot about the retail industry. After that I worked at a beach resort in Mexico where I enjoyed working as part of a team and improved my spoken Spanish.
Through the variety of positions I have held, I have learned important interpersonal skills, improved my knowledge of Spanish and have gained extensive computing skills. I feel the job you are offering will enable me to put these skills into practice.
I would enjoy the opportunity to discuss my suitability for the role in more detail in person, and I can be available for an interview at your convenience.
Sincerely,
Brad Arnoldson

5

Ask the students to write their own résumé and job application email for a job as a summer camp counselor. Tell them to follow the tips on writing a résumé and to check their work thoroughly for appropriate language before they give it to you for checking.

Writing

Workbook page 47
Writing a job application email
Formal expressions
Appropriacy

Further practice material

Need more classroom practice activities?

Photocopiable resource materials in the Teacher's Presentation Kit / Extra Resources

Need more tests?

Test Generator
Teacher's Presentation Kit / Extra Resources / Tests

Need more on important teaching concepts?

Key concepts in *American Inside Out Evolution* pages xxi-xxxvi

Need student self-study practice?

Workbook pages 44-47

Need more information and ideas?

American Inside Out Evolution website www.macmillan.com.br/americaninsideoutevolution

Need to check what your students can do by the end of this unit?

Self-evaluation checklists on pages xxxix-xlvi

12 Home *Overview*

Section	Aims	What the students are doing
Reading & Vocabulary SB page 124	Reading for specific information Houses	Discussing dream houses. Reading an article about two unusual houses and discussing which one they prefer. Completing collocations.
Grammar SB page 125	Participle clauses	Completing a table with sentences containing participle clauses. Rewriting sentences using participles.
Vocabulary SB page 128	Furnishings	Matching furnishings to rooms. Discussing furnishings.
Speaking & Listening SB page 128	Fluency practice Listening for detail	Looking at pictures of rooms and discussing them and the people who might own them. Listening to a psychologist talking about what our rooms say about us and matching interpretations to rooms.
Grammar SB page 129	Nouns and quantity expressions	Completing extracts from descriptions of rooms. Completing sentences with appropriate endings. Choosing the correct verb form in sentences about quantity.
Speaking: anecdote SB page 129	Fluency practice	Talking about their favorite room.
Reading & Speaking: SB page 130	Reading for specific information Fluency practice	Reading an extract from *Sons and Lovers* by D. H. Lawrence and answering questions. Putting a character's morning routine in the correct order. Talking about the relationship between the characters in the story.
Listening & Vocabulary SB page 130	Listening for specific information Morning routines	Listening to people from different countries talking about what they have for breakfast. Matching food items to people. Talking about daily routines and breakfast habits.
Language for Life SB page 132	Saying hello and goodbye	Completing expressions for saying goodbye in a conversation. Matching phrases with appropriate responses. Writing a conversation.
Life Skills SB page 132	Influencing Others	Dealing with different opinions. Learning expressions to use when agreeing, disagreeing, and expressing one's opinion.
Vocabulary Extra SB page 133	Get it right	Completing statements with *actual* / *actually* or *current* / *currently*. Choosing the verb or verb phrase that doesn't belong. Underlining the correct alternative. Categorizing nouns as countable or uncountable. Identifying the common error in sentences and identifying ones they commonly make. Finding examples of correct usage in their dictionaries.

12 Home *Teacher's notes*

Warm up

Write on the board *Home is where the heart is.* Ask the students what they think this saying means and whether or not they agree with it. Ask them what home means to them. Perhaps get them to complete the sentence *Home is where ...*

Reading & Vocabulary (SB page 124)

1

- Pairwork. Explain the concept of a "dream" or ideal house. Go through the list of possibilities with the class, and then ask them to discuss in pairs how they imagine their dream house. Make it clear that they should use their own ideas and not confine themselves to those in the book. Then ask the pairs to report back to the class.
- Focus attention on the two pictures on pages 126 and 127. Ask the students not to read the article yet, but to think about which of the features listed they would expect each house to have.
- When they've finished predicting the features of each house, ask them to read the article and find out if they were right.

ANSWERS:
The houseboat is on the coast.
The treehouse is eco-friendly, in the middle of nowhere, and has amazing views.

Language note

Vocabulary: house
There are some differences between American and British English when describing types of homes or accommodations. For example:
Am E *apartment* = Br E *flat*
Am E *apartment building* or *condominium* (for a small group of apartments, each owned by the occupier) = Br E *block of flats*
Am E *a row house* or *town-house* = Br E *a terraced house*
Am E *a house on one level* = Br E *bungalow*
bungalow = a house that is small and compact, usually on one level

2

Put the students into pairs and ask them to discuss which of the two houses they'd prefer to live in. Make sure they give their reasons, and encourage them to report back to the class.

3

- Pairwork. Ask the students to try to complete the collocations without looking at the article.
- When they've done as many as they can, allow them to look at the article again and check their answers.
- Ask the students to discuss their answers to the questions and report back to the class on their ideas.

ANSWERS:
a living
b air
c fuels
d door
e dark / black

Grammar (SB page 125)

Participle clauses

1

- Go through the sentences in the table with the class. Ask the students to identify the relative clauses in the sentences in column 2. Then ask them to find two appropriate sentences from the article on pages 126 and 127 to complete the table.
- Check answers with the class and go through the information on participle clauses in the margin.

ANSWERS:
1 We found the perfect houseboat, designed by a famous architect.
2 There is a growing group of people working towards having a simpler life.

Language note

Grammar: participle clauses
(See Student's Book page 150.)

2

- Go through the example with the class and then ask the students to work individually to rewrite the remaining sentences. Allow them to compare answers in pairs before checking with the class.
- Ask the students to discuss with a partner whether any of the sentences are true for them.

ANSWERS:
a My apartment building, built in the 1990s, is modern.
b My own apartment, located on the top floor, is very light and airy.

c Every morning I am woken up by the sun streaming through my window.
d My bedroom is full of souvenirs collected on my travels.
e The neighbors living across from us are very friendly.

3 Grammar Extra 12, Part 1

Ask the students to turn to Grammar Extra 12, Part 1 on page 150 of the Student's Book. Here they'll find an explanation of the grammar they've been studying and a further exercise to practice it.

ANSWERS:
1
a That man speaking very loudly is my cousin.
b The people living on my street are very friendly.
c The glasses kept in that cabinet are very expensive.
d The rooms overlooking the back of the house are the best.
e The pizza sold in that place is the best!

Vocabulary (SB page 128)

1

- Point out that the headings in the table are all rooms in a house. Ask the students to work in pairs and to decide which of the furnishings listed in the box they'd expect to find in each room. Point out that some may appear in more than one room.
- Allow them to compare their answers with other pairs before checking with the class. Find out if anyone has any of these items in an unusual place in their own home.

POSSIBLE ANSWERS:
In the kitchen: a dustpan and brush; an ironing board; a sink; dish towels; a tumble dryer
In the bathroom: a shaving outlet; a shower curtain; a towel rail; a sink
In the living room: candlesticks; a fireplace; a mantelpiece; ornaments; patterned wallpaper
In the hallway: coat hooks; a doormat

Language note

Vocabulary: things you find in a house
Differences between British and American English:
Am E *drapes* = Br E *curtains*
Am E *mailbox* = Br E *letterbox*
Am E *dish towel* = Br E *tea towel*

2

- Ask the students to read the lists of items and decide which part of a room they'd associate with each group. Then check with the class and make sure everyone understands all the items. (*Parquet* is a kind of wooden flooring made up of small blocks that fit together.)
- Ask the students to check all the items in Exercises 1 and 2 that they have in their homes. Find out who has the most items.

ANSWERS:
a a floor
b a window
c a wall
d a front door

Speaking & Listening (SB page 128)

1

- Pairwork. Go through the instructions and the questions with the class. Ask them to discuss the questions in pairs, giving as much detail as possible. With weaker classes, you might like to begin by simply getting the students to describe what they can see in the pictures.
- Ask the pairs to report back to the class on their opinions. Write on the board any adjectives they come up with to describe the kinds of people they think the rooms belong to.
- Pairwork. Read the following instructions as if you were the examiner.
Student A. Look at these two pictures. They show two different living rooms. Compare the pictures and say what kind of person you think each room belongs to. (Allow about 1 minute.)
Student B. Which room do you like best and why? (Allow about 20 seconds.)
- You could then have the students change roles and use the same pictures to repeat the activity. Better still, find two more pictures of contrasting rooms from a magazine or brochure, i.e. two different kitchens or two different bedrooms. Use the same instructions as above with the new pictures.

2 2.44-2.45

- Go through the sentences with the class and then ask them to decide which room each interpretation matches. Allow them to compare their ideas in pairs or small groups before you play the recording.
- Play the recording for the students to check their ideas. Encourage them to say whether they agree or disagree with the psychologist's assessment. Then ask them to turn to *Additional Material* section and read what the people who own the rooms think.

ANSWERS:
2
a Room 1
b Room 1
c Room 2
d Room 2
e Room 1
f Room 2

2.44

Room 1

This is obviously a family room. The couch is big and comfortable, but the use of colors suggests that both comfort and style are important. I imagine a small family with a young child sitting on the couch to watch a movie or listen to a story. There are several cushions which may look attractive, but nine times out of ten, they don't make seats more comfortable. I'd say that this apartment belongs to a family with a sense of style, who want a beautiful living space.

So with that in mind I imagine they would have chosen the brightly colored furniture and the rest of the matching decor together.

The room has a neutral palette with some splashes of yellow around the room on the cushions, the lamp stand, and the picture on the wall. The big glass door adds to the brightness of the room.

The room is very tidy and I imagine that, like many families nowadays, both partners pitch in with housework in the evenings and on weekends.

I think the people who live here are sociable young professionals who enjoy entertaining, but like to keep a tidy home and would get upset if someone spilled wine on the rug.

2.45

Room 2

This one's more difficult to guess because there are very few clues here about the type of person who lives in it. I think it's a man because there are hardly any personal objects on display - for instance there aren't any family pictures around the place.

There's plenty of evidence to suggest that a successful career person lives here. There is a stylish leather and chrome armchair which is probably Italian design and worth a lot of money – whoever lives here certainly has good taste which may indicate that this person works in a creative field such as advertising or the media.

There isn't really enough furniture to make this look like a home, which suggests someone who spends most of his time traveling might live here. I think this is somebody who doesn't actually spend much time at home and when he does, he's obsessively neat. You only have to look at how his books are organized on the shelves to see that he likes things to be in order. The minimalism suggests that he wants to be ready to pack his bags and leave at short notice.

He has little time to socialize, except in a working context, and probably never entertains at home.

Grammar (SB page 129)

Nouns and quantity expressions

1

- Focus the students' attention on the information in the margin. Point out that some of the quantity expressions can be used with both countable and uncountable nouns, but there are some that can only be used with one type.
- Pairwork. Ask the students to work in pairs to complete the extracts. Check answers before asking them to put the quantifiers in a logical order.

ANSWERS:

a There are
b There are
c There are
d There is
e There is

Logical order: **c, b, e, a, d**

Language note

Grammar: nouns and quantity expressions
(See Student's Book page 150.)

2

Pairwork. Ask the students to complete the sentences with the appropriate endings. Check answers before asking them to identify the meaning of the quantifiers in bold. Draw their attention to the difference in meaning between *few* and *a few*.

ANSWERS:
a 2
b 1
c 1
d 2

a a little, a few
b little
c few

3

Ask the students to work individually to complete the sentences so that they are true for them. Then tell the students to compare and discuss their sentences in pairs.

4

- Do the first one as an example with the class, and then ask the students to choose the correct forms.
- Check answers before asking the students to change the statements to make them true for their own home town or city. Also point out that they should add two more statements of their own before comparing their answers with a partner.

ANSWERS:
a isn't
b 's
c are
d 's
e are
f 's

5 Grammar Extra 12, Part 2

Ask the students to turn to Grammar Extra 12, Part 2 on page 150 of the Student's Book. Here they'll find an explanation of the grammar they've been studying and further exercises to practice it.

ANSWERS:
2
1 are
2 much
3 few
4 plenty of
5 little
6 Some of
7 hardly any
8 a lot of

3
Students' own answers.

Speaking: anecdote (SB page 129)

For more information about how to set up, monitor, and repeat anecdotes, see pages xix to xx in the Introduction.

- Go through the instructions and the questions with the class. Give the students a minute or two to decide which room they're going to talk about. Then ask them to look at the questions and think about their answers to them. Allow them to make notes of what they're going to say and how they're going to say it, but discourage them from writing a paragraph that they can simply read aloud. Go around, monitoring and giving help where necessary.
- Pairwork. Put the students in pairs and ask them to take turns telling their partner about their favorite room. Encourage them to ask each other follow-up questions to get further information. Then ask some pairs to report back to the class about what they found out.

Reading & Speaking (SB page 130)

1

Tell the students that they're going to read an extract from a famous novel by D. H. Lawrence called *Sons and Lovers*. Ask the students to look at the picture of the kitchen on page 131 and to work individually to write three adjectives describing the room and three adjectives describing the life of the people who might live there. Allow them to compare their answers with a partner, and then have a class discussion of their impressions.

Cultural notes

- **D. H. Lawrence** /ˈdi eɪtʃ ˈlɔrəns/ (1885–1930)
  British novelist, poet, and painter. The son of a miner, Lawrence was encouraged by his mother to become a teacher. The semi-autobiographical *Sons and Lovers* (1913) was his third novel and established his reputation as an author ready to explore issues relating to emotion and human intimacy, subjects that at the time were regarded as taboo.
- ***Sons and Lovers***
  This novel was written in 1913 and tells the story of Paul Morel, a boy born in a mining community in central England. His complex relationship with his mother and his troubled relationships with his father and with other women, dominate the story.

2

Give the students plenty of time to read the extract to find out if their ideas were correct. Then ask them to find the answers to the questions.

ANSWERS:
a Morel gets up at 5:00 a.m. (sometimes earlier) and the text implies he goes to work at 6:00 a.m.
b For breakfast, he has tea, toasted bacon, and a thick slice of bread with drops of fat from the bacon. For lunch, he has two thick slices of bread-and-butter and cold tea with no milk or sugar.
c He loves having breakfast alone ("... he sat down to an hour of joy").

3

Encourage the students to try to put the routine in order without looking back at the text. When they've finished, allow them to read the extract again to check their answers.

ANSWERS:
Correct order: 1, 9, 3, 2, 5, 7, 8, 6, 4

Extra activity

Ask the students to write sentences describing their own morning routine. They could then mix these up and get a partner to try to put them back in the right order.

4

- Groupwork. Go through the questions with the class, and then ask them to discuss them in small groups.

- When they've finished, encourage them to report back to the class on their ideas, and then ask them to turn to *Additional Material* section and to read the summary to check their ideas. Find out if anything surprised them.

Listening & Vocabulary (SB page 130)

1

Make sure the students can form the questions they'll need to find out the information. Give them a few minutes to mingle and ask each other their questions. They should then report back to the class on what they found out.

2

Pairwork. The students look at the list of food and drink items and answer the questions with a partner. Encourage them to report back to the class on their discussion.

Cultural note

Miso soup /ˈmisoʊ ˈsup/
A flavorful soup from Japan containing miso paste, tofu, and konbu (seaweed). It usually accompanies a meal of rice, fish, and Japanese pickles.

3 2.46–2.48

- Ask the students to say which items they think are typically eaten in each country.
- Play the recording for them to check their answers.

ANSWERS:
USA: eggs, bacon, toast, pancakes, orange juice, coffee
GERMANY: jelly, cereal, cold meat, bacon, ham, cheese, bread rolls, coffee, eggs, tea
JAPAN: green tea, rice, miso soup, omelet, pickled vegetables, grilled fish, seaweed

2.46 (I = Interviewer; L = Lizanne)

I: Lizanne, you're from the USA. What do you have for breakfast?
L: Uh, eggs, bacon, pancakes, and some toast on the side.
I: And what to drink?
L: Usually we start with orange juice and have a lot of coffee.
I: And your eggs – how do you like them done?
L: Sunny side up.
I: What does that mean?
L: That means that the yolk is facing upward – it hasn't been turned over.
I: Thank you.

2.47 (I = Interviewer; N = Nicola)

I: Nicola, you're from Germany. Tell me about breakfast. What do you have for breakfast?
N: Well, in Germany it's different. Some people like jelly or cereals, but the typical breakfast is, of course, with cold meat like salami, bacon, or ham, and cheese. And we always have hot bread rolls and coffee. But I don't like coffee very much. And, of course, boiled eggs – they are very important in Germany and very typical, with salt or pepper.
I: You don't drink coffee for breakfast. What do you like?
N: I like to drink tea.

2.48 (I = Interviewer; M = Michiko)

I: Michiko, what do you have for breakfast? What do you have to drink for breakfast?
M: We drink green tea for breakfast.
I: OK, and what about, what do you eat?
M: We eat rice, miso soup, pickled vegetables, uh, grilled fish – like salmon, and a Japanese omelet, and seaweed.
I: What, what do you have in the Japanese omelet? What does that ...
M: A Japanese omelette is sweet, and it's different from the Western omelet.
I: And miso soup. What is in that?
M: Miso soup is a salty soup, which often has seaweed, vegetables, and tofu.

4

Ask the students to discuss their perfect breakfast in pairs. Encourage them to report back to the class on their discussion.

Language for Life (SB page 132)

1 2.49

- Ask the students to look at the picture and to say what time it is and what they think the two people might be saying (it's night and they're saying goodbye). Explain that there are many different ways of saying goodbye in English.
- Ask the students to read the conversation and complete it with the words in the box. Allow them to compare their answers in pairs or small groups.
- Play the recording for them to check their answers. Point out that Ann and Bob are probably in love, so they don't really want to say goodbye at all; that is why they're taking such a long time saying it!

ANSWERS:
1 better
2 good
3 inviting
4 for
5 so

6 regards
7 will
8 Call
9 have to
10 Take
11 you
12 safely
13 Love
14 too
15 yourself
16 already

2.49
Ann: I'd better be going.
Bob: It was good to see you.
Ann: Thank you for inviting me.
Bob: Thanks for coming.
Ann: Well, so long.
Bob: Give my regards to your family.
Ann: I will.
Bob: Call me.
Ann: OK. I really have to be going.
Bob: Take care.
Ann: See you.
Bob: Drive safely.
Ann: Love you.
Bob: Me too.
Ann: Take care of yourself.
Bob: Missing you already!

2 2.50

- Pairwork. Put the students in pairs and ask them to match the phrases with appropriate responses.
- Check answers and then get the students to identify which phrases are ways of saying hello and which are ways of saying goodbye.
- Play the recording for them to check and repeat the useful phrases. When they've done this chorally, ask for individual repetition of the phrases.

ANSWERS:
a 3
b 10
c 7
d 6
e 4
f 1
g 9
h 8
i 5
j 2

2.50
a Imagine seeing you here!
Oh, I come here all the time.
b You have to come and stay again soon.
I'd love to.
c Good to see you again! You haven't changed a bit.
Neither have you. As beautiful as ever.
d Have a safe trip!
Thanks. I'll call when I get there
e Long time no see!
Yes, it must be over a year.
f What have you been up to?
Not much. The usual.
g Thank you for everything.
You're most welcome.
h Hi, how are you doing?
Fine, thanks. How about you?
i We've got to get together again soon.
Absolutely, that would be great.
j Keep in touch.
I will.

Life Skills (SB page 132)

Dealing with Different Opinions

1 2.51

Students will listen to a psychologist talking about positive attitude and suitable expressions to use when dealing with different opinions or ideas.

2.51 **(I = Interviewer; P = Psychologist)**
I: What are some of your suggestions for dealing with differences?
P: When we are faced with differences in opinions or ideas, it is important to have the right attitude. I have five simple suggestions. Firstly, be respectful. Never shame or put someone down for their point of view. We should always listen and respond respectfully. Secondly, if there is disagreement, try to communicate face to face. Nonverbal communication like body language and tone of voice can help to make a message clearer and avoid misunderstandings. Thirdly, if you are going to have a difficult conversation, a change of scene is advisable. Taking the conversation to a neutral space can help to diffuse a tense discussion. Next, find common ground. Sometimes a disagreement may be on only one or two points. Find points you agree on and build up from there. Finally, sometimes we need to agree to disagree when we cannot find common ground. In these cases, we can disagree respectfully.
I: Can you also suggest some useful expressions to be used in such situations?
P: Yes. In these situations it is important to know how to express your opinion, agree and disagree effectively. To express your opinion, you can start by saying "My opinion is that ..." or "To my mind ...", then complete

according to the situation. If you want to agree with someone, you can say "I share your view" or "Fair enough". Pay attention to the intonation I used here. Depending on how you say it, your interlocutor could get a different message, so you must sound positive. When disagreeing you can use "I take a different view" or "I see what you are saying, but that argument does not hold water", and complete your argument. Sometimes, when you don't agree, you could simply make an alternative suggestion or present an alternative point of view by saying "How about ...". These are just some suggestions, there're many other phrases which can be used in these situations, some of which you probably already know. If used with the correct intonation, these phrases can be very effective.

2

POSSIBLE ANSWERS:

SITUATION	**WHAT ATTITUDE WOULD YOU ADOPT** (answers may vary)	**WHAT WOULD YOU SAY?** (answers may vary)
Your colleague thinks you should hire an outside contractor for a job. This way, it would be easier to manage the project. You think the work should be done in-house because the material is too confidential to be handled by anyone outside the company.	Be respectful, find common ground, face to face communication.	*I see what you are saying, but that argument does not hold water.* This is a highly confidential project and we can't trust anyone outside of the company with this information. *To my mind,* the safest approach is to do this internally.
Your friend loves onions on her pizza but you hate them. You don't object to any other ingredient. The pizza place can make customized orders, such as ingredients on only half the pizza.	Be respectful, agree to disagree.	*Fair enough. Why don't we* order the pizza with onions on only half? That way we both get what we want.
You haven't seen your friends for a long time. They want to go meet up to go bowling. You don't mind bowling, but you'd rather go dancing.	Be respectful, find common ground.	*How about* we go bowling first and then go dancing after?

Vocabulary Extra (SB page 133)

Get it right

1-5

The first five exercises of this section are based on some of the most common learner errors at this level. The exercises are intended for the students to test themselves and then check their answers in the dictionary extracts at the side. Go through the information at the top of the page with the class, and then ask the students to work individually to do the first five exercises and then to check their answers. When checking with the class, ask the students to respond to the personal response questions after some of the exercises.

ANSWERS:

1

a current
b currently
c actual
d current, actually
e actually

2 afford (because it is never followed by a verb in the *-ing* form)

3

a with my parents
b of children
c politics
d competitions
e for products

4

All of them are uncountable.
The noun *advice* is interchangeable with any of the other nouns.

5

a decrease <u>in</u> crime
b dependent <u>on</u> their husbands
c difference <u>in</u> grammar
d increase <u>in</u> violent crime
e reason <u>for</u> poverty
f a solution <u>to</u> this problem

6

Ask the students to look in their own dictionaries to find example sentences that show the correct usage of six words or structures that they often use incorrectly.

Further practice material

Need more classroom practice activities?

Photocopiable resource materials in the Teacher's Presentation Kit / Extra Resources

Need more tests?

Test Generator
Teacher's Presentation Kit / Extra Resources / Tests

Need more on important teaching concepts?

Key concepts in *American Inside Out Evolution* pages xxi-xxxvi

Need student self-study practice?

Workbook pages 48-51

Need more information and ideas?

American Inside Out Evolution website www.macmillan.com.br/americaninsideoutevolution

Need to check what your students can do by the end of this unit?

Self-evaluation checklists on pages xxxiv-xlvi

Review D *Teacher's notes*

These exercises act as a check of the grammar and vocabulary that the students have learned in Units 10–12. Use them to find any problems that students are having, or anything that they haven't understood and that will need further work.

Grammar (SB page 134)

1

This exercise reviews relative clauses from Unit 10. When checking answers, ask the students to identify whether the relative clauses are defining or non-defining.

ANSWERS:
a who **b** which **c** who **d** who **e** which

2

This exercise reviews cleft sentences from Unit 10.

ANSWERS:
- **a** What really annoys me is people who talk at the theater. / What really annoys me at the theater is people who talk.
- **b** What I like about Connie is her sense of humor.
- **c** What I feel like eating tonight is steak and fries.
- **d** The thing I can't stand about summer is the mosquitoes.
- **e** What I'd really like to do is watch TV.

3

This exercise reviews future forms from Unit 11.

ANSWERS:
1. 'm having
2. isn't going to be
3. might not get
4. 'm not going to tell
5. 'll help
6. 'll have to support
7. starts
8. 'll have left
9. 'll be starting

4

This exercise reviews future forms and future time clauses from Unit 11.

ANSWERS:
1. 've finished
2. 've done
3. 've organized
4. do
5. 've done/'d done
6. won't be
7. don't get
8. 'll be
9. is
10. 'm going to tell

5

This exercise reviews participle clauses from Unit 12.

ANSWERS:
- **a** My house, situated in the middle of town, was built one hundred years ago.
- **b** These ornaments, given to me by my grandmother, are very valuable.
- **c** The cat sitting on the windowsill had kittens last year.
- **d** Those children playing volleyball are my brothers and sisters.
- **e** The people living around here are really nice.

Vocabulary (SB page 135)

1

This exercise reviews words for looking at and seeing from Unit 10.

> **ANSWERS:**
> **a** staring
> **b** gazing
> **c** caught sight
> **d** spot
> **e** make out
> **f** notice

2

This exercise reviews educational expressions from Unit 11.

> **ANSWERS:**
> **1** pay
> **2** got
> **3** going on
> **4** fail
> **5** applied for
> **6** studied
> **7** won

3

This exercise reviews exaggerated language from Unit 11. Make sure the students understand that they have to modify some of the pronouns.

> **ANSWERS:**
> **a** took my breath away
> **b** in seventh heaven
> **c** at the end of my rope
> **d** on its last legs
> **e** at death's door
> **f** dying for a drink

Pronunciation (SB page 135)

1

Remind the students that the boxes show the syllables of a word and the large boxes indicate the stressed syllables. Here they're being asked to classify words according to how many syllables they have and where the main stress falls. Encourage them to say each word aloud to get a feeling for what sounds right.

2 2.52

Ask the students to underline the stressed syllable in each of the words in the table. Then play the recording for them to check their answers. Play it a second time for them to listen and repeat.

ANSWERS:
1 and 2

A: □□□	**B:** □□□□	**C:** □□□□
advertise	absolutely	epitomize
evidence	disappointing	experience
ornament	education	relationship
thoroughly	understanding	nostalgically

Further practice material

Need more classroom practice activities?

Photocopiable resource materials in the Teacher's Presentation Kit / Extra Resources

Need more tests?

Test Generator
Teacher's Presentation Kit / Extra Resources / Tests

Need more on important teaching concepts?

Key concepts in *American Inside Out Evolution* pages xxi-xxxvi

Need more information and ideas?

American Inside Out Evolution website www.macmillan.com.br/americaninsideoutevolution

Notes

Notes

Notes

Notes

Notes